Testimonials from organizations that have used this methodology

UK Food Manufacture with 4,000 FTEs with Factories in 10 Locations

I was specifically concerned with the business's sole focus on short-term outputs, as opposed to medium- and long-term inputs, which I saw as predictors of future performance. I was also concerned at the lack of teamwork and confusing terminology (in-company slang), which created division, confusion, and a bit of a blame culture. Needing some inspiration, I read up on business improvement theory and came across David's work.

We asked a senior manager to lead the change program working with, and mentored by, David. This took the form of a series of sessions where the manager and David, working with a number of key stakeholders, participated in a small number of workshops and project planning meetings, the culmination of which was a full rollout of the KPI methodology across the business.

David, using webinar technology, was able to deliver the training in 2.5-hour sessions to multiple locations simultaneously, with breakout sessions where groups could germinate, share, and develop their ideas. The webinar sessions helped garner buy-in from the executives and helped deliver results quickly. Alongside this steering group, we established a KPI team to do the heavy lifting and to ensure the intent was cemented into daily working patterns. This KPI team remains today, providing the entire business with KPI reporting on a daily basis.

I would recommend this methodology to all CEOs who are seeking to more easily see the granular performance of their business. We've moved from being a backward-looking business, where teams politick and mark their own homework, to a more lithe and forward-looking company with live and objective reporting that guides us to focus on the things that are important and we can control.

Mike Snell, Managing Director, IPL

Having an external and objective guide in the shape of David's work was instrumental in launching our KPI Office. Utilizing an external and objective view allowed us to approach the implementation with much more empathy and ensure a smoother entry into the cadence of the business.

Having an external mentor and sounding board was crucial for a right first-time implementation. This was our first and only venture into launching a KPI venture, something David had done countless times.

We implemented pretty much exactly to David's guide, and I'd suggest that the implementation is agnostic to the nature of the business you are running.

The three hardest things in the project that we overcame were (1) gaining cultural acceptance that we needed to introduce better measurement, (2) turning the business into a "receive, not run" reporting culture, and (3) identifying a data visualization platform that was easy to implement.

Our KPI team now consists of five analysts who operate a business partner model whereby each analyst partners with a division. Their tasks are threefold: (1) provide the required measures for that column of the org to succeed, (2) provide easy to interpret and visualise insight into their current performance, and (3) collaborate with their business partners on creating actions to improve performance using the aforementioned data and insight.

The main benefit we have seen from the KPI project has been educating the business that measurement is not a bad thing. In fact, the achievement we are most proud about is that we now have a culture where people want to be measured.

Jordan Steane, KPI Team Leader, IPL

Global Consumer Finance Business

I first became aware of David's KPI methodology some years ago in the UK. When we were planning for our recent annual executive offsite, we wanted to engage in a different way with KPIs and David's methodology came to mind. Our executives originate from both large and small financial organizations and we'd all seen different approaches to KPIs in our prior professional lives. What we all really wanted to do this time was try to break from the backward-looking measures of the past and instead identify measures that informed our chosen future.

David brought a refreshing approach to the identification and implementation of relevant and tailored KPIs that you and your teams can engage with.

I would recommend this methodology to all executives who are looking to break free from KPIs that have previously delivered poorer performance outcomes than you and your teams deserve.

Cameron Small, Group CFO

I was brought in to lead and implement this particular project after our global executive had spent nearly two days at an executive offsite getting an overview of David's methodology and ascertaining the corporate CSFs pertinent to our particular business. I was joined by a colleague who was an L&E professional working in our head office Human Resources team. Although we were based in different countries and had never previously met, we managed to build and maintain team camaraderie through daily communication and frequent video calling.

The CSFs were the backbone to the overall project. When we presented them to employees around the world, we found they resonated with all regions and all lines of business. It was certainly easier to build a framework when the starting point was communal, and knowing the executive had invested valuable time in determining the CSFs added tremendously to buy-in.

David was instrumental in training our two-person KPI leadership team. He co-presented with us on the first two workshops (Australia and Korea) where we instructed on the methodology and gathered performance measures from all participants. We took over presenting from that point for the remainder of our global workshops and found the templates provided were particularly helpful. David had done a tremendous job in imparting his knowledge and instilling confidence in us.

David's KPI book (third edition) was our reference manual. We used it as a guide when questions and thoughts came out of the crowd that we struggled to handle – the topic was always covered in the book.

Throughout the project I found David's mentoring useful and would recommend that all KPI team leaders access a suitable external mentor.

We followed the process as laid out in the KPI book with the exception that we ultimately determined we could successfully implement fewer KPIs in our organization and still significantly increase monitoring of our performance outside of historical financial metrics.

The three hardest things in the project that we overcame were (1) buy-in from all senior leadership, which was necessary to ensure success, (2) inconsistencies with systems and processes among our operating regions, as our growth was mainly via acquisitions vs organic, and (3) ensuring the project got top attention given all the challenges facing the organization and competing priorities for time.

The KPI team has now grown with multiple KPI Champions in each global operating region/line of business and our main tasks ahead are refining the dashboard and continuing to implement some of our newest performance measures that are an innovative way of managing the organization.

Susan MacDonald, KPI Team Leader

Feedback from Other Users

We worked with David Parmenter's methodology since 2013. The "winning KPIs" methodology works extremely well alongside the implementation of "lean" in our business. I wholeheartedly recommend this book and methodology to those who have been tasked with developing KPIs that can change behaviors and deliver a broad range of improved business results.

Louise O'Connell, Strategy and Performance Manager, Nelson Management Limited

David's methods for the development and implementation of KPIs is straightforward, clear, and above all else, practical. Anyone interested in implementing KPIs for the first time in his or her organization will find this book an invaluable resource.

Suzanne Tucker, CEO, The CFO Edge, Inc.

David's KPI methodology is easy to understand and share and facilitates the identification and implementation of KPIs in any business. His approach drives improvement in operational performance.

Scott Hodge, President and Performance Architect, Associates in Management Excellence

Key Performance Indicators

Key Performance Indicators

Developing, Implementing, and Using Winning KPIs

Fourth Edition

DAVID PARMENTER

WILEY

Published by John Wiley & Sons, Inc., Hoboken, New Jersey.
Published simultaneously in Canada.

For general information on our other products and services or for technical support, please contact our Customer Care Department within the United States at (800) 762-2974, outside the United States at (317) 572-3993, or fax (317) 572-4002.

Wiley publishes in a variety of print and electronic formats and by print-on-demand. Some material included with standard print versions of this book may not be included in e-books or in print-on-demand. If this book refers to media such as a CD or DVD that is not included in the version you purchased, you may download this material at http://booksupport.wiley.com. For more information about Wiley products, visit www.wiley.com.

Library of Congress Cataloging-in-Publication Data

Names: Parmenter, David, author.
Title: Key performance indicators : developing, implementing, and using winning KPIs / David Parmenter.
Description: Fourth edition. | Hoboken, New Jersey : John Wiley & Sons, Inc., [2020] | Includes index.
Identifiers: LCCN 2019024533 (print) | LCCN 2019024534 (ebook) | ISBN 9781119620778 (hardback) | ISBN 9781119620792 (ePDF) | ISBN 9781119620822 (ePub)
Subjects: LCSH: Performance technology. | Performance standards. | Organizational effectiveness.
Classification: LCC HF5549.5.P37 P37 2020 (print) | LCC HF5549.5.P37 (ebook) | DDC 658.3/125—dc23
LC record available at https://lccn.loc.gov/2019024533
LC ebook record available at https://lccn.loc.gov/2019024534

Cover Design: Wiley
Cover Image: © Jurik Peter/Shutterstock

Printed in the United States of America

V10013915_091319

Contents

About the Author

D AVID PARMENTER'S work on KPIs is recognized internationally as a breakthrough in understanding how to make performance measures work. His commitment to Kaizen (continuous improvement) has led to this fourth edition of this best selling book.

David has worked for Ernst & Young, BP Oil Ltd, Arthur Andersen, and PricewaterhouseCoopers, and is a fellow of the Institute of Chartered Accountants in England and Wales.

He is a regular writer for professional and business journals. His performance management topics encompass replacing the annual planning process with quarterly rolling planning, reporting performance, and leadership and management issues.

He is also the author of *The Financial Controllers and CFO's Toolkit: Lean Practices to Transform The Finance Team* (Third edition), *Key Performance Indicators for Government and Non Profit Agencies: Implementing Winning KPIs*, and *The Leading-Edge Manager's Guide to Success* (all from Wiley). He can be contacted via parmenter@waymark.co.nz. His website, www.davidparmenter.com, contains many implementation toolkits, papers, articles, and freeware that will be useful to readers.

David is an international presenter having delivered keynote addresses, workshops and pay-to-view webinars to thousands of attendees in 32 countries. He is known for his thought-provoking and lively sessions, which have led to substantial change in many organizations.

Acknowledgments

I would like to acknowledge all the medical staff at Capital & Coast District Health Board, Wellington, whose dedication is greatly assisting my wife in her battle against cancer. Their professionalism and teamwork had a profound impact on me, and lessons gathered have filtered into my work.

This book has been influenced by the readers and clients who have had faith in this methodology and embedded it into their enterprises. Their feedback on earlier chapter drafts has been invaluable.

A special thanks goes to my wife, Jennifer, and my researcher Ahad, who have assisted me in the important quality assurance steps.

As an author, my views have been shaped by the great writers of the past. To all those referenced in this book I am so grateful that you shared you wisdom to us all.

In my journey I have been guided by a cluster of mentors whose advice and direction has been most valuable. These include Reg Birchfield, Jeremy Hope, Harry Mills, Nathan Donaldson, Robert Russell, and Christoph Papenfuss.

I must also thank all those readers who, after reading this edition, decide to do something in their organization. I hope this book and accompanying templates help you leave a profound legacy. It is my fervent hope that we together can change the way leading organizations around the world measure, manage, and improve performance for the benefit of all concerned.

Overview

Every performance measure has a dark side, a negative consequence, an unintended action that leads to inferior performance. I suspect that well over half the measures in an organization may well be encouraging unintended negative behavior.

The Introduction explores the burning platform in performance management: how old, broken bureaucratic methods are being used that limit the longevity of organizations. It suggests a way forward, blazed by some modern organizations and documented by the paradigm shifters (Drucker, Welch, Collins, et al.).

Key learning points from the Introduction include:

1. Every performance measure has a dark side and why over half of your measures may be destroying value.
2. The three major benefits of ascertaining an organization's critical success factors and the associated performance measures.
3. The importance of measuring at the top of the cliff.
4. Examples of measures that are often confused as KPIs and dysfunctional measures that, if used, will damage an organization.
5. Performance with KPIs should be seen as a requirement, a "ticket to the game" and not worthy of additional reward.
6. Why a KPI project has to be run in-house.
7. The steps CEOs need to take to get performance measurement to work in their organizations.
8. The foolishness of setting year-end targets when you cannot see into the future.
9. Guidelines as to the chapters the Board, CEO, KPI team, and team coordinators should read.
10. Why owners of my previous editions should buy the fourth edition.
11. The variety of electronic material that is available for free and for a fee to help the KPI team get started.

Introduction

Why You Should Be Interested in This Book

Many organizations fail to achieve their potential because they lack clarity regarding the more important things to do. These organizations have not distinguished their critical success factors (CSFs) from the myriad known success factors. This lack of clarity means that often staff members will schedule their work based around their team's priorities rather than the priorities of the organization. As Exhibit I.1 shows, even though an organization has a strategy, teams often are working in directions very different from the intended course.

Performance, in many organizations, is thus a rather random exercise, like the weekend golfer who is lucky to win the Saturday competition every 10 years. This does not need to be the case, as truly great organizations know their CSFs, communicate them to their staff and use the CSFs, as this book suggests, as the source for all their measures.

Changing this

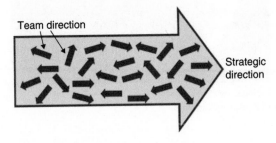

Exhibit I.1 Discord Between Teams' Efforts and the Organization's Strategy

Steve Jobs believed that few in management thought deeply about why things were done. He came up with this quote, which I want to share with you. I believe it should be on every wall and in front of every work area.

Your time is limited, so don't waste it living someone else's life. Don't be trapped by dogma—which is living with the results of other people's thinking. Don't let the noise of others' opinions drown out your own inner voice.[1]

From my observations, the failure rate for key performance indicators (KPIs) and balanced scorecard projects is "off the scales." KPIs, in many organizations, are a broken tool. The KPIs are often a random collection, prepared with little expertise, signifying nothing at best, and wasteful, distracting, and counterproductive at worst.

This fourth edition is a major rewrite that incorporates: "lessons learned" from some major implementations using this methodology; a more concise KPI methodology with clear, fresh implementation guidance; insights into how other areas of performance management can be rectified.

Unintended Behavior: The Dark Side of Performance Measures

Source: NASA, https://www.nasa.gov/multimedia/imagegallery/image_feature_1633.html. Photo courtesy of Fernando Echeverria.

Performance measures are like the moon: they have a dark side, promoting an unintended action that leads to inferior performance. I suspect well over half the measures in an organization may well be encouraging unintended negative behavior.

Dean Spitzer's *Transforming Performance Measurement: Rethinking the Way We Measure and Drive Organizational Success*[2] was one of the first books to focus on the unintended consequences of performance measures.

Example: City Train Service

A classic example is provided by a city train service that had an on-time measure with some draconian penalties targeted at the train drivers. The train drivers who were behind schedule learned simply to stop at the top end of each station, triggering the green light at the other end of the platform, and then to continue the journey without the delay of letting passengers on or off. After a few stations, a driver was back on time, but the customers, both on the train and on the platform, were not so happy.

Management needed to realize that late trains are not caused by train drivers, just as late planes are not caused by pilots. The only way these skilled people would cause a problem would be either arriving late for work or taking an extended lunch when they are meant to be on duty.

Lesson: Management should have been focusing on controllable events that led to late trains. The measures that would assist with timely trains would include:

- Signal failures not rectified within __ minutes of being reported. These failures should be reported promptly to the CEO, who will make the phone call to the appropriate manager (receiving these calls on a regular basis would be career-limiting).
- Planned maintenance that has not been implemented should be reported to the senior management team on a weekly basis, keeping the focus on completion.

Example: Accident and Emergency Department

The National Health Service in the UK has set a four-hour target to treat all patients who turn up for treatment at accident and emergency (A&E). The A&E are measured on the time from patient registration to being seen by a house doctor. Hospital staff soon realized that they could not stop patients registering with minor ailments, but they could delay the registration of patients in ambulances as they were receiving good care from the paramedics.

The nursing staff thus began asking the paramedics to leave their patients in the ambulance until a house doctor was ready to see them, thus improving the "average time it took to treat patients." Each day there would be a parking lot full of ambulances and some circling the hospital. This created a major problem for the ambulance service, which was unable to deliver an efficient emergency service.

Lesson: Management should have been focusing on the timeliness of treatment of critical patients, and thus they only needed to measure the time from registration to consultation of these critical patients. Nurses would have treated patients in ambulances as a priority, the very thing they were doing before the measure came into being. Far too often we do not sort out the wheat from the chaff.

Example: Fast Food Service

A fast food chain wanted to reduce the chicken waste so they held a competition. They would fly the winning manager and their family to a well-known resort. A restaurant manager who was under performing and feeling the pressure, both at home and work, saw the competition as the opportunity to rectify both issues. The manager got the shifts to assemble and explained his plan. "I want you to take the chicken out of the freezer when you receive an order and not before." "But boss, that will lead to huge queues both in the restaurant area and in the drive through," his supervisors explained. "Do not worry, we will only do this for the week of the competition."

The manager won the chicken waste award and was hailed in the head office as a hero, and an example of what was possible. Until the next week's revenue numbers came in. All the customers caught up in the long queues had taken their custom elsewhere. When head office investigated, they were flabbergasted. "How could you think of such a change to procedure?," they asked. "I delivered your zero waste you wanted," replied the unrepentant manager.

Lesson: Tying a reward to an important measure will lead to gaming. Low chicken waste should be treated "as a ticket to the game."

Some Common Measures to Avoid

Measuring sales staff against a predetermined gross revenue target. Sales staff are legendary at meeting their targets at the expense of the company, offering discounts, extended payment terms, selling to customers who will never pay; you name it, they will do it to get the commission.

Tying pay to low inventory levels. Stores maintaining low inventory to get a bonus and having production shut down because of stockouts.

Measuring completion of case load. Experienced caseworkers in a government agency will work on the easiest cases and leave the difficult ones to the inexperienced staff because they are measured on cases closed. This has led to tragic circumstances.

Capacity utilization rate. This is an anti–lean performance measure that prompts plant supervisors to maximize long runs, producing items for stock rather than for actual customer demand.

Delivery in full on time on all deliveries. Using this measure on all dispatches no matter how insignificant they are will lead to cherry picking by staff. It is only human nature to tackle the easy, nonimportant dispatches first, putting the major, more complex, deliveries at risk.

It is thus imperative that before a measure is used, it is:

- Discussed with the relevant staff: "If we measure this, what will you do?"
- Piloted before it is rolled out.
- Abandoned if its dark side creates too much adverse performance.

"People will do what management inspects, not necessarily what management expects."

As Spitzer says, "People will do what management inspects, not necessarily what management expects."

The Three Major Benefits of Ascertaining an Organization's Critical Success Factors

There are three major benefits of ascertaining an organization's critical success factors and the associated performance measures:

1. A clarity of purpose, from aligning the daily staff actions to the organization's critical success factors.
2. Improving performance through having few and more meaningful measures.
3. Creating wider ownership, empowerment, and fulfillment at all levels of the organization.

A Clarity of Purpose from Aligning the Daily Staff Actions to the Organization's Critical Success Factors

Before measures are developed, you need to know what is important in the organization to get right day in, day out. Every organization on planet earth, seeking outstanding performance, needs to know what its critical success factors are and have these communicated to staff.

If the CSFs of the organization are clarified and communicated, staff members will be able to align their daily activities closer to the strategic direction of the organization, as shown in Exhibit I.2.

This behavioral alignment is often the missing link between good and great organizations. CSFs and their associated KPIs are the only things that truly link day-to-day performance in the workplace to the organization's strategy. In the past people thought that because monthly budgets were linked to the annual planning process, which in turn was linked to the five-year plan, which in turn was linked to the strategic plan, strategy was linked to day-to-day activities. It looked good on paper, as shown in Exhibit I.3, but never worked in practice.

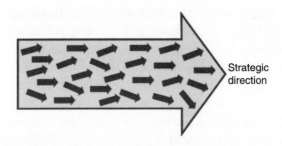

Exhibit I.2 Alignment of Teams' Efforts and the Organization's Strategy

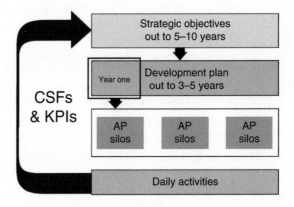

Exhibit I.3 Linkage of CSFs and KPIs to the Strategic Objectives
Note: AP= annual planning.

Measures That Help Create Alignment

I have extracted some of the measures that are included in the appendix to this book.

1. Measuring any exception that relates to delivery in full on time to key customers including:
   - Late deliveries over two hours late to key customers—reported intraday to the CEO
   - Incomplete deliveries to key customers—reported intraday to the CEO
   - Late planes in the sky over two hours late—reported intraday to the CEO

- Late projects which have passed their original deadline—reported weekly to the executive team
- Complaints from our key customers that have not been resolved within __ hours—reported intraday to the executive team
- Key customer service requests outstanding for more than 48 hours—reported intraday to the executive team

2. Measures that relate to recruiting the right people all the time
   - Key position job offers that are over 48 hours old and have not yet been accepted by the chosen candidate—reported daily to the executive team
   - Names of shortlisted candidates for whom the next round of interviews has yet to be scheduled—reported daily to the executive team

3. Measures that relate to staff satisfaction
   - Number of planned CEO recognitions for next week/two weeks—reported weekly to the CEO
   - Number of initiatives implemented after staff satisfaction survey—reported weekly to the executive team post survey
   - Key staff who have handed in their notice today—reported intraday to the CEO.

Improving Performance through Having Fewer and More Meaningful Measures

Performance measures can and should have a profound impact on performance because they:

- Tend to make things happen; it helps people see progress and motivates action.
- Increase visibility of a more balanced performance and focus attention on what matters.
- Increase objectivity—Dean Spitzer[3] points out that staff actually like measuring and even like being measured, but they do not like being judged subjectively.
- Improve your understanding, your decision making, and execution—Spitzer illustrates that you will not be able to execute well, consistently, without measurement. Measurement can improve your business

intuition and significantly increase your "decision-making batting average."

- Improve consistency of performance over the long term.
- Facilitate feedback on how things are going, thereby providing early warning signals to management.
- Help the organization become future-ready by encouraging timely feedback, looking forward by measuring future events (e.g., a CEO should look weekly at the list of celebrations, or recognitions, scheduled for the next two weeks), encouraging innovation, abandonment of the broken, and supporting winning management habits such as recognition, training, and mentoring.

Creating Wider Ownership, Empowerment, and Fulfillment in All Levels of the Organization

Performance measures communicate what needs to be done and help staff understand what is required. They enable leaders to give the general direction and let the staff make the daily decisions to ensure progress is made appropriately. This shift to training and trusting staff to make the right calls is very much the Toyota way. Any incorrect decision is seen as a fault in training rather than with the individual.

The delegation of authority to the front line is one of the main foundation stones of this KPI methodology (see Chapter 3, Background to the Winning KPI Methodology). This issue was discussed at great length in Jeremy Hope's book *The Leader's Dilemma*.[4]

I have yet to meet a person who desires failure or finds failure rewarding. Where measures are appropriately set, staff will be motivated to succeed.

The Burning Platform in Performance Management

There is a burning platform in many organizations, and it is called performance management. Old, broken bureaucratic methods are being used that limit the longevity of the organization. These dubious performance management methods enable managers to take actions that produce short-term illusionary gains at the expense of the organization's longevity. In fact, the more successful managers are at the "short-term game" the higher they climb up the corporate tree helping themselves to ever-increasing annual bonuses.

If Martians landed and inspected our methods, they would wonder how we ever managed to get to the moon, let alone land a rover on Mars. It is testament to the great people working against such a system.

Over the forty years I have been observing and studying performance management, I have come to the conclusion that the major performance management issues are not only common in most organizations, but they are also being amplified as big data and new wave technology lead us to an ever-growing reporting regime of meaningless measures. The sparse progress in those forty years indicates that these issues appear to be locked in each organization's DNA.

While the list of failed performance management practices is daunting, it is still worth understanding them and selecting a sound starting point. I will address the major performance management issues and supply a reference to explore the long-term fixes.

	Failed performance management practices (**the bolded statements have been further explored in this introduction**)	Books offering workable solutions
A lack of clarity on performance measurement	**No formal education on performance measurement**	This book
	Confusion on what KPIs are and what they can and should do	
	Too many of the wrong measures	
	Measuring far too much at the bottom of the cliff	
	Calling all measures KPIs	
	Linking measures to performance Pay Schemes	
	Using external consultants to deliver a KPI or balanced scorecard project	
	A lack of CEO and senior management commitment to KPIs	

	Operating without ascertaining the organization's critical success factors	This book
A lack of clarity of purpose	Believing that a long-drawn-out strategy process will galvanize action	Jack Welch's *Winning* Chan Kim and Renée Mauborgne's *Blue Ocean Shift*
	Allowing a self-serving culture to override the publicly stated values	Jeremy Hope's *The Leader's Dilemma*
	Allowing short-term thinking to override the greater good	
A regime that nurtures the status quo	**A failure rate with projects that matches the failure rate of race horse ownership**	Jack Welch's *Winning* Tom Peters' *Thriving on Chaos* Henry Mintzberg, *No More Executive Bonuses* (*Sloan Management Review*, November 2009). Elizabeth Haas Edersheim's *The Definitive Drucker*
	Allowing innovation to be stifled by bureaucracy	
	A lack of commitment to getting recruitment right the first time	
	Executive salary setting and redundancy pay-outs	
	Reliance on outdated management practices	
Old, broken command-and-control bureaucratic processes	Allowing growth in the layers of bureaucratic management	Jeremy Hope's *The Leader's Dilemma* Tom Peters' *Thriving on Chaos*
	A focus on centralization	
	Setting annual targets when you cannot see into the future	
	Fixation on annual planning processes when it should be a continuous process	
	A reporting regime designed to further support the top-heavy bureaucracy	
	A lack of trust that business unit will deliver without oversight	

A trail of failed IT implementations	Installing a silver bullet, an untried IT system installed by a team of external consultants	Elizabeth Haas Edersheim's *The Definitive Drucker*
A misguided belief that the lean movement is only for manufacturers	A lack of understanding and adoption of continuous flow	Jeffrey Liker's *The Toyota Way*
	A lack of abandonment	Elizabeth Haas Edersheim's *The Definitive Drucker*

Reference Reading Offering Workable Solutions

The solutions to these performance management failings can be found in these great books. It is interesting to note that only two of them are recent publications for good reason. Management failings are common no matter how technology has changed and like a good wine these books have aged well.

Jeremy Hope's book *The Leader's Dilemma: How to Build an Empowered and Adaptive Organization Without Losing Control.*[5] In the book, Hope outlines how 21st-century organizations such as Whole Foods Market (United States), American Express (United States), Statoil (Norway), HCL Technologies (India), Telenor (Norway), Southwest Airlines (United States), Ahlsell (Sweden), Toyota, General Electric, W.L. Gore & Associates (United States), Swenka Handelsbanken (Sweden), John Lewis Partnership (UK), Leyland Trucks (UK), Nucor Steel (United States), and Tomkins (UK) have radically changed performance management practices.

Tom Peters' book *Thriving on Chaos: Handbook for a Management Revolution.*[6] Although written in 1987 it is just as valid today. It contains many case studies and practical steps to implement. Every chapter in the book has a summary of the key learning points on the left hand side of the first page. I have copied the technique in this book.

Jack Welch's *Winning.*[7] Where do you start to analyze the leadership traits of Jack Welch? The CEO who took General Electric (GE) from being worth $10 billion to $500 billion. *Forbes* magazine crowned him the best business leader of the 20th century. I consider Jack Welch a "paradigm shifter." His book, written with Susy Welch, *Winning* is a must read.

Chan Kim and Renée Mauborgne's *Blue Ocean Shift: Beyond Competing.*[8] This is the practical implementation book that follows on from their *Blue Ocean Strategy* and is the quintessential book on the topic of exploring new opportunities. The writers discovered it is easier to find new areas of business (blue oceans) than fight tooth and nail for a dwindling market (red oceans). Cirque du Soleil is an example of blue ocean thinking. Dance, opera, and circus were merged together into a great new spectacle where there were few competitors. If you are looking to get out of the red oceans, this book is for you.

Jeffrey Liker's *The Toyota Way*[9] explains what makes Toyota so special. How in Toyota every employee is expected to reflect each day "What could I do better tomorrow?" and come up with at least one innovation per month, no matter how small. The Toyota average, internationally, is 10 innovations per employee per year. If you want to learn more on continuous improvement (Kaizen), this is the book to read.

Elizabeth Haas Edersheim's summary of Drucker's work, *The Definitive Drucker: Challengers for Tomorrow's Executives—Final Advice from the Father of Modern Management.*[10] The greatest book ever written on Drucker's work and that includes his own books. I consider Peter Drucker to be the Leonardo da Vinci of management—I believe he will be better understood and respected 400 years from now. All managers and leaders should devour this book and refer to it constantly.

No Formal Education on Performance Measurement

Management, who have yet to receive formal education on performance measurement, are running organizations in both the private and public sectors. Unlike accounting and information systems, where rigorous processes have been formulated, discussed, and taught, performance measurement has been left an orphan of business theory and practice.

The fix: Chapter 12, Implementation Case Studies and Lessons, references the major books in performance measurement.

Confusion on What KPIs Are and What They Can and Should Do

The 2018 *MIT Sloan Management Review* and Google's cross-industry survey[11] asked senior executives to explain how they and their organizations are using KPIs in the digital era. It is probably the largest survey on this topic with more than 3,200 senior executives providing feedback and supported by in-depth interviews with 18 selected executives and thought leaders.

This study found that the measurement leaders, the highest-performing group, in the survey sample:

- *Look to KPIs to help them lead—to find new growth opportunities for their company and new ways to motivate and inspire their teams.*
- *Treat their KPIs not simply as "numbers to hit" but as tools of transformation.*
- *Use KPIs to effectively align people and processes to serve the customer and the brand purpose.*

However, this study lost its way when it confirmed a common misunderstanding by defining KPIs as:

The quantifiable measures an organization uses to determine how well it meets its declared operational and strategic goals.

This definition is flawed on several counts:

1. Measuring progress on the journey to reaching the strategic goals is done by periodic reporting, which will seldom lead to profound alignment of people and processes.
2. It makes the time-honored mistake that all measures are KPIs. How can this be? In the study, the writers acknowledged that "most companies do not deploy KPIs rigorously for review or as drivers of change. In practice, KPIs are regarded as 'key' in name only; the most prevalent attitude toward them seems to be one of compliance, not commitment." The words "key" and "performance" are linked together so that the measure is one that will lead to customer delight and improved financial performance.
3. Reporting progress against goals is necessary, typically done monthly, and is not the real driver for alignment that we seek. I have yet to see

a monthly report that ever created any change. We need 24/7, daily, and weekly warning flags which encourage timely corrective action and thus the monthly progress report should only confirm what we already know.

The fix: Chapter 1, The Great KPI Misunderstanding, clarifies what KPIs are and what they are not.

Too Many of the Wrong Measures

Organizations using the balanced scorecard approach frequently end up with 200–300 measures. I believe an organization only needs up to 100 measures, around 10 KPIs and key result indicators (KRIs) and 80 performance indicators (PIs) and result indicators (RIs). These terms are explained in Chapter 1. Chapters 3 and 6 explain the need for a center of expertise to be established within the organization to design and test measures before they are used.

As has been pointed out to me by Peter Rafferty, we do not just have data lakes; we have data swamps, and his comment on this is very illuminating.

With ever more data (I don't like the term big data), we have ever increasing data swamps. Data "lakes" are more organized. It's VERY easy for people to wade into their swamps and pull out measures for all manner of things: activities, milestones, outputs, and a million things that aren't KPIs. Worse, these all get reported ad nauseam in reports and on cluttered dashboards. Worse yet, organizations—or their consultants making money on it—pride themselves on making up measures. Heck, I saw a bar chart two weeks ago that had a measure of number of measures, not kidding.

Peter Rafferty, Transport Consultant, Gannett Fleming

Many companies are working with the wrong measures. Frequently, the task of finding measures is a task carried out at the last minute by staff members who do not have a clue about what is involved in finding a measure that will create the appropriate behavioral response. Chapter 8 discusses the rules to follow when designing measures.

Another quote, which I received recently, sums this up beautifully.

KPIs should be developed as if scarcity was a key consideration; as if every KPI used comes with a high cost. Asking "If we could only measure or indicate one thing ... what would it be?" is a great place to start in determining KPIs as you find what is really important. Developing KPIs is most effective if there is discussion across the business on what is essential and resist the temptation to measure too many things.

Michael Clark, Founder of Evergood Equestrian Association

The fix: Organizations that have used this methodology have been able to limit the number of performance measures.

Measuring Far Too Much at the Bottom of the Cliff

For far too long organizations have relied too much on "bottom of the cliff" monthly measures that are too late to change events. It is clearly better to catch problems early on rather than measure their impact in the monthly report. Where you need change to occur, 24/7, daily, or weekly measurement has a far better chance to prompt corrective action to take place.

I do not believe there is a monthly KPI on this planet. If a performance indicator is key to the well-being of an organization, surely you would measure it as frequently as possible. This theme is further developed in Chapter 1.

The fix: Organizations that have used this methodology have been able to focus more performance measures into intraday, daily, and weekly measures.

Calling All Measures KPIs

It is a myth to consider all performance measures to be KPIs. Chapter 1, The Great KPI Misunderstanding, explains that there are four types of measures split into two groups. Here are some common measures that are incorrectly called KPIs.

Return on capital employed: This measure has never been a KPI as it cannot be tied down to a manager; it is a result of many activities under different managers. Can you imagine the reaction if a GM was told one morning by the CEO, "Pat, I want you to increase the return on capital employed today." This measure is a key result indicator and is ideal for reporting progress to the board.

Net promoter score: The likelihood of a referral is a result of the many interactions with the customer and is a good key result indicator, ideal for reporting progress to the board. However, instead of looking at this measure management we need to be measuring, on a daily basis, selected measures from the initial touch that we have from our marketing and sales engagements, the delivery and invoicing of a service or product, the service experience, and the way we maintain an ongoing relationship with them.

Revenue per employee: A useful ranking tool when comparing many retail stores with each other providing that you split the stores into leagues, the large stores in prime locations to the stores in small towns with low foot traffic. Again, it is a result indicator, a result of foot traffic, recent promotions, recent competitors' actions, season buying patterns, and the weather.

Economic value added (EVA): A measure dreamed up to take account of the opportunity cost of equity, which is useful as long as the reader understands the measure. It is used periodically and is a result indicator. To arrive at EVA requires a series of adjustments to be made to restate the net profit after tax, including charging economic depreciation and excluding certain noncash adjustments.

Customer satisfaction rate or index: A measured derived from a survey of customers. It has never been a KPI, as it is measured too infrequently, does not tell you what to fix, and often includes all customers when it should be targeted at the profitable customers.

Employee satisfaction rate or index: Like the customer satisfaction measure, it has never been a KPI as it is measured too infrequently and is a result of many events in the past. The KPI that should be measured weekly after the report is out is "How many of the survey recommendations have been implemented?" This KPI has a life of six to eight weeks, after which it is often too late to make the changes. It is far better to run these surveys three to four times a year based on a statistical sample, sharing the results with all staff.

The fix: Chapter 1, The Great KPI Misunderstanding, explains that there are four types of measures split into two groups.

Linking Measures to Performance Pay Schemes

Far too frequently ill-conceived, unfair, and dysfunctional performance-related pay schemes divert wealth into the senior management's pockets at the expense of the long-term viability of the organization.

> *But despite hundreds of research studies over 50 years that tell us that extrinsic motivation* (behavior that is driven by external rewards such as money, fame, grades and praise) *doesn't work, most leaders remain convinced that financial incentives are the key to better performance.*
>
> ***Jeremy Hope***[12]

Performance bonuses give away billions of dollars each year based on methodologies to which little thought has been applied. Who are the performance bonus experts? What qualifications do they possess to work in this important area other than prior experience in creating the mayhem we currently have?

Which bright spark advised the hedge funds to pay a $1 billion bonus to fund managers who create a paper gain that may never eventuate into cash when the stock market turns ugly? These schemes are flawed from the start; "super" profits were being paid out, there is no allowance made for the cost of capital, that in certain markets a fool can make money, and often does, and the bonus schemes are typically only "high side" focused.

A study by consultants William Mercer concluded that most individual merit or performance-based pay plans share two attributes: they absorb vast amounts of management time and resources, and they make everybody unhappy.[13]

In a recent HBR study,[14] conducted on nearly 1,300 private sector organizations, covering some targeted interviews and 14,000 completed questionnaires the survey found:

- Where there were low to medium levels of employee participation in profit-related pay, there was a lower level of job satisfaction, organizational commitment, and trust in management.
- Share ownership among staff had a direct negative relationship with job satisfaction, and no significant relationship with employees' commitment and trust in management.

Yet when we look at most profit-related pay schemes, we find they are heavily stacked toward the senior executive team, and these are often doubled up with share options that give away large, unseen sums to the executive team. One study found that the average US corporation gives around 75 percent of stock options to the top five executives.[15] There are a number of issues with this: first, around 70 percent of the stock price is driven by industry factors;[16] second, it disenfranchises most employees; and last, it distributes an obscene amount of wealth from shareholders to these executives.

Henry Mintzberg believes the incentive system cannot be fixed and should be scrapped altogether.[17] Jensen and Murphy[18] have showed that there is virtually no link between how much CEOs were paid and how well their companies performed.

A common feature of the many failed KPI projects I have heard about is that the cart was put in front of the horse; management was going for a quick fix for the wrong reasons. KPIs were being set up so management could have a hook to hang the bonus structure on. One of the greatest myths of performance measurement is that by linking pay to performance measures you will increase performance. You will merely increase the manipulation of these important measures, undermining them so much that they will become *key political indicators*.

KPIs are a special performance tool, and it is imperative that these are not included in any performance-related pay discussions. KPIs, as defined in Chapter 1, are too important to be gamed by individuals and teams to maximize bonuses. Performance with KPIs should be a "ticket to the game" and not worthy of additional reward.

The balanced scorecard has been manipulated whether it is tied to annual performance bonus or not. As Spitzer says, "The ultimate goal is not the customer—it's often the scorecard." Spitzer has heard executives, when being candid, saying, "We don't worry about strategy; we just move our numbers and get rewarded."

The fix: Organizations including American Express (United States), Dupont (United States), Southwest Airlines (United States), General Electric, Groupe Bull (France), John Lewis Partnership (UK), Leyland Trucks (UK), Marshall Industries (United States), Nucor Steel (United States), Swenka Handelsbanken (Sweden), and Whole Foods Market (United States) have transformed their performance-related pay schemes. To read more, access my working guide on the foundation stones of performance-related pay schemes from www.davidparmenter.com.

> Only when the chief executive officer is passionate and knowledgable about measurement will you have the opportunity to get twenty-first-century measurement to work effectively and efficiently.

Using External Consultants to Deliver a KPI or Balanced Scorecard Project

Peter Drucker observed that many new initiatives failed as the wrong people were leading them. When we recruit a new employee or consultant to undertake a major project, there will be much uncertainty among staff and management. Staff will be wondering, What is going to happen with my job? Are my favorite tasks about to disappear? What effect is this going to have on my pay?

These doubts, along with the added insult of the Porsche Carrera in the visitors' car park, often leads to stonewalling any potential project progress. There may be some staff and management who will do their utmost to make the consultant fail. The consultant, in such circumstances, is given as much chance of success as a mountaineer solo climbing Mount Everest. It can be done but only by a freak of nature.

Instead, Drucker advised that you find a project manager in your organization who holds the highest stack of IOUs. This is one of the seven foundation stones as explained in Chapter 3. Implementing critical success factors and their associated measures has to be managed by an in-house KPI team, schooled and coached by an experienced mentor (a consultant). Where consultants outnumber in-house sourced team members failure is sure to follow.

The fix: Organizations that have used this methodology have implemented their CSFs and associated measures using an in-house team.

A Lack of CEO and Senior Management Commitment to KPIs

As Dean Spitzer[19] argues, one of the fundamental issues of the implementation of performance measurement is measurement leadership. "Only when the chief executive officer (CEO) is passionate and knowledgeable about measurement will you have the opportunity to get twenty-first-century measurement to work effectively and efficiently." Only when the CEO is prepared to be the figurehead of KPI project will it work.

I am hopeful that if you are a CEO and are reading this introduction, you may be sharing with me the opinion that traditional performance management techniques have well and truly broken down.

Like an ocean liner on a journey where the crew on the bridge are constantly measuring distance and direction, CEOs likewise need to evaluate "Are we on the right journey?" "How are we progressing?" and "What needs to be improved to aid our progress?"

Due to your workload as the chief executive officer (CEO), I doubt whether you will have time to read much of this book. That is not such a problem, as I explain in this letter.

Letter to the CEO

David Parmenter, Writer, Speaker, Facilitator
Helping organizations measure, report, and improve performance
PO Box 10686, Wellington, New Zealand
(+64 4) 499 0007
www.davidparmenter.com
30 September 2019

Dear CEO,

Re: Invitation to put winning key performance indicators in your organization

I would like to introduce you to a process that will have a major impact on your organization. It will link you and your staff to the key activities in the organization that have the most impact on the bottom line. If implemented successfully, the CSF and KPI project will have a profound impact, leaving a major legacy.

I would like to wager that you have not carried out an exercise to distinguish your organization's critical success factors from the many success factors you and your senior management team talk about on a regular basis.

I would also point out that much of the reporting you receive, whether it is financial or on performance measures, does not aid your daily decision-making process. The reason for this is because much of

---

the information you receive is monthly data, received far too late to affect any change.

I recommend that you read the following chapters of this book:

Introduction—this covers the major benefits of getting the KPIs right.

Chapter 1, The Great KPI Misunderstanding—this explains the background to a new way of looking at KPIs, considered by many to be a breakthrough in understanding KPIs.

Chapter 2, Myths of Performance Measurement—the reasons why performance measures may not be working in your organization.

Chapter 3, Background to the Winning KPI Methodology.

Chapter 4, Leading and Selling the Change—this chapter will be useful to all managers who are trying to sell an idea.

Chapter 5: Getting the CEO and Senior Management Team Committed to the Change.

Chapter 6: Up-Skill In-House Resources to Manage the KPI Project.

Having read these chapters I am sure you will want to support the winning KPI project with commitment and enthusiasm. My KPI book, *Key Performance Indicators: Developing, Implementing, and Using Winning KPIs*, is designed to be a working manual for the KPI team.

Request your PA to access a recording of me delivering "The Late Planes in the Sky KPI" story. There are a number of recordings on my website. Please invest 20 minutes listening to it as the recording will illustrate the potential of a KPI.

I am hopeful that this book will help your KPI team achieve a significant improvement in performance. I look forward to hearing about your progress.

Kind regards,
David Parmenter
parmenter@waymark.co.nz
P.S. Please feel free to ring me +64 4 499 0007

The fix: Organizations where the CEO has shown measurement leadership and attended the two-day CSF workshop have been successful with their KPI project implementation.

Operating without Ascertaining the Organization's Critical Success Factors

When visiting an organization, I always look around at the walls. If I am unable to see posters with the critical success factors (CSFs), I know immediately that the organization does not have this clarity. I believe that not knowing your organization's CSFs is like going to soccer's World Cup without a goalkeeper, or, at best, an incompetent one.

The definition I use for the CSFs is

The list of issues or aspects of organizational performance that determine ongoing health, vitality, and well-being.[20]

The fix: How to ascertain your organization's CSFs is covered in Chapter 7, Finding Your Organization's Critical Success Factors. The process has been road tested in many organizations leaving a profound legacy.

Allowing Short-Term Thinking to Override the Greater Good

As Professor Tom Johnson points out, "A finance orientated growth strategy is the belief that profitability improves by taking steps aimed at increasing revenue and cutting costs. While such steps embody impeccable arithmetic logic, they ignore the reality that long-term profitability results from satisfied customers and focused operations."[21]

Arie de Geus[22] has discovered that long-term organizations did not see themselves as primarily economic units to produce profits and value for the entrepreneur and the shareholder. They saw themselves as living systems composed of other living systems.

The drive to meet short-term sales targets and gain substantial bonuses has led to some classic problems. GM and Ford have decimated their brands by heavily discounting cars to get volume. It has become so prevalent that it is now expected by customers.

The large multinationals who drive their business each quarter to meet a predetermined target, ignoring comparing their performance to the marketplace, are like lemmings running toward the cliffs and the abyss.

In fact, it may be a natural phenomenon that organizations over a certain size are eventually doomed to fail as they suffer from many of the harmful issues listed here.

The fix: Toyota sets a shining example of how a large corporation can put the long term above the needs of the immediate future.

A Failure Rate with Projects That Matches the Failure Rate of Race Horse Ownership

Far too many projects are started in organizations due to our addiction for the new and our boredom with projects that appear to be grinding to a halt. Managers would far rather let a project die than risk committing to it and finding out they now have a failure tag around their neck.

Projects are started without an understanding of how to sell and lead change, resulting in management and staff eventually killing off the project as their "default future" vision was not challenged and changed.

The fix: How to solve the completion dilemma and selling change is covered in this book.

Setting Annual Targets When You Cannot See into the Future

All forms of annual targets are doomed to failure. Far too often management spends months arguing about what is a realistic target, when the only sure thing is that it will be wrong. It will be either too soft or too hard. How can you set an annual sales target unless you can see into the future?

The striving to meet the quarter-end and year-end numbers by fair means or foul, by taking on excessive risk that seldom is taken into account, has led to the demise of once noble institutions that had survived for multiple decades, such as Northern Rock, Lehman Brothers, Merrill Lynch, and Bear Sterns. These organizations would have had a different future if executives had looked at performance differently.

Far too frequently organizations end up paying incentives to management when in fact they have lost market share. In other words, rising sales did not keep up with the growth rate in the marketplace. As Jeremy Hope[23] points out, not setting an annual target beforehand is not a problem as long as staff members are given regular updates about how they are progressing against their peers and the rest of the market. Jeremy Hope argues that if you do not know how hard you have to work to get a maximum bonus, you will work as hard as you can.

Jack Welch[24] when at General Electric rewarded subsidiaries who in a difficult trading year sold less than previous years but had managed to increase their market share.

The fix: Progressive organizations around the world, such as Whole Foods Market (USA), American Express, (USA), Statoil (Norway), Ahlsell (Sweden), General Electric, W.L. Gore & Associates (USA), Swenka Handelsbanken (Sweden), and Tomkins (UK), have moved away from the annual planning cycle to a rolling quarterly planning process.

The fix: The work of Jeremy Hope clearly spells out an alternative solution.

Suggested Chapter Reading by Reader Designation

This book is a resource for anyone in the organization involved with the development and use of KPIs. It is desirable that all KPI project team members, the external project facilitator, team coordinators, and local facilitators (if required) have their own copy to ensure all staff follow the same plan. Team members are expected to take the book with them when meeting staff and management, as they will be able to clarify issues by using examples from the book.

Exhibit I.4 Recommended Reading

	Section title	Board	CEO and SMT	KPI project team, external facilitator	Team coordinators
	Introduction	✓	✓	✓	✓
Stage 1: Getting the enterprise committed to the change and up-skilling an in-house KPI team					
Chapter 1	The Great KPI Misunderstanding	✓	✓	✓	✓
Chapter 2	The Myths of Performance Measurement	✓	✓	✓	✓

(continued)

Exhibit I.4 (*Continued*)

	Section title	Board	CEO and SMT	KPI project team, external facilitator	Team coordinators
Chapter 3	Background to the Winning KPI Methodology		✓	✓	✓
Chapter 4.	Leading and Selling the Change		✓	✓	
Chapter 5	Getting the CEO and Senior Management Committed to the Change		✓	✓	
Chapter 6	Up-Skill In-House Resources to Manage the KPI Project		✓	✓	
Stage 2: Ascertaining the operational critical success factors (the aspects that need to be done well day-in day-out)					
Chapter 7	Finding Your Organization's Operational Critical Success Factors			✓	✓
Stage 3: Determining measures and getting them to work					
Chapter 8	Characteristics of Meaningful Measures			✓	✓
Chapter 9	Designing and Refining Measures			✓	✓
Chapter 10	Reporting Performance Measures			✓	✓
Chapter 11	Ongoing Support and Refinement of KPIs and CSFs			✓	✓

Exhibit I.4 (*Continued*)

	Section title	Board	CEO and SMT	KPI project team, external facilitator	Team coordinators
Chapter 12	Implementation Case Studies and Lessons			✓	
Appendix	Performance Measures Database			✓	

Note: SMT = senior management team

The recommended reading is set out in Exhibit I.4.

Why Owners of My Previous Editions Should Buy the Fourth Edition

When I wrote the first edition, I deliberately cocooned myself from outside influences other than my experiences and the KPI manual.[25] Since 2007 I have been an avid reader of performance management and measurement literature and have met thousands of people through my keynote addresses and workshops. This additional knowledge has combined to produce this fourth edition.

With my advancing years has come, I hope, some wisdom. In writing this edition I have experienced a number of Aha! moments that I hope will add some extra clarity. The layout and structure of the chapters has gone through a substantial upgrade.

The book has been improved by:

- Simplifying and refining the Winning KPI process into three concise stages
- Reorganizing chapters to make the book easy to use and removing duplication
- Refining the "Leading and selling the change" process by incorporating more reference to the psychology of change resistance
- A list of dysfunctional measures to avoid

- A new chapter on the characteristics of meaningful measures
- Incorporating new methods I have used in more recent KPI implementations
- Developing new diagrams, templates, and exercises to assist the KPI team with the implementation
- An improved performance measures database

Since the last edition I have invested a large amount of time to advance the winning KPI methodology. It is available to you for a small investment of money and a large investment of your time. The new simplified approach is summarized in Exhibit I.5.

Exhibit I.5 A Summary of the New Simplified Approach

Task	Description
1.1 Sell the KPI project to the CEO, the senior management team, and the organization's oracles. (See Chapters 4 and 5.)	The project starts off with a well-practiced elevator pitch, followed by a compelling presentation and then a focus group workshop to get the green light from the organization's oracles.
1.2 Locate an external facilitator to mentor the KPI team. (See Chapter 5.)	An external facilitator will help guide the organization with regard to timings, selection and size of KPI team, and what needs to be abandoned to make room for the KPI project.
1.3 Train a small KPI team. (See Chapter 6.)	The external facilitator helps train a small in-house KPI team and ensures that the KPI team leader has a cluster of mentors supporting them. Working with the organization's oracles, the KPI team develops a blueprint for the implementation that will cover where the KPI project will be piloted.
1.4 Sell the KPI project to all employees to encourage their participation in the two-day performance measures workshops. (See Chapter 4.)	Employees who are to attend the two-day performance measures workshop need to be convinced that it is an important exercise worthy of their participation.

Exhibit I.5 *(Continued)*

Task	Description
2.1 Locate the existing success factors and desired external outcomes from documentation and interviews. (See Chapter 7.)	Determine what your organization's success factors and desired external outcomes are.
2.2 Run the two-day critical success factors workshop to ascertain the critical success factors. (See Chapter 7.)	Map the sphere of influence each success factor has to ascertain to understand which ones have the most significant impact. These are the critical success factors. Present these to all staff.
3.1 Run the two-day performance measures workshops to train all the remaining relevant staff to develop meaningful measures. (See Chapters 8 and 9.)	Select representatives across the organization to attend a two-day workshop to be trained in the methodology, as well as how and why the organization has chosen its CSFs. Attendees will be shown how to design appropriate measures from the CSFs and how to get a mix of past, current, and future measures.
3.2 Refine the measures after the performance measures workshops. (See Chapter 9.)	KPI team will delete duplicated and inferior indicators, remove those measures where the cost of data extraction is greater than the derived benefit, and reword all indicators to improve their understanding.
3.3 Hold a performance measures gallery to weed out dysfunctional and poor measures. (See Chapter 9.)	Hold a "measures gallery" where staff are invited to share their views on the measures that have been displayed on the walls of the project team's room.
3.4 Ask all teams to select their team performance measures from the finalized database of measures. (See Chapter 9.)	Teams select the relevant measures and indicate their selection in the database.

(continued)

Exhibit I.5 (*Continued*)

Task	Description
3.5 Find the key result indicators (KRIs) and the key performance indicators (KPIs). (See Chapter 9.)	Ascertain the eight to twelve KRIs that will be reported to the Board to show how the organization is performing. Ascertain the winning KPIs, ensuring they have the seven characteristics discussed in Chapter 1. Commence the testing of the KPIs in three designated areas.
3.6 Design the reporting framework. (See Chapter 10.)	The intraday, daily, weekly, monthly, and quarterly progress reports are designed utilizing best practice visualization techniques. Utilize existing technology so that the CEO can receive intraday updates on a smart phone and laptop.
3.7 Help facilitate the appropriate use of the selected performance measures by all the teams in the organization. (See Chapter 11.)	For several months, the KPI team will be required to ensure the reporting of measures is prepared on time and correctly and that corrective actions are undertaken where necessary. There will need to be a program to roll out KPI training to existing and new staff.
3.8 Refine CSFs and associated measures after one year of use. (See Chapter 11.)	A review should be undertaken to assess what modifications, if any, are needed to the existing CSFs and measures.

PDF Toolkit

With all my books there is a heavy focus on implementation. The purpose of this book is to prepare the route forward for the KPI team, to second-guess the barriers the finance team will need to cross and set out the major tasks they will need to undertake. Naturally, each implementation will reflect the organization's culture, future-ready status, and the level of commitment from the CEO, the in-house KPI team, and the organization's staff.

The PDF toolkit is to be read and used in conjunction with *Key Performance Indicators: Developing, Implementing, and Using Winning*

KPIs (fourth edition). The location of the templates is indicated in the relevant chapters with this icon:

To support your implementing the strategies and best practices in this book, the following electronic media are available:

- Webcasts and recorded presentations (see www.davidparmenter.com/ webcasts). Some of these are free to everyone, and some are accessed via a third party for a fee.
- A PDF download of the checklists, draft agendas, questionnaires, and worksheets referred to in the chapters are available from kpi .davidparmenter.com/fourthedition. The website will refer to a word from a specific page in this book that you need to use as a password to access these for free.
- The electronic versions of all the forms, instructions, templates, and most of the report formats featured in the book can be purchased from www.davidparmenter.com.
- For small to medium-sized enterprises (SMEs) I have developed two special toolkits consisting of electronic versions of all the forms, instructions, templates, and most of the report formats. One tailored to suit SMEs with 100–250 full-time employees (FTEs) and one for SMEs with less than 100 FTEs. These toolkits are available from kpi.david parmenter.com/fourthedition.

For example, the PDF includes the following to support this introduction:

- Overview of Toyota's 14 management principles
- Overview of the advice from paradigm shifters such as Peter Drucker, Jim Collins, Jack Welch, Tom Peters, Gary Hamel, Jeremy Hope relevant to a KPI project
- "Getting the Right Consultants on the Bus" by David Parmenter, Finance Management Faculty, ICAEW, December 2013

Notes

1. Steve Jobs's 2005 Stanford Commencement Address, "Your Time Is Limited, So Don't Waste It Living Someone Else's Life," (www.huffingtonpost.com).

2. Dean R. Spitzer, *Transforming Performance Measurement: Rethinking the Way We Measure and Drive Organizational Success* (New York: AMACOM, 2007).

3. Dean R. Spitzer, *Transforming Performance Measurement: Rethinking the Way We Measure and Drive Organizational Success* (New York: AMACOM, 2007).

4. Jeremy Hope, *The Leader's Dilemma: How to Build an Empowered and Adaptive Organization without Losing Control* (San Francisco: Jossey-Bass, 2011).

5. Jeremy Hope, *The Leader's Dilemma: How to Build an Empowered and Adaptive Organization without Losing Control* (San Francisco: Jossey-Bass, 2011).

6. Tom Peters, *Thriving on Chaos: Handbook for a Management Revolution* (New York: Harper Perennial 1988).

7. Jack Welch and Suzy Welch, *Winning* (New York: HarperBusiness, 2005).

8. Chan Kim and Renée Mauborgne, *Blue Ocean Shift: Beyond Competing—Proven Steps to Inspire Confidence and Seize New Growth* (New York: Hachette Books, 2017).

9. Jeffrey K. Liker, *The Toyota Way* (New York: McGraw-Hill, 2003).

10. Elizabeth Haas Edersheim, *The Definitive Drucker: Challenger for Tomorrow's Executives—Final Advice from the Father of Modern Management* (New York: McGraw-Hill, 2006).

11. Michael Schrage and David Kiron, "Leading with Next-Generation Key Performance Indicators." The 2018 *MIT Sloan Management Review* and Google's cross-industry survey, Research Report.

12. Jeremy Hope and Robin Fraser, *Beyond Budgeting: How Managers Can Break Free from the Annual Performance Trap* (Boston: Harvard Business Review Press, 2003).

13. Jeffrey Pfeffer, "Six Dangerous Myths About Pay," *Harvard Business Review* (May–June 1998): 109–119.

14. Chidiebere Ogbonnaya, Kevin Daniels, and Karina Nielsen, "How Incentive Pay Affects Employee Engagement, Satisfaction, and Trust," *Harvard Business Review*, Digital Article (March 2017).

15. Fast Company Staff, "I No Longer Want to Work for Money" (www.fastcompany.com, February 2007).

16. J. C. De Swann and Neil W. C. Harper, "Getting What You Pay for with Stock Options," *McKinsey Quarterly*, no. 1 (2003).

17. Henry Mintzberg, "No More Executive Bonuses," *Sloan Management Review* (November 2009).

18. Michael C. Jensen and Kevin J. Murphy, "CEO Incentives—It's Not How Much You Pay, But How," *Harvard Business Review*, no. 3 (May–June 1990): 138–153.

19. Dean R. Spitzer, *Transforming Performance Measurement: Rethinking the Way We Measure and Drive Organizational Success* (New York: AMACOM, 2007.

20. AusIndustries, *Key Performance Indicators Manual: A Practical Guide for the Best Practice Development, Implementation and Use of KPIs* (Business & Professional Publishing, 1999). Now out of print.

21. H. Thomas Johnson, "Financial Results Are a By-Product of Well-Run Human-Faced Organizations," *The Leading Edge*, February 18, 2010, p. 462.

22. Randall Rothenberg, "Arie de Gerus: The Thought Leader Interview," *Strategy and Business*, Issue 23 (2001).

23. Jeremy Hope, *The Leader's Dilemma: How to Build an Empowered and Adaptive Organization without Losing Control* (San Francisco: Jossey-Bass, 2011).

24. Jack Welch and Suzy Welch, *Winning* (New York: HarperBusiness, 2005).

25. AusIndustries, *Key Performance Indicators Manual: A Practical Guide for the Best Practice Development, Implementation and Use of KPIs* (Aus-Industries, 1996). Now out of print.

Key Performance Indicators

Overview

Many companies are working with the wrong measures, many of which are incorrectly termed key performance indicators (KPIs). It is a myth to consider all performance measures to be KPIs. This chapter explores how the four types of performance measures differ with examples of each type. The seven characteristics of KPIs are defined. The confusion over whether measures are lead or lag indicators is addressed. The questions *How many measures should we have?* and *How many of each measure type?* are answered. The importance of timely measurement is also covered.

Key learning points from the chapter are:

1. Clarity over the different types of measures, *result indicators* and *performance indicators*
2. The definition of a KPI
3. British Airways late planes KPI story
4. The seven characteristics of KPIs
5. The 10/80/10 rule
6. The lead or lag debate is finally buried
7. The need to have more *current-* and *future*-oriented measures that act like a fence at the top of the cliff
8. Avoid measuring too much and measuring too late

CHAPTER 1

The Great KPI Misunderstanding

For far too long organizations have measured too much, with the cost often outweighing the benefit of the measurement. They have relied too much on financial measures and have used "bottom of the cliff" monthly measures that are too late to change events. Added to this mix is often a balanced scorecard, driven by consultants, at great expense and populated by measures designed by managers to keep the boss happy. A mess of epic proportions.

> There are four types of performance measures, and thus it is a myth to consider all measures as KPIs.

The Four Types of Performance Measures

From my research over the past 30 years I have come to the conclusion that there are four types of performance measures, and thus it is a myth to consider all measures as KPIs. These four measures are in two groups: *result indicators* and *performance indicators*.

I use the term *result indicators* to reflect the fact that many measures are a summation of more than one team's input. These measures are useful in looking at the combined teamwork but, unfortunately, do not help management fix a problem, as it is difficult to pinpoint which teams were responsible for the performance or nonperformance.

Performance indicators, on the other hand, are measures that can be tied to a team or a cluster of teams working closely together for a common purpose. Good or bad performance is now the responsibility of one team. These measures thus give clarity and ownership.

With both these measures some are more important, so we use the extra word "key." Thus, we now have two measures for each measure type:

1. Key result indicators (KRIs) give the board an overall summary of how the organization is performing.

2. Result indicators (RIs) tell management how teams are combining to produce results.

3. Performance indicators (PIs) tell management what teams are delivering.

4. Key performance indicators (KPIs) tell management how the organization is performing 24/7, daily, or weekly in their critical success factors, and by taking action management is able to increase performance dramatically.

Many performance measures used by organizations are result indicators and it is thus, no wonder, why reporting these measures has not improved performance. First, I will describe each type of measure.

Key Result Indicators

What are key result indicators (KRIs)? KRIs are measures that often have been mistaken for KPIs. The common characteristics of these measures is that they are the result of many actions carried out by many teams over a period of time, hence the use of the term "result," and they are good summary measures, hence the term "key." These key result indicators should be reviewed typically at the bimonthly or quarterly board meetings giving the board an understanding as to how the organization is progressing with its strategy. KRIs are always a past measure.

Key result indicators are of little use to management as they are reported too late to change direction, nor do they tell you what you need to do to improve these results. You know you have a KRI when the CEO is the person ultimately responsible for the measure. For the private sector, key result indicators would include:

- Net profit before tax
- Net profit on key product lines

- Customer satisfaction (by customer group, showing the trend over an 18-month period)
- Return on capital employed
- Employee satisfaction (by groups showing the trend over an 18-month period)

For government and nonprofit agencies these measures would also include:

- Availability of the major services that are offered, e.g., average waiting time for service
- On-time implementation of infrastructure projects
- Membership numbers (for professional organizations)

Separating KRIs from other measures has a profound impact on reporting, resulting in a separation of performance measures into those impacting governance and those impacting management. Accordingly, an organization should have a Board Dashboard consisting of up to 10 KRIs for the board, and a series of management reports reporting progress in various intervals during the month depending on the significance of the measure. These reports are illustrated in Chapter 10.

Result Indicators

Result indicators (RIs) summarize the activity of more than one team. They are good to review as an overview of how teams are working together. The difference between a key result indicator and a result indicator is simply that the key result indicator is a more overall and more important summary of activities that have taken place.

When you look at a financial measure, you will note that you have assigned a value to various activities that have taken place. In other words, financial indicators are a result of activities. I thus believe all financial performance measures are RIs. Daily or weekly sales analysis is a very useful summary, but it is a result of the effort of a number of teams: from the sales team to the teams involved in manufacture, quality assurance, and dispatch. Financial indicators are useful but mask the real drivers of the performance. To fully understand what to increase or decrease, we need to look at the activities that created the financial indicator.

5

Key performance indicators (KPIs) are those indicators that focus on the aspects of organizational performance that are the most critical for the current and future success of the organization.

Result indicators look at activity over a wider time horizon. They not only measure quarterly and monthly results but also weekly, daily activities, and future planned events. For the private sector, result indicators that lie beneath KRIs could include:

- Sales made yesterday
- Number of initiatives implemented from the recent customer satisfaction survey
- Number of planned initiatives to be implemented next month to improve the timeliness of _____
- Number of initiatives implemented from the staff survey
- Number of employees' suggestions implemented in the past 30 days
- In-house courses scheduled to be held within three weeks where attendee numbers are below target
- Number of managers who have not attended leadership training (reported quarterly, by manager level)
- Number of staff trained to use specified systems (key systems only)

For government and nonprofit agencies, result indicators would also include:

- Weekly hospital bed utilization
- Percent coverage of [Enterprise Name]'s supported services
- Number of people on treatment/tested for [Disease Name 1], [Disease Name 2], and for [Disease Name 3]
- Grants achieving their public health targets as per grant agreements
- Percentage of investments covering low-income, high disease-burdened countries

Key Performance Indicators

Key performance indicators (KPIs) are those indicators that focus on the aspects of organizational performance that are the most critical for the current and future success of the organization.

KPIs are rarely new to the organization. Either they have not been recognized, or they were gathering dust somewhere unknown to the current management team. KPIs can be illustrated by two examples.

Example: An Airline KPI

My favorite KPI story is about a senior British Airways official who set about turning British Airways (BA) around in the 1980s by reportedly concentrating on one KPI.

The senior BA official employed some consultants to investigate and report on the key measures he should concentrate on to turn around the ailing airline. They came back and told the senior BA official that he needed to focus on one critical success factor (CSF), the timely arrival and departure of airplanes. The consultants must have gone through a sifting process sorting out the success factors that were critical from those that were less important. Ascertaining the five to eight CSFs is a vital step in any KPI exercise, and one seldom performed. In Exhibit 1.1 the CSFs are shown as the larger circles in the diagram.

The senior BA official was, I am sure, initially not impressed, as everybody in the industry knows the importance of timely planes.

However, the consultants then pointed out that this is where the KPIs lay, and they proposed that he focus on a late plane KPI. He was notified,

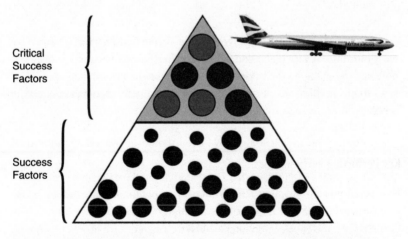

Critical
Success
Factors

Success
Factors

Exhibit 1.1 The Importance of Knowing Your Critical Success Factors

wherever he was in the world, if a BA plane was delayed over a certain time. The BA airport manager at the relevant airport knew that if a plane was delayed beyond a certain "threshold," they would receive a personal call from the senior BA official (let's call him Sam). I imagine the conversation going like this:

> *"Pat, it's Sam on the phone. I am ringing up about BA135 that left Kennedy Airport over two and a quarter hours late, what happened?" Pat replies, "There is an easy explanation to this late plane Sam. The system will tell you that the plane was late leaving Hawaii. In fact, it was one and three quarters hours late and everything was in order at our end except an elderly passenger got lost in the duty-free shopping area. We had to offload their bags and, as you can see, we did it in record time, only half an hour—a time I wish to celebrate with my team next week!"*
>
> *"Pat, how long have you worked for British Airways?"*
>
> *Pat, now realizing this conversation is not going well, responded, "About 30 years, Sam."*
>
> *"In fact, Pat, it is 32. So, with 32 years of experience with us you are telling me that with six hours of advance notice that the plane was already late, you and your team could do nothing to reduce the delay, and instead you added half an hour to an already late plane. Quite frankly Pat, I am disappointed, as you and your team are better than this!"*

Pat and many others employed by the airline had the "not invented by us" syndrome. A late plane created by another BA team was their problem not ours. Pat gathered the troops the next day and undertook many proactive steps to ensure they recaptured the lost time, no matter who had created the problem. Actions such as:

- Doubling up the cleaning crew, even though there was an additional external cost to this.
- Communicating to the refueling team which planes were a priority.
- Providing the external caterers with late-plane updates so they could better manage re-equipping the late plane.
- Staff on the check-in counters asked to watch out for at-risk customers and chaperone them to the gate.

■ Not allowing the business class passenger to check in late, yet again. This time saying, "Sorry Mr. Carruthers, we will need to reschedule you as you are too late to risk your bags missing this plane. It is on a tight schedule. I am sure you are aware that the deadline for boarding passed over 30 minutes ago."

The BA managers at the relevant airport knew that if a plane was delayed beyond a certain threshold, they would receive a personal call from Sam. It was not long before BA planes had a reputation for leaving on time.

The late-planes KPI worked because it was linked to most of the critical success factors for the airline. It linked to the "delivery in full and on time" critical success factor, namely the "timely arrival and departure of airplanes," and it linked to the "timely maintenance of planes" critical success factor.

It is interesting that Ryanair, a low-cost Irish airline, has a major focus on timeliness of planes. They know that is where they make money, often getting an extra European flight each day out of a plane due to their swift turnaround and their uncompromising stand against late check-in. They simply do not allow customers to get in the way of their tight schedules.

The late-planes KPI affected many aspects of the business. Late planes:

1. Increased cost in many ways, including additional airport surcharges and the cost of accommodating passengers overnight as a result of planes having a delayed departure due to late-night noise restrictions.
2. Increased customer dissatisfaction leading to passengers trying other airlines and changing over to their loyalty programs.
3. Alienated potential future customers as those relatives, friends, or work colleagues inconvenienced by the late arrival of the passenger avoided future flights with the airline.
4. Had a negative impact on staff development as they learned to replicate the bad habits that created late planes.
5. Adversely affected supplier relationships and maintenance scheduling.
6. Increased employee dissatisfaction, as they were constantly firefighting and dealing with frustrated customers.

Example: A Distribution Company KPI

A distribution company's chief executive officer (CEO) realized that a critical success factor for the business was for trucks to leave as close to capacity as possible. Where trucks were sent out underweight, he would ring them.

KPIs have seven
characteristics.

"Pat, it's Sam on the phone. I am ringing up about the truck that was sent to Alice Springs yesterday with only ten tons on it. What happened?" Pat replies, "There is an easy explanation. We had agreed to a delivery date, and there was no other freight going to that town. I am a stickler for ensuring we deliver every item on time to customers, Sam."

"Pat, you have worked for us for 12 years and are one of our most experienced dispatchers, and you know that making calls to customers to optimize our truck fleet is the most important part of your job. I am disappointed, Pat, as I know you are better than this!"

In both examples the impact on profitability was significant, and staff members did their utmost to avoid a career-limiting phone call from the CEO. (Both these examples are provided in greater detail in my webcast, "Introduction to Winning KPIs," which can be accessed via www.davidparmenter.com.)

The Seven Characteristics of KPIs

From extensive analysis and from discussions with over 3,000 participants in my KPI workshops, covering most organization types in the public and private sectors, I have concluded that KPIs have seven characteristics, as set out in Exhibit 1.2.

Exhibit 1.2 The Seven Characteristics of KPIs

Nonfinancial	Nonfinancial measures (e.g., not expressed in dollars, yen, pounds, euros, etc.)
Timely	Measured frequently (e.g., 24/7, daily, or weekly)
CEO focus	Acted upon by the CEO and senior management team
Simple	All staff understand the measure and what corrective action is required
Team based	A team can be phoned, and they will accept responsibility, and can take action to improve measure
Significant impact	Major impact on the organization's critical success factors
Limited dark side	Have been tested to ensure that they have a positive impact on performance, with any unintended consequence being of minor significance

Non financial. When you put a dollar, yen, pound, or euro sign on a measure, you have already converted it into a result indicator (e.g., daily sales are a result of activities that have taken place to create the sales). The KPI lies deeper down. It may be the number of visits to contacts with the key customers who make up most of the profitable business.

Timely. KPIs should be monitored 24/7, daily, or perhaps weekly for some. A monthly, quarterly, or annual measure cannot be a KPI, as it cannot be key to your business if you are monitoring it well after the horse has bolted. I have yet to see a monthly performance measure improve performance.

CEO focus. All KPIs will have the CEO's constant attention with daily calls being made to the relevant staff enquiring about exceptions or recognizing their outstanding performance. Staff will perceive talking about poor performance with the CEO, on a regular basis, as career-limiting and will take innovative steps to prevent recurrences.

Simple. A KPI should tell you what action needs to be taken. The British Airways late-planes KPI communicated immediately to everyone that there needed to be a focus on recovering the lost time. Cleaners, caterers, baggage handlers, flight attendants, and front desk staff would all work some magic to save a minute here and a minute there while maintaining or improving service standards.

Team based. A KPI is deep enough in the organization that it can be tied to a team. In other words, the CEO can call someone and ask, "Why did this happen?" and that manager will take on the responsibility to fix the issue. Return on capital employed has never been a KPI, because the CEO would get nowhere saying to a GM, "Pat, I want you to increase the return on capital employed today."

Significant impact. A KPI will affect a number of the organization's critical success factors. In other words, when the CEO, management, and staff focus on the KPI, the organization scores goals in many directions.

Limited dark side. All measures have a dark side, an unintended consequence where staff will take some remedial actions that will be contrary to the desired intentions. Before becoming a KPI, a performance measure needs to be tested to ensure that it helps teams to align their behavior in a coherent way to the benefit of the organization. The possible unintended consequence associated with measuring all the selected KPIs being checked to ensure they are not major or of significance.

11

For the private sector, key performance indicators that fit the characteristics I have proposed could include:

- Number of CEO recognitions planned for next week or the next two weeks—reported weekly to the CEO
- Staff in vital positions who have handed in their notice in the last hour—reported within one hour to the CEO
- Late deliveries to key customers—reported daily to the CEO
- Key position job offers issued to candidates that are more than three days outstanding—reported daily to the CEO
- List of late projects, by manager, reported weekly to the senior management team—reported weekly to the CEO
- Number of vacant places at an important in-house course—reported daily to the CEO in the last three weeks before the course is due to run
- Number of initiatives implemented after the staff-satisfaction survey—reported weekly to the CEO for up to two months after survey
- Number of innovations planned for implementation in the next 30, 60, or 90 days—reported weekly to the CEO
- Number of abandonments to be actioned in the next 30, 60, or 90 days—reported weekly to the CEO
- Complaints from key customers that have not been resolved within two hours—reported 24/7 to CEO and GMs
- Key customer enquiries that have not been responded to by the sales team for over 24 hours—reported daily to the GM
- Date of next visit to major customers by customer name—reported weekly to CEO and GMs

For government and nonprofit agencies, key performance indicators could also include:

- Emergency response time over a given duration—reported immediately to the CEO
- Number of confirmed volunteers to be street collectors for the annual street appeal—reported daily to the CEO in the four to six weeks before the appeal day
- Date of next new service initiative—reported weekly to the CEO

12

Performance Indicators

Performance indicators (PIs) are those indicators that are nonfinancial (otherwise they would be result indicators) that can be traced back to a team. The difference between performance indicators and KPIs is that the latter are deemed fundamental to the organization's well-being. Performance indicators, although important, are thus not crucial to the business. The performance indicators help teams to align themselves with their organization's strategy. Performance indicators complement the KPIs; they are shown on the organization, division, department, and team scorecards.

> An organization, with over 500 FTEs, will have about 10 KRIs, up to 80 RIs and PIs, and 10 KPIs.

For the private sector, performance indicators could include:

- Abandonment rate at call center—callers giving up waiting
- Late deliveries to other customers (excluding key customers)
- Planned abandonments of reports, meetings, processes that are no longer functioning
- Number of innovations implemented by each team/division
- Sales calls organized for the next week, two weeks, and so forth
- Number of training hours booked for next month, months two and three, and months four to six—in both external and internal courses

For government and nonprofit agencies, performance indicators could also include:

- Number of media coverage events planned for next month, months two to three, and months four to six
- Date of next customer focus group
- Date of next research project into customer needs and ideas

Number of Measures Required: The 10/80/10 Rule

How many measures should we have? How many of each measure type? What time frames are they measured in? To answer these questions, I devised, more than 10 years ago, the 10/80/10 rule, as illustrated in Exhibit 1.3. I believe an organization with over 500 FTEs will have about 10 KRIs, up to 80 RIs and PIs, and 10 KPIs. These numbers are the upper limits and, in many cases, fewer measures will suffice.

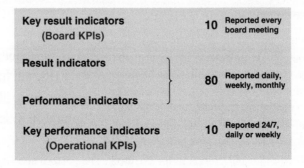

Exhibit 1.3 The 10/80/10 Rule for the Number of Measures

For smaller organizations, the major change would be a reduction in the number of RIs and PIs. Reporting up to 10 KRIs to the board or governing body is entirely logical. We do not want to bury them in too much detail. A Board Dashboard can easily be designed to show these KRIs along with a summary financials all on one fan-fold (A3) page, as shown in Chapter 10.

For many organizations, 80 RIs and PIs will at first appear totally inadequate. Yet, on investigation, you will find that separate teams are actually working with variations of the same indicator, so it is better to standardize them (e.g., a "number of training days attended in the past month" performance measure should have the same definition and the same graph).

When we look at the characteristics of KPIs one will see that these measures are indeed rare and that many organizations will operate very successfully with no more than 10 KPIs. Kaplan and Norton[1] recommend no more than 20 KPIs and Hope and Fraser[2] suggest fewer than 10 KPIs. KPI project teams may, at first, feel that having only 10 KPIs is too restrictive and thus increase the number of KPIs to 30 or so. With careful analysis, that number will soon be reduced to the 10 suggested, unless the organization is composed of many businesses from very different sectors. If that is the case, the 10/80/10 rule can apply to each diverse business, providing it is large enough to warrant its own KPI rollout.

As explained in Chapter 2, it is a myth that the more measures there are, the better performance measurement will be. In fact, as has no doubt been witnessed by many readers, the reverse is true. I believe the 10/80/10 rule is a good guide, as it appears to have withstood the test of time.

14

Difference between KRIs and KPIs and RIs and PIs

During workshops, one question emerges time and time again: "What are the differences between KRIs and KPIs, and RIs and PIs?" Exhibits 1.4 and 1.5 clarify these differences.

Exhibit 1.4 Difference between KRIs and KPIs

KRIs	KPIs
Can be financial or nonfinancial (e.g., return on capital employed and customer satisfaction percentage).	Nonfinancial measures (not expressed in dollars, yen, pound, euros, etc.).
Measured monthly, bimonthly, and quarterly.	Measured frequently (e.g., 24/7, daily, or weekly).
Reported at the board meetings as a good summary of progress to date (e.g., seen as an outcome measure).	Available to all staff so action can be taken.
It does not help staff or management because nowhere does it tell you what you need to fix.	All staff understand the measure and what corrective action is required.
Commonly, the only person responsible for a KRI is the CEO.	Responsibility can be tied down to a team or a cluster of teams working closely together.
A KRI is designed to summarize progress in a particular area. Tends to focus on the external critical success factors as seen through the board members' eyes.	Significant impact (e.g., it impacts on more than one internal critical success factor).
A KRI is a result of many activities managed through a variety of performance measures.	Focuses on a specific activity.
Normally reported by way of a trend graph covering at least the past 15 months of activity.	Normally reported by way of an intranet screen indicating activity, person responsible, past history, so that a meaningful phone call can be made.

Exhibit 1.5 Difference between RIs and PIs

RIs	PIs
Can be financial and nonfinancial.	Mainly nonfinancial measures (not expressed in dollars, yen, pound, euros, etc.).
Measured more frequently as monthly or sometimes quarterly measures.	Measured more frequently as daily, weekly, biweekly, or monthly.
Designed to summarize overall performance by a collection of diverse teams.	Tied to a discrete activity, and thus to a team, or a cluster of teams who work closely together.
A result of more than one activity.	Focuses on a specific activity.
Does not tell you what you need to do more or less of.	All staff understand what action is required to improve performance.
Normally reported in a division/ department scorecard summarizing various team performance.	Normally reported in a team scorecard.

When sorting through measures I use the following simple set of rules:

1. If it is a financial indicator—it can never be a KPI.
2. If the time period is longer than a week—it can never be a KPI.
3. If you cannot find a manager to phone who will accept responsibility for performance—it can never be a KPI.

The Lead and Lag Confusion

Many management books that cover KPIs talk about lead and lag indicators; this merely clouds the KPI debate. Using the new way of looking at performance measures, we dispense with the terms *lag* (outcome) and *lead* (performance driver) indicators. At my seminars, when the audience is asked, "Is the late-planes-in-the-air KPI a lead indicator or a lag indicator?" the vote count is always evenly split. The late plane in the sky is certainly both a lead and a lag indicator. It talks about the past, and it is about to create a future problem when it lands. Surely this is enough proof that the labeling of measures as lead-and-lag indicators is misleading and should be included among the myths of performance measurement.

Lead-and-lag labeling of measures is misleading.

Have a Mix of 60 Percent Past, 20 Percent Current, and 20 Percent Future-Oriented Measures

Key result indicators replace outcome measures, which typically look at past activity over months or quarters. PIs and KPIs are now characterized as past, current, or future measures; see Exhibit 1.6.

Past measures are those that look at historic events—activity that took place last week, last month, last quarter, and so on. PIs and KPIs are now characterized as past-, current-, or future-focused measures. Typically, most measures fit into this category. Ideally while they will always be the more dominant, they should not exceed 60 percent of the total number of measures.

Current measures refer to those monitored 24/7 or daily (e.g., late/incomplete deliveries to key customers made yesterday). While most organizations have some current measures, they need to extend the number to around 20 percent of the total number of measures.

Future measures are the record of an agreed future commitment when an action is to take place (e.g., date of next meeting with key customer, date of next product launch, date of next social interaction with key customers). Typically, these have not been measured in the past. I recommend that you have up to 20 percent of your measures in this category.

In your organization, you will find that your KPIs are either past measures (where the KPI relates to last week's activity) current (where it is referring to yesterday's or today's activity)—or future-oriented measures (e.g., a list, by key customer, of the dates of the next planned sales visits).

Most organizational indicators are measuring events of the past month or quarter. All measures that look back beyond a week, as already mentioned, cannot be and never were KPIs.

In workshops, I ask participants to write a couple of their major past measures and then restate the measures as current and future measures. Try this on your organization, please take five minutes to restate three measures used in your organization.

The lead/lag division of measures did not focus adequately on current or future-oriented measures. Entities that want to create a better alignment

Exhibit 1.6 Past/Current/Future Performance Measures Analysis

Past measures (past week/two weeks/month/quarter).	Current measures (real-time/today/yesterday).	Future measures (next week/month/quarter).
Number of late planes last week/last month.	Planes more than two hours late (updated continuously).	Number of initiatives to be commenced in the next month, two months to target areas that are causing late planes.
Percentage of **on-time delivery** (show progress over past 18 months)	Late deliveries/incomplete deliveries to key customers. Cancellation of order by key customer.	Number of initiatives planned within next three months to **increase on-time delivery** to customers.
Monthly sales by key customer. Sales last month in new products. Percentage of **sales** that have arisen from cross-selling among business units.	**Sales** made yesterday. Key customer **inquiries** that have not been responded to by the sales team within ___ hours. Complaints from our key customers that have not been resolved within two hours, reported to the CEO.	Date of next visit to key customers (by customer name, reported to CEO). Number of initiatives planned within next three months to **increase sales staff time in front of customers.** Date of next initiative to attract targeted **new customers.** Number of improvements to new products to be implemented in next month, months two and three.
Number of managers trained in **recruiting** practices. Number of **candidates** that come from employee referrals. **Turnover of new hires** within one year.	Key position job offers that are over 48 hours old and have not yet been accepted by the chosen candidate. Job applications from potential **candidates,** which have not been responded to within three days of receipt.	Names of shortlisted **candidates** for whom the next round of interviews has yet to be scheduled.

of staff activities with the organization's critical success factors will need to be monitoring more current and future measures.

Monitoring the activity taken now about the organizing of future actions to occur will help focus staff on what is expected of them. *Current* and *future* measures are often the fence at the top of the cliff. They are in place, so that we do not have to report inferior performance at month-end (the body at the bottom of the cliff). In other words, current and future measures help make the right future happen. In Exhibit 1.7 are some useful future measures that will work in most organizations.

All these future measures would be reported in a weekly update given to the CEO. Although CEOs may let a couple of weeks pass with gaps appearing on these updates, they will soon start asking questions. Management would take action, prior to the next meeting, to start filling in the gaps to ensure they avoided further uncomfortable questioning.

Exhibit 1.7 Examples of Common Future Measures

Future innovations	To encourage future innovations it is desirable to measure the number of new innovations that will be fully operational in the next month, month two, and month three by department.
Future key customer events	To maintain a close relationship with our key customers, a list should be prepared with the next agreed social interaction (e.g., date agreed to attend a sports event, a meal, the opera, etc.).
Future PR events	To maintain the CEO's profile it is desirable to monitor the public relations events that have been organized in the next one to three, four to six, seven to nine months.
Future recognitions	To maintain staff recognition, the CEO needs to monitor the formal recognitions planned next week/next two weeks by themselves and their direct reports.
New products	The CEO needs to maintain an active watch on the planned date of the next product launch to prevent unnecessary date slippage.
Disaster planning	The CEO needs to ensure that the organization is ready for a disaster by monitoring the date of **next environmental disaster** clean-up practice exercise.
Staff satisfaction	The CEO needs to ensure staff satisfaction surveys are carried out at least three times a year. By monitoring the date of next planned **staff satisfaction** survey the CEO has the ability to bring the date forward.
In-house training	To re-enforce the commitment that every manager should have to in-house training the CEO needs to know, on a weekly basis, all the managers that do not have any staff registered to attend the **in-house courses** scheduled in the upcoming weeks.
Health and safety	The CEO needs to ensure a constant focus on health and safety by monitoring the date of the next **health and safety** audit.

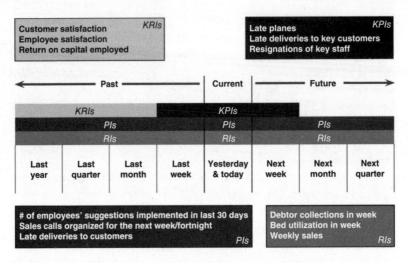

Exhibit 1.8 The Differences in the Four Measures and the Time Zones

A KPI provided to management that is more than a few days old is useless.

The differences in the four measures and the past, current, and future time periods are further explained in Exhibit 1.8. KRIs are summaries of past performance, principally monthly trend analysis over 18 months. KPIs focus on activity in the past week, yesterday, and today, and that planned for the next week and the next two weeks. PIs and RIs will be heavily weighted to the past; however, we do need at least 20 percent of measures to be current- or future-focused.

Importance of Timely Measurement

Before proceeding further, we will look at the importance of timely measurement. It is essential that measurement be timely. Today, a KPI provided to management that is more than a few days old is useless. KPIs are prepared in real time, with even weekly ones available by the next working day. The suggested reporting framework of performance indicators is set out in Exhibit 1.9.

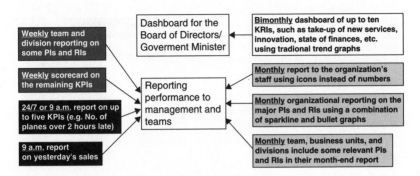

Exhibit 1.9 Suggested Reporting Framework

Frequently, staff working for government and nonprofit agencies tell me that we do not have any measures that we need to monitor frequently. I beg to differ. Review the Appendix for examples of measures that will be useful for all sectors.

Some of the KPIs will be updated daily or even 24/7 (as in the British Airways case), whereas the rest of the KPIs will be reported weekly. Performance measures that focus on completion should be included. A common weekly KPI, for organizations where finishing is a problem, is the reporting to the senior management team of all important projects and reports that are running late. Such reporting will revolutionize project and task completion in your organization.

The RIs and PIs will be reported in various time frames from daily, weekly, and fortnightly to monthly. The KRIs, which are best used to report performance to the board, will, therefore, be based around the timing of the board meeting.

Where Are You in Your Journey with Performance Measures?

The checklist in Exhibit 1.10 is designed to assess your progress with performance measures. It will help you assess how far you are on the journey.

Exhibit 1.10 Assessing Your Progress with Performance Measures Checklist

Knowledge of the critical success factors	Is it covered?
1. Senior management has a common understanding of the organization's success factors.	☐ Yes ☐ No
2. The organization has identified the critical success factors.	☐ Yes ☐ No
3. The critical success factors have been communicated to all staff and are impacting positively on the setting of daily priorities.	☐ Yes ☐ No
Existing KPI implementation	
1. Teams have been trained in designing measures.	☐ Yes ☐ No
2. The KPI team vet all measures before they are approved.	☐ Yes ☐ No
3. The KPIs were implemented based around a methodology such as a Balanced Scorecard, PuMP, Winning KPIs.	☐ Yes ☐ No
4. Teams have selected measures from an approved list of measures.	☐ Yes ☐ No
5. Measures have been derived from the identified critical success factors.	☐ Yes ☐ No
6. There is an awareness that not all measures are KPIs.	☐ Yes ☐ No
7. There are no more than 100 measures in the organization.	☐ Yes ☐ No
How KPIs are operating	
1. Measures are carefully vetted to ensure they promote appropriate action and all those measures that are damaging performance are removed.	☐ Yes ☐ No
2. There is a mix of past, current, and future measures.	☐ Yes ☐ No
3. The performance measures reporting follows best practice graphical presentation rules.	☐ Yes ☐ No
4. There are fewer than 10 KPIs in the organization and these are monitored frequently 24/7, daily, or weekly.	☐ Yes ☐ No
5. KPIs are not linked to pay; performance with KPIs is deemed as a given, e.g., seen as a "ticket to the game."	☐ Yes ☐ No

Your score:

Under 5: A complete visit to performance measurement is in order. This book and accompanying download materials will assist you to sell the change and commence the project.

Between 5 and 10: Some good progress has been made. This book will assist you with improvements.

Over 10: You should write a case study and I will feature it.

Notes

1. Robert S. Kaplan and David P. Norton, *The Balanced Scorecard: Translating Strategy into Action* (Cambridge: Harvard Business Press, 1996).
2. Jeremy Hope and Robin Fraser, *Beyond Budgeting: How Managers Can Break Free from the Annual Performance Trap* (Cambridge, MA: Harvard Business Press, 2003).

Overview

Since humans first walked the plains in search of food, myths have been central to their beliefs. These myths having no scientific basis just hearsay. Many management practices, still used in the 21st century, are corrupted by ill-informed beliefs. In this chapter, I explore the myths surrounding performance measurement that have given rise to this dysfunctional situation.

This chapter will ensure that there is a better understanding about how currently held beliefs can limit the usefulness of performance measures and in particular, the KPIs.

Key learning points from the chapter include:

1. The myths surrounding performance measures
2. Tying remuneration to KPIs will encourage manipulation of these measures
3. The damaging nature of year-end targets
4. Delegating a KPI project to a consulting firm will lead to failure
5. The myths surrounding The Balanced Scorecard (BSC) Methodology that limit the scorecard's effectiveness
6. The dangers of the BSC strategy mapping
7. Cascading measures down an organization is a damaging process
8. The primary use of performance measures is to support the organization's critical success factors rather than help implement strategies

CHAPTER 2

The Myths of Performance Measurement

I have become increasingly aware that key performance indicators (KPIs) in many organizations are a broken tool. Measures are often a random collection prepared with little expertise, signifying nothing. KPIs should be measures that link daily activities to the organization's critical success factors (CSFs), thus supporting an alignment of effort within the organization in the intended direction. I call this alignment the El Dorado of management.

The Myths Surrounding Performance Measures

Poorly defined KPIs cost the organization dearly. Some examples are measures gamed by the senior executive's to increase their bonuses to the detriment of the organization; teams encouraged to perform tasks that are contrary to the organization's strategic direction; costly "measurement and reporting" regimes that lock up valuable staff and management time; and a six-figure consultancy assignment resulting in a "door stop" report or a poorly functioning balanced scorecard.

Myth #1: Most Measures Lead to Better Performance

Every performance measure can have a negative consequence or an unintended action that leads to inferior performance. Over half the measures

25

in an organization may well be encouraging unintended negative behavior. In order to make measures work, one needs to anticipate the likely human behavior that will result from its adoption, and endeavor to minimize the potential negative impact.

This myth has been covered in the unintended behavior—the dark side of performance measures section of the introduction.

Myth #2: All Measures Can Work Successfully in Any Organization, at Any Time

Contrary to common belief, it is a myth to think that all measures can work successfully in any organization, at any time. The reality is that there needs to be, as Spitzer has so clearly argued, a positive "context of measurement" for measures to deliver their potential. To this end, I have established seven foundation stones that need to be in place in order to have an environment where measurement will thrive. These seven foundation stones are explained at length in Chapter 3. They are:

1. Partnership with the staff, unions, and third parties
2. Transfer of power to the front line
3. Measure and report only what matters
4. Source all KPIs from the organization's critical success factors
5. Abandon processes that do not deliver
6. Appointment of a home-grown KPI team leader
7. Organization-wide understanding of the winning KPIs definition

Myth #3: All Performance Measures Are KPIs

Throughout the world, from Iran to the United States and back to Asia, organizations have been using the term *KPI* for all performance measures. No one seemed to worry that the term KPIs had not been defined by anyone. Thus, measures that were truly key to the enterprise were being mixed with measures that were completely flawed. Let's break the term down. *Key* means key to the organization, and *performance* means that the measure will assist in improving performance. There are in fact four types of performance measure. These are explained in Chapter 1.

Myth #4: By Tying KPIs to Remuneration You Will Increase Performance

It is a myth that the primary driver for staff is money and that an organization must design financial incentives in order to achieve great performance. Recognition, respect, and self-actualization are more important drivers. In all types of organizations, there is a tendency to believe that the way to make KPIs work is to tie KPIs to an individual's pay. But when KPIs

> When KPIs are linked to pay, they create key political indicators (not key performance indicators).

are linked to pay, they create key political indicators (not key performance indicators), which will be manipulated to enhance the probability of a larger bonus.

KPIs should be used to align staff to the organization's critical success factors and to show 24/7, daily, or weekly how teams are performing. They are too important to be manipulated by individuals and teams to maximize bonuses. KPIs are so important to an organization that performance in this area is a given or, as Jack Welch says, "a ticket to the game."[1]

Performance bonus schemes are often flawed on a number of counts. This is addressed in a working guide that can be accessed from www .davidparmenter.com.

Myth #5: We Can Set Relevant Year-End Targets

It is a myth that we know what good performance will look like before the year starts, and thus it is a myth that we can set relevant annual targets. In reality, as former CEO of General Electric Jack Welch says, "it leads to constraining initiative, stifling creative thought processes and promotes mediocrity rather than giant leaps in performance."[2] All forms of annual targets are doomed to failure. Far too often management spends months arguing about what is a realistic target, when the only sure thing is that it will be wrong. It will be either too soft or too hard.

I am a follower of Jeremy Hope's work. He and his co-author Robin Fraser were the first writers to clearly articulate that a fixed annual performance contract was doomed to fail. Far too frequently organizations end up paying incentives to management when in fact they have lost market share. In other words, rising sales did not keep up with the growth rate in the marketplace. As Hope and Fraser point out, not setting an annual target beforehand is not a problem as long as staff members are given regular updates about how they are progressing against their peers and the rest of the market. Hope argues that if you do not know how hard you have to work to get a maximum bonus, you will work as hard as you can.

Myth #6: Measuring Performance Is Relatively Simple, and the Appropriate Measures Are Obvious

There will not be a reader of this book who has not, at some time in the past, been asked to come up with some measures with little or no guidance. Organizations, in both the private and public sectors, are being run by management who have not yet received any formal education on performance measurement. Many managers have been trained in the basics of finance, human resources, and information systems. They also have been ably supported by qualified professionals in these three disciplines. The "lost soul" is performance measurement, which has only scant mention in the curriculum of business degrees and in professional qualifications obtained by finance, human resources, and information systems professionals.

Performance measurement has been an orphan of business theory and practice. While writers such as Deming, Whetley and Kellner-Rogers, Hamel, Hope, and Spitzer have for some time been pointing out the dysfunctional nature of performance measurement, it has not yet permutated into business practice. Performance measurement is worthy of more intellectual rigor in every organization on the journey from average to good and then to great performance.

The appointment of a chief measurement officer was first mentioned by Dean Spitzer,[3] who is an expert on performance measurement. The person appointed to the role as chief measurement officer would be part psychologist, part trainer, part salesperson, and part KPI project manager. They would be responsible for running the two-day workshop to ascertain the critical success factors, the designing and refining of the performance measures, the designing of the reporting systems, and the ongoing support. This person would report directly to the CEO and have a status befitting the diverse blend of skills required for this position.

Myth #7: KPIs Are Financial and Nonfinancial Indicators

I firmly believe that all KPIs in countries as diverse as Canada, the United States, the United Kingdom, and Romania are nonfinancial. In fact, I believe that there is not a financial KPI on this planet.

Financial measures are a quantification of an activity that has taken place; we have simply placed a value on the activity. Thus, behind every financial measure is an activity. Many financial measures will be result indicators, a summary measure. It is the activity that you will want more or less of. It is the activity that drives the dollars, pounds, or yen. Thus, financial measures cannot possibly be KPIs.

When you put a pound or dollar sign to a measure, you have not dug deep enough. Sales made yesterday will be a result of sales calls made previously to existing and prospective customers, advertising, product reliability, amount of contact with the key customers, and so on. I group all sales indicators expressed in monetary terms as result indicators.

Myth #8: You Can Delegate a KPI Project to a Consulting Firm

For the past 15 years or so, many organizations have commenced performance measure initiatives, and these have frequently been led by consultants. Commonly, a balanced scorecard approach has been adopted based on the work of Kaplan and Norton. The approach, as I will argue, is too complex and leads to a consultant-focused approach full of very clever consultants undertaking this exercise with inadequate involvement of the client's staff. Although this approach has worked well in some cases, there have been many failures.

> KPI projects are in-house projects that need to be run by skilled individuals who know the organization and its success factors.

All projects that impact many of the organization's staff must be led by a skilled in-house team who are trusted, well networked, have IOUs they can call on and know how the the organization works. Thus, having an in-house KPI project team is one of the seven, non negotiable, foundation stones explained in Chapter 3. They have been unburdened from the daily grind to concentrate on this important project. In other words, these staff members have moved their family photographs, the picture of the 17-hand stallion, or their beloved dog and have put them on their desks in the project office,

29

leaving the daily chore of firefighting in their sphere of operations to their second-in-charge, who has now moved into the boss's office, on a temporary basis of course!

The Myths around the Balanced Scorecard

The groundbreaking work of Kaplan and Norton[4] brought to management's attention the fact that an organization should have a balanced strategy, and its performance needs to be measured in a more holistic way, in a balanced scorecard (BSC). Kaplan and Norton suggested four perspectives from which to review performance: financial, customer, internal process, and learning and growth. There was an immediate acceptance that reporting performance in a balanced way made sense and a whole new consultancy service was born. Unfortunately, many of these balanced scorecard initiatives have failed for reasons set out below.

BSC Myth #1: The Balanced Scorecard Was First Off the Blocks

Hoshin Kanri business methodology, a balanced approach to performance management and measurement, was around well before the balanced scorecard. It has been argued that the BSC originated from a westernized adaptation of the Hoshin Kanri model.

As I understand it, translated, Hoshin Kanri means a business methodology for direction and alignment. This approach was developed in a complex Japanese multinational, where it is necessary to achieve an organization-wide collaborative effort in key areas.

One tenet behind Hoshin Kanri is that all employees should incorporate into their daily routines a contribution to the key corporate objectives. In other words, staff members need to be made aware of the critical success factors and then prioritize their daily activities to maximize their positive contribution in these areas.

In the traditional form of Hoshin Kanri, there is a grouping of four perspectives. It is no surprise that the balanced scorecard perspectives are mirror images, as shown in Exhibit 2.1. An informative paper on the comparison between Hoshin Kanri and the balanced scorecard has been written by Witcher and Chau,[5] and it is well worth reading.

Exhibit 2.1 Similarities between Hoshin Kanri and Balanced Scorecard Perspectives

Hoshin Kanri	Balanced Scorecard
Quality objectives and measures	Customer focus
Cost objectives and measures	Financial
Delivery objectives and measures	Internal process
Education objectives and measures	Learning and growth

BSC Myth #2: There Are Only Four Balanced Scorecard Perspectives

For almost 20 years the four perspectives listed in Kaplan and Norton's original work (Financial, Customer, Internal Process, and Learning and Growth) have been consistently reiterated by Kaplan and Norton and others through to present time. I recommend that these four perspectives be increased by the inclusion of two more perspectives (Staff Satisfaction, and Environment and Community) and that the Learning and Growth perspective be reverted back to its original name, Innovation and Learning, as presented in Exhibit 2.2.

Exhibit 2.2 The Suggested Six Perspectives of a Balanced Scorecard

FINANCIAL Asset utilization, sales growth, risk management, optimization of working capital, cost reduction	CUSTOMER FOCUS Increasing customer satisfaction, targeting customers who generate the most profit, getting close to noncustomers	ENVIRONMENT AND COMMUNITY Employer of first choice, linking with future employees, community leadership, collaboration
INTERNAL PROCESS Delivery in full on time, optimizing technology, effective relationships with key stakeholders	STAFF SATISFACTION Right people on the bus, empowerment, retention of key staff, candor, leadership, recognition	INNOVATION AND LEARNING Innovation, abandonment, increasing expertise and adaptability, learning environment

BSC Myth #3: The Balanced Scorecard Can Report Progress to Both Management and the Board

One certainly needs to show the minister or board the state of progress. However, it is important that governance information be shown rather than management information. The measures that should be reported to the board are key result indicators.

We need to ensure the "management-focused" performance measures (KPIs, result indicators, and performance indicators) are only reported to management and staff.

BSC Myth #4: Measures Fit Neatly into One Balanced Scorecard Perspective

When an organization adopts the balanced scorecard, which is certainly a step in the right direction, staff members are frequently in a dilemma over measures that seem to influence more than one balanced scorecard perspective. Where do I put this measure? Debates go on, and often resolution is unclear.

Measures do not fit neatly into one or another perspective. In fact, when you get a measure that transcends a few perspectives, you should get excited as you are zeroing in on a possible KPI. To illustrate this point, let's look at where late planes in the sky should be reported. Should it be in the customer, financial, or internal process perspective? In fact, this measure affects all six perspectives as shown in Exhibit 2.3.

BSC Myth #5: Indicators Are Either Lead (Performance Driver) or Lag (Outcome) Indicators

I am not sure where the lead/lag labels came from, but I do know that they have caused a lot of problems and are fundamentally flawed. These labels assume that a measure is either about the past or about the future. It ignores the fact that some measures, in particularly KPIs, are both about the past and the future.

I have lost count of the number of times I read Kaplan and Norton's[6] original masterpiece to try and understand the lead/lag indicators argument until I realized my difficulty in understanding lead/lag indicators was a result of flawed logic.

Exhibit 2.3 How Late Planes Impact Most If Not All Six Perspectives

Measure	Financial	Customer satisfaction	Staff satisfaction	Innovation and learning	Internal process	Environment and community
				Perspectives		
Late planes in the sky over two hours late	✓	✓	✓	✓	✓	Possible

> Strategy mapping, in the wrong hands, can give birth to a monster.

I have presented to thousands of people on KPIs and I always ask, "Is the late-planes-in-the-air KPI a lead or a lag indicator?" The vote count is always evenly split. It has clearly arisen out of past events and will have a major impact on future events—the late arrival will make the plane leave late. I recommend that we dispense with the terms "lag" (outcome) and "lead" (performance driver) indicators. We should see measures as either a *past, current* (yesterday's or today's activities—the here and now), or *future* measure (monitoring now the planning and preparation for events/actions that should occur in the future), as discussed in Chapter 1.

BSC Myth #6: "Cause and Effect" Strategy Mapping Is a Valid Process

If strategy maps help management make some sense out of their strategy, then as a working document, they must be useful. However, I am concerned with the "simplified" use of cause-and-effect relationships, a major component of strategy mapping, as illustrated in Exhibit 2.4. I believe it has led to the demise of many performance measurement initiatives. From these oversimplified relationships come the strategic initiatives and the cascading performance measures. Strategy mapping, in the wrong hands, can give birth to a monster.

The "cause-and-effect" diagrams of strategic mapping, where initiatives/success factors neatly fit into a balanced scorecard perspective and create one or possibly two cause-and-effect relationships, is full of intellectual thought signifying nothing in many cases. It seems to argue that every action or decision has an effect elsewhere in the organization, that you can boil down "cause-and-effect" relationships to one or two relationships. Jeremy Hope believed that strategy maps are seductive models of how we like to think organizations work and are dangerous weapons in the wrong hands. He summed it up beautifully in his whitepaper "Hidden Costs":

> *If you think an organization is a machine with levers that you can pull and buttons that you can press to cause a predictable action and counter-action elsewhere (as in a car engine), then cause-and-effect is an idea that works.*
>
> **Jeremy Hope, "Hidden Costs" whitepaper, 2004**

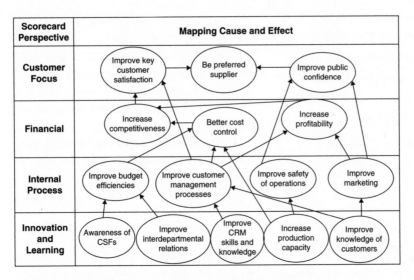

Scorecard Perspective	Mapping Cause and Effect

Exhibit 2.4 Strategy Mapping of the Balanced Scorecard

These strategy map diagrams are flawed on a number of accounts:

- Success factors do not fit neatly within a perspective; the more important they are the more perspectives they impact, and hence some success factors would need to be drawn across the whole page of a strategy map. This is clearly too untidy for the "strategy map" designers.
- If you are bright enough, you can argue a totally different causal route for your arrows in your strategic mapping. Every action a company takes has myriad impacts. To restrict oneself to one or two relationships in strategy mapping is at best too simplistic, at worst totally naive.
- When I ask attendees to map the impact of late planes on the success factors of an airline, they come up with at least twenty impacts. Strategy mapping cannot cope with multiple relationships and thus cannot cope with the reality of day-to-day business.

Cascading measures down an organization was probably the most damaging process used in the balanced scorecard approach.

- Actions that employees take, on a daily basis, are influenced by many factors; they cannot be simplified into one or two causal impacts. The secret is to understand those employee actions. These actions can be noted from observation or from interviews. "If we measure _____ what will it promote you to do." These actions will never be correctly identified by BSC consultants.

BSC Myth #7: Measures Are Cascaded Down the Organization

Cascading measures down an organization was probably the most damaging process used in the balanced scorecard approach. The approach assumes that by analyzing a measure such as "return on capital employed" you could break it down in myriad measures relevant to each team or division.

It also assumes that each and every team leader with minimal thought processes would arrive at relevant performance measures. Kaplan and Norton ignored the crucial facts that the team leaders and the senior management team need to know about the organization's critical success factors and the potential for the performance measure to have a "dark side," an unintended consequence.

Having first ascertained the organization's CSFs it is thus best to start the balanced scorecard *from the ground up* at the team level within the operations, level 4 in Exhibit 2.5. It is at the operational team level that KPIs will be found. Find me an accounting team with a winning KPI! Like many support functions, their team will work with PIs and RIs. This sends a clear message: finish the monthly and annual accounts quickly and spend more time helping the teams who are working directly on the organization's KPIs.

By cascading up, not down, CEOs are saying that finding the right measures that link to the CSFs is important. It is the El Dorado of management when you have every employee, every day, aligning themselves with the organization's CSFs. Very few organizations have achieved this alignment, this magical alignment between effort and effectiveness, Toyota being a shining light.

BSC Myth #8: Performance Measures Are Mainly Used to Help Manage Implementation of Strategic Initiatives

The balanced scorecard approach sees the purpose of performance measures as helping implement the strategic initiatives. It is argued that in order to implement the strategies you report and manage the performance measures that best reflect progress, or lack of it, within the strategic initiatives.

I do not believe performance measures are on this planet to implement strategies. Performance measures are here to ensure that staff members spend their working hours focused primarily on the organization's critical success factors.

> I do not believe performance measures are on this planet to implement strategies. Performance measures are here to ensure that staff members spend their working hours focused primarily on the organization's critical success factors.

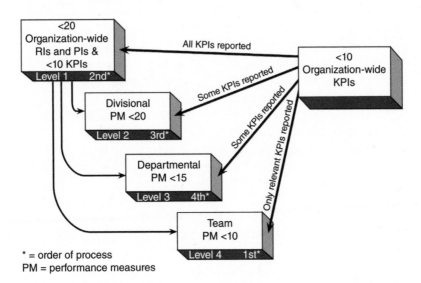

Exhibit 2.5 Interrelated Levels of Performance Measures in an Organization

Notes

1. Jack Welch and Suzy Welch, *Winning* (New York: Harper Business, 2005).
2. Ibid.
3. Dean R. Spitzer, *Transforming Performance Measurement: Rethinking the Way We Measure and Drive Organizational Success* (New York: AMACOM, 2007).
4. Robert S. Kaplan and David P. Norton, *The Balanced Scorecard: Translating Strategy into Action* (Cambridge: Harvard Business Press, 1996).
5. Barry J. Witcher and Vinh Sum Chau, "Balanced Scorecard and Hoshin Kanri: Dynamic Capabilities for Managing Strategic Fit," *Management Decision* 45, no. 3 (2007): 518–538.
6. Robert S. Kaplan and David P. Norton, *The Balanced Scorecard: Translating Strategy into Action* (Cambridge: Harvard Business Press, 1996).

Overview

Organizations often begin to develop a KPI system by immediately trying to select KPIs without the preparation that is indicated in the three-stage Winning KPI Methodology. This chapter provides an overview of the three stages and discusses the seven foundation stones that need to be laid before we can successfully develop and utilize key performance indicators (KPIs) in the workplace.

I explain the seven foundation stones, which are: (1) partnership with the staff, unions, and third parties; (2) transfer of power to the front line; (3) measure and report only what matters; (4) only source performance measures from the critical success factors; (5) abandon processes that do not deliver; (6) appointment of a home-grown KPI team leader; (7) organization-wide understanding of the winning KPIs definition.

Key learning points from the chapter include:

1. The three stages of the winning KPIs process
2. The seven foundation stones of the winning KPIs process
3. Empowerment of the organization's employees, particularly those in operations, is vital to the success of a KPI project
4. Each measure should have a linkage to a success factor or critical success factor
5. The main purpose of performance measures is to ensure that staff spend their working hours focused primarily on the organization's critical success factors
6. Importance of Peter Drucker's advice on "Abandonment" and "Never give a new job to a new person"
7. Implementing the Winning KPI methodology in a small to medium-sized enterprise

CHAPTER 3

Background to the Winning KPI Methodology

M any organizations that have operated with key performance indicators (KPIs) have found the KPIs made little or no difference to performance. In many cases this was due to a fundamental misunderstanding of the issues. Organizations often begin to develop a KPI system by immediately trying to select KPIs without the preparation that is indicated in the three-stage implementation plan. Like painting the outside of the house, 50 percent of a competent job is in the preparation. Establishing a sound environment in which KPIs can operate and develop is crucial. Once the organization understands the process involved and appreciates the purpose of introducing KPIs, the building phase can begin.

Winning KPI Methodology

The implementation difficulties were first grasped by a key performance indicator manual developed by the Australian Government Department "AusIndustries" as part of a portfolio of resources for organizations pursuing international best practices. This book has adopted many of the approaches of the KPI manual, which was first published in 1996. The KPI manual was the first book to recognize that:

- A project needs foundation stones. There were originally four, and these have now increased to seven.

- There are 12 important steps in the original KPI manual, see Exhibit 3.1. These were adopted in the first two editions of my book.
- However, under pressure from readers to further simplify them, I have thus compacted them now into three stages, see Exhibit 3.2, albeit the twelve steps still exist in their entirety.
- You need to invest resources to sell the change to senior management and the rest of the organization. This edition emphasizes the need to sell the change through the emotional drivers of the intended audience.
- The critical success factors are the key driving force behind performance measures. This has been further refined with the branding of operational critical success factors.
- KPIs are at the work-face, improving operations benefiting the financial, customer, internal process, innovation & learning, Environment & community and staff BSC perspectives.
- Readers need templates to move forward swiftly. This edition continues the tradition of endeavoring to second-guess all the main templates a KPI project team would need.

The Original 12-Step Process

In the first two editions of my KPI book I talked about a 12-step process that should be put into an organization with over 500 FTEs within a 16-week timeframe, as seen in Exhibit 3.1.

The Three-Stage Winning KPIs Process

I was asked by clients to further simplify the process, and I used the opportunity of the fourth edition to rethink the approach to make it more user-friendly. The new model incorporates all the original twelve steps in a three-stage process, illustrated in Exhibit 3.2.

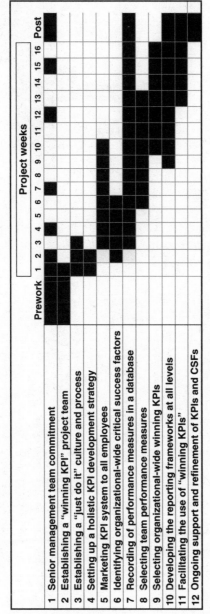

Exhibit 3.1 Twelve-Step Implementation of a 16-Week Timeline

43

Stage	Task	pre	1	2	3	4	5	6	7	8	9	10	11	12	13	14	15	16	post
1 Getting the enterprise committed to the change and up-skilling an in-house KPI team.	1.1 Sell the KPI project to the CEO, the senior management team, and the organization's oracles	■	■																
	1.2 Locate an external facilitator to help select, train, and mentor the KPI team	■	■																
	1.3 Train a small KPI team			■	■														
	1.4 Sell the KPI project to all employees who are to attend the two-day performance measures workshops							■											
2 Ascertaining the operational critical success factors.	2.1 Locate the existing success factors and desired external outcomes from documentation and interviews			■	■														
	2.2 Run the two-day critical success factor (CSF) workshop to ascertain the CSFs						■												
	3.1 Run the two-day performance measures workshops to train the selected staff to develop meaningful measures								■	■	■								
	3.2 Refine the measures after the performance measures workshops							■	■	■	■	■	■	■					
	3.3 Hold a performance measures gallery to weed out dysfunctional and poor measures												■						
3 Determining measures and getting them to work.	3.4 Ask all teams to select their team performance measures from the finalized database of measures														■				
	3.5 Find the key result indicators (KRIs) and the key performance indicators (KPIs)									■	■								
	3.6 Design the reporting framework									■	■	■	■	■	■	■	■		
	3.7 Facilitate the appropriate use of the selected performance measures by all the teams in the organization																	■	■
	3.8 Refine CSFs and associated measures after one year of use																		■

Exhibit 3.2 The Three-Stage Process

An Overview of the Three Stages

Before readers venture into the detail, I wish to overview the three stages of the Winning KPI Methodology, which are described in Chapters 4 to 11.

Stage 1: Getting the enterprise committed to the change and up-skilling the in-house KPI team	All major project implementations are deeply affected by the success or failure in leading and selling the change. Chapter 4, which outlines John Kotter's model of leading change, emphasizes the importance of selling by emotional drivers of the intended audience, and sets out the steps required in this stage.
	The senior management team must be committed to developing and driving through the organization KPIs and any balanced scorecard that includes them. In addition, timing is everything. This project must find a suitable window where the senior management team will have time to commit to the change process. Chapter 5 outlines the steps required in this stage.
	The success of a KPI project rests with trained home-grown staff who have been reassigned so that they are full time on the project. Chapter 6 covers the importance of selecting an in-house person to lead the KPI team and explains the reasons why an external recruitment to run the KPI team is doomed to fail.
Stage 2: Ascertaining your organization's operational critical success factors	Critical success factors (CSFs) are operational issues or aspects that need to be done well day-in and day-out by the staff in the organization. Chapter 7 looks at the differences between CSFs and external outcomes, highlights the importance of the CSF by indicating that it is a missing link in management theory, explains that an organization has typically five to eight CSFs, shows how CSFs are the origin of all performance measures, and explains how an organization goes about ascertaining them. Chapter 12 covers case studies on CSF workshops and some common critical success factors and their likely measures.
Stage 3: Determining measures and getting the measures to drive performance	Many performance measures are created from a flawed process. Chapter 8 examines common reasons why organizations get their measures radically wrong and how to design appropriate measures. Chapter 9 outlines all the tasks that need to be performed during a performance measures workshop. Chapter 9 also outlines the tidy-up process on the performance measure database, and how to select the KPIs and KRIs.
	Chapter 10 looks at the reporting framework that needs to be developed at all levels within the organization and shows how KPIs are refined to maintain their relevance and a variety of reporting templates.

Seven Foundation Stones of the Winning KPIs Process

Success or failure of the KPI project is determined by the presence or absence of these seven foundation stones.

There are seven foundation stones that need to be laid before we can successfully develop and utilize key performance indicators (KPIs) in the workplace. When building a house, you need to ensure that the whole building is undertaken on a solid foundation. Success or failure of the KPI project is determined by the presence or absence of these seven foundation stones; see Exhibit 3.3 below. They are so important that I can guarantee you will have limited success without them in place. I have witnessed far too many projects where well-meaning and talented individuals have compromised these foundation stones only to later suffer the fate of an underperforming KPI platform.

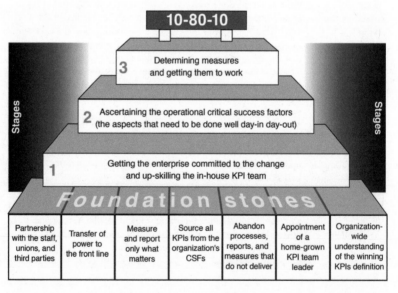

Exhibit 3.3 The Seven Foundation Stones in the Winning KPI Methodology

"Partnership with the Staff, Unions, and Third Parties" Foundation Stone

The successful pursuit of performance improvement requires the establishment of an effective partnership among management, local employee representatives, unions representing the organization's employees, employees, major customers, and major suppliers.

Implications of the "partnership" foundation stone include:

Recognition of the need for change	Recognition by all stakeholders that significant organizational and cultural change requires a mutual understanding and acceptance of the need for change and knowledge on how change should be implemented.
Consultative arrangements	Commitment to the establishment and maintenance of effective communication between all interested and affected parties.
Involving key customers and key suppliers	Extension of the notion of partnership to include and involve the organization's key customers and key suppliers.

If you want to improve satisfaction with your major customers, would it not make sense to sit down with them and ask, "What should we measure to better manage the delivery of our products and services to you?" If you want your key suppliers' performance to improve, would you not visit them and discuss your expectations?

Example: An Airline Working with Its Suppliers

When team members were discussing how to improve performance with late planes that were about to land, they soon realized how important their key suppliers were. Instead of calling their cleaners and aviation fuel supplier numerous times each day, saying, "Please treat these planes as a priority," they simply gave their key suppliers read-only access to their late-planes screen. They said, "Whenever a plane is over, say, one hour late, you have our preapproved authority to speed the process up." The cleaners doubled the cleaning crew and thus halved the cleaning time, and the aviation fuel supplier had its staff awaiting the plane's arrival so refueling could commence as soon as it was safe to do so.

"Transfer of Power to the Front Line" Foundation Stone

> Successful performance improvement requires empowerment of the organization's employees, particularly those in the operational front line.

Successful performance improvement requires empowerment of the organization's employees, particularly those in the operational front line. Although this has been discussed in many management books, the leading authors in this area are Peter Drucker, Gary Hamel, Tom Peters, and Robert Waterman. I recommend that the reader become familiar with their work.

Implications of the "transfer of power" foundation stone include:

Effective two-way communication	The embracing of effective and honest top-down and bottom-up communications. Meaning that staff can challenge the status quo and give observations that may well be the last thing they want to hear (e.g., no longer is the messenger of bad news shot; now they are acknowledged).
Empowerment	The empowerment of employees to take immediate action to rectify situations that are negatively impacting KPIs (e.g., able to authorize the doubling of cleaning staff to speed turnaround time for an anticipated late plane.)
Devolving responsibility	Giving teams the responsibility to select their performance measures and to make performance improving decisions.
Training	Training staff on; why the organization's CSFs should drive daily activities; designing and refining measures; and how progress should be graphically reported.
Agile methodologies	Adoption of Lean and Agile methodologies such as stand-up scrum meetings, Kanban Boards and Kaizen.
Awareness of learning difficulties	Additional support for those employees with literacy, numeracy, or other learning-related difficulties.

Example: Empowerment at a Car Manufacturer

Leading car manufacturers have long realized the importance of empowerment. When staff members on the production line see a quality defect, they place a tag on it. If they have time, they will start to fix it. The next operator, on the production line, spots the tag, and, after completing designated tasks, also carries on with the rectification work.

If the operator realizes that the fault cannot be fixed before it will be covered over by the installation of the next panel, he or she simply pulls the "cord" to stop production in that section. Management then organizes the fixing of the fault and restarts the line. They investigate whether the decision to stop the line was correct. If not, they see it as a failure of the training, not the fault of the individual, and simply discuss the matter with the staff concerned. The ability of staff to stop a production line without consultation is a high-level form of empowerment. The key to the success of this method is that staff members are not only empowered to stop the production line, but also feel confident to make this decision.

"Measure and Report Only What Matters" Foundation Stone

It is critical that management ensure that performance is measured and reported in a way that promotes appropriate action. Organizations should be reporting events on a daily/weekly/monthly basis, depending on their significance, and these reports should cover the critical success factors.

> Each measure should have a reason for existing, a linkage to a success factor or critical success factor.

Implications of the "measure and report" foundation stone include:

Measures to have a reason to exist	We should measure only what we need to. Each measure should have a reason for existing, a linkage to a success factor or critical success factor.
Leads to action	What gets reported should be followed by action. The chief executive officer has to commit to making phone calls: "Pat, why did BA235 leave 2.5 hours late?"

49

Lean reporting	There needs to be a major revamp of reporting embracing the lean movement. It needs to be more concise, timely, efficient to produce, and focused on decision making.
Data visualization	Reporting should be prepared in accordance with the work of Stephen Few; the leading writer in data visualization space.
Bottom-up process	Organizational performance measures will be developed in response to the performance measures developed by teams, e.g., a bottom-up process.

> It is the critical success factors and their associated performance measures that link daily activities to the organization's strategies.

A practical exercise to highlight the waste in reporting is to ask the chief executive officer to request all staff and management to provide one copy of every report they worked on last month. A person is designated to gather the reports, to ensure all management and staff have sent in their reports, and to weed out the duplications. In some organizations, the pile will be over four feet high. Put all the papers in a see-through container, and then make a container a quarter of the size and announce that this is the total amount of reporting allowed.

Example: Unnecessary Reporting in a Government Department

I once saw a pile of reports on a finance manager's desk. When I asked what they were, he said they were the budget holder's month-end reports. "What do you use them for?" I asked. There was a silence, and then he replied in a low tone, "I do not use them. I call the relevant budget holder if I need an explanation of a major variance." Hundreds of hours of budget-holder time were wasted each month when they could have been better spent getting home at a reasonable hour.

"Source All KPIs from the Organization's Critical Success Factors" Foundation Stone

Critical success factors should be the source of all performance measures that really matter: the KPIs. It is the critical success factors and their associated performance measures that link daily activities to the organization's strategies. The critical success factors impact 24/7 on the business; therefore, it is important to measure how the staff in the organization are aligning their daily activities to these critical success factors.

> The main purpose of performance measures is to ensure that staff members spend their working hours focused primarily on the organization's critical success factors.

I believe the main purpose of performance measures is to ensure that staff members spend their working hours focused primarily on the organization's critical success factors. The traditional balanced scorecard approach, however, sees the purpose of performance measures as helping to monitor the implementation of the strategic initiatives. There is, thus, a significant difference in how measures are produced in "winning KPIs" methodology and that of the traditional balanced scorecard approach. This will be explained in subsequent chapters.

Implications of the "source of KPIs" foundation stone include:

Importance of CSFs	An organization's critical success factors are more fundamental to an organization than its strategic initiatives. An organization can still succeed without a well-formulated strategy, and many do.
Primary role of measures	The primary role of performance measures is to help the workforce focus on the critical success factors of the business, day-in and day-out. Other methodologies see the primary purpose of performance measures as monitoring the implementation of strategic initiatives.

CSFs come first	Before KPIs can be found, the critical success factors must be determined in the process outlined in Chapter 7. If a measure is not linked to a critical success factor, it will not be a KPI and is unlikely to be very important to the organization and, therefore, should be screened for potential abandonment.
Linkage to CSFs	The key performance indicators, performance indicators, result indicators, and key result indicators that an organization is using should all be linked to either a critical success factor or a success factor. The database of measures that an organization utilizes should record this linkage.

"Abandon Processes That Do Not Deliver" Foundation Stone

> Of all of Peter Drucker's legendary insights, "abandonment" stands head and shoulders above them all.

The need for this foundation stone came about as a result of my voracious interest in reading Peter Drucker's work, especially Elizabeth Haas Edersheim's interpretation.[1] I knew that if I absorbed his work, I would be able to improve my understanding of performance management.

Of all of Peter Drucker's legendary insights, "abandonment" stands head and shoulders above them all. He saw abandonment as the vital source, the fountain of innovation. Abandonment is a sign that management is recognizing that some initiatives will never work as intended and that it is better to face this reality sooner rather than later. It is essential that the organization have freed up enough time to give the KPI project the time and commitment it requires.

Implications of the abandonment foundation stone include:

Hold an abandonment day each month	Create an abandonment day each month during which teams report back to the organization on what they have agreed to abandon. Other teams have 24 hours to appeal the abandonment.
Measure the abandonment rate	Make heroes of the teams who embrace abandonment the most.

Abandon all dysfunctional performance measures	In some circumstances, it would be worth abandoning all performance measures in an organization and restarting the exercise basing performance measures on the critical success factors. Some measures will no doubt be reinstated, but many will remain discarded.
Abandon reports	Abandon reports that are completed the same way they were last month and the month before, with nobody reading them. Every report should have a small box, on the front page, explaining how it is relevant to the organization's critical success factors and strategy.
Abandon meetings	Abandon meetings that generate a little or no follow-up action where the primary purpose is the meeting itself. They just fall off the to-do list over time. Every meeting should have a clear statement explaining why it is in existence, a record of what action it has taken, and the cost per hour to the organization.
Abandon broken-down balanced scorecards	Abandon the existing balanced scorecard and any balanced scorecard software if the scorecard is not working. The scorecard application may be able to be recycled by the KPI project team.
Abandon projects	Review the current projects schedule for projects that are no longer appropriate or needed.
Abandon performance-related pay linkage to annual targets	If you can see into the future setting annual targets works. In reality annual targets, will either be too easy or too hard. Performance related pay should be linked to relative measures. This is discussed in a working guide available on www.davidparmenter.com.
Abandon the annual planning process	The annual planning process, as it is currently set up, is only an annual political event serving no purpose. Visit www.davidparmenter.com for an explanation of quarterly rolling planning.
Abandon performance reviews	Annual or twice-yearly performance reviews—nobody likes receiving them, the managers hate preparing them, and they do not help with remuneration. Managers should be giving regular feedback to their staff, and this should occur at least once a month.

"Appointment of a Home-Grown KPI Team Leader" Foundation Stone

There needs to be a new approach to measurement that is done by staff who have been suitably trained: an approach that is consultative, promotes partnership between staff and management, and finally achieves behavioral alignment to the organization's critical success factors and strategic direction. I have been working with performance measures for many years and have spent untold hours endeavoring to unlock their secrets. Over the years one thing has become abundantly clear: you need a measurement expertise in-house. Dean Spitzer[2] suggests that a new position be established called a "chief measurement officer." I have drafted a job description for the KPI team leader/CMO and included it in the PDF toolkit supporting Chapter 6.

Implications of the chief measurement officer foundation stone include:

Full-time responsibility	In most of the implementations I have observed, my advice to appoint a KPI team leader and make him or her, where possible, full time, has been compromised due to workload commitments. In every case this has delayed progress and put the project on the back foot. For organizations with over 250 full-time staff, this position should and must be full time. In small organizations, this duty must be at least half the workload with much daily operational activity reassigned so that the incumbent has a chance to focus and create some momentum in the project.
In-house appointment	Peter Drucker said, "Never give a new job to a new person."[3] We need to appoint an in-house person as the KPI project team leader. Someone who is well respected in the organization, has had success implementing projects, and has a pile of "I owe you" favors that they can call upon when help is required. Staff, who are concerned about the change, are more likely to support the KPI initiative when it is led by a trusted in-house appointee.

	Drucker observed that many new initiatives failed as the wrong people were leading them. When we recruit a new employee or consultant to undertake a new job or project, such as the introduction of the balanced scorecard into the organization, there will be much uncertainty among staff and management. Staff will be wondering what is going to happen with their jobs, whether their favorite tasks are about to disappear, and what effect the change is going to have on their pay.
	These doubts, along with the added insult of the consultant's Porsche Carrera in the visitors' car park, often leads to stonewalling any potential project progress. There may be some staff and management who will do their utmost to make the consultant fail. The consultant, in such circumstances, is given as much chance of success as a mountaineer solo-climbing Mount Everest. It can be done, but only by a freak of nature.
Direct reporting line to the CEO	The position would report directly to the CEO, as befits the knowledge and diverse blend of skills required.

Performance measurement is worthy of more intellectual rigor in every organization that is on the journey from average to good and finally to great. The chief measurement officer would be part psychologist, part teacher, part salesperson, and part project manager. Only when we have this level of expertise within the organization can we hope to move away from measurement confusion to measurement clarity.

> "Never give a new job to a new person."
> —Peter Drucker

"Organization-Wide Understanding of the Winning KPIs Definition" Foundation Stone

I have realized that unless the organization embraces the new definition of what a KPI is and what it is not, the progress will be limited very quickly. I have repeatedly found that once the organization has held the two-day critical-success-factor workshop, staff who have gone back to their offices soon start to call all measures KPIs again. It is vital that the senior management team, led by the CEO, communicate the new meaning of a KPI and that all breaches of the term "KPI" are quickly picked up and corrected by staff and managers.

Implications of the "organization-wide KPIs definition" foundation stone include:

KPI definition	*Key performance indicators* focus on the aspects of organizational performance that are the most critical for the current and future success of the organization.
KPIs are organizational based	Teams will only have KPIs in their area if a KPI is significant to the organization.
KPIs are operationally focused	Most measures used by teams will be PIs and RIs. Head office teams such as Finance and IT are unlikely to have a KPI as these are largely in operations.
Two groups of measures	The understanding of the two groups of measures, *result indicators* and *performance indicators*, will need to be conveyed to all managers in training sessions. Staff will need to be able, with the help of the KPI team, to segregate measures into KRIs, RIs, PIs, and KPIs.

Implementation Variations and Shortcuts for Small to Medium-Sized Enterprises

The tasks outlined in this book are designed around organizations with over 250 FTEs. To assist KPI team leaders of SMEs with less than 250 FTEs, I have included additional guidelines here and in subsequent chapters.

Implementing the Winning KPI Methodology in a Small to Medium-Sized Enterprise (100–250 Employees)

For organizations with between 100 to 250 full-time equivalents the three-stage process can be truncated into a shorter time frame. The major time savings are that:

1. The senior management team have in many cases driven the process from the beginning. Thus, with the CEO on board from the start organizing the critical success workshop is much quicker.
2. The KPI team is often selected based on who appears to be most capable with the methodology based on their performance in the CSF workshop.
3. Some of the tasks outlined in this book can be merged together; these have been highlighted in the implementation kit that can be acquired from www.davidparmenter.com.
4. The lower staff numbers mean that fewer workshops are necessary.

The seven foundations stones are still very relevant, particularly the need for the KPI project leader to be freed of other duties. Otherwise delays and failure await. Organizations with between 100 to 250 full-time equivalents can purchase a modified and truncated set of templates from www.davidparmenter.com.

The impact of the truncation can be seen in Exhibit 3.4.

Implementing the Winning KPI Methodology in a Small Enterprise with Less than 100 Employees

For organizations with less than 100 full-time equivalents the three-stage process can be further truncated. The major time savings are that:

1. The owners are often running the business and the decision to start organizing the critical success workshop can be very quick.
2. There is often only one person who can run the project, and if workload cannot be cleared, the project should be delayed.
3. Some of the tasks outlined in this book can be merged together; these have been highlighted in subsequent chapters.
4. The CSF and performance measure workshops are merged together.

The seven foundation stones are still very relevant, and where the person responsible to lead the KPI project is not freed of other duties, delays and implementation failures await. Organizations with less than 100 staff can purchase a modified and truncated set of templates from www.davidparmenter.com.

The impact of the truncation can be seen in Exhibit 3.5.

Exhibit 3.4 The Truncated Three-Stage Process for SMEs with 100–250 FTEs

Stage	Task	pre	1	2	3	4	5	6	7	8	9	10	post
1 Getting the enterprise committed to the change and up-skilling an in-house KPI team	1.1 Selling the KPI project to the CEO, the senior management team and the organization's oracles	■											
	1.2 &1.3 Locate an external facilitator to help select, train and mentor the KPI team		■	■							■		■
	1.4 Selling the KPI project to all employees to encourage their participation in the two-day workshop					■							
2 Ascertaining the operational critical success factors	2.1 Locate the existing success factors and desired external outcomes from documentation and interviews			■	■								
	2.2 & 3.1 Combine the critical success factors and the performance measures workshops two-days for those attending				■								
	3.1 Run one-day performance measures workshops to train other staff, who did not attend the two-day workshop, to develop meaningful measures						■						
	3.2 Refining the measures after the performance measures workshops							■					
	3.3 Hold a performance measures gallery to wean out any dysfunctional and poor measures								■				
3 Determining measures and getting them to work	3.4 Ask all teams to select their team performance measures from the finalized database of measures									■	■		
	3.5 Find the key result indicators (KRIs), and the key performance indicators (KPIs)									■			
	3.6 Design the reporting framework										■	■	
	3.7 Facilitate the appropriate use of the selected performance measures by all the teams in the organization											■	
	3.8 Refine CSFs and associated measures after one year of use												■

58

Stage	Task	pre	1	2	3	4	5	6	post
1 Getting the enterprise committed to the change and up-skilling an in-house KPI team	1.1 Selling the KPI project to the CEO / owner	■	■						
	1.2 Owner asks the selected staff to clear their diary for the two-day workshop		■						
	1.3 KPI project lead trains themselves with possible help from an external facilitator			■					
2 Ascertaining the operational critical success factors	2.1 Locate the existing success factors and desired external outcomes from documentation and interviews			■					
	2.2 Combine the critical success factors and the performance measures workshop into two-days				■				
3 Determining measures and getting them to work	3.1 Refining the measures after the performance measures workshops					■			
	3.2 Hold a performance measures gallery to wean out any dysfunctional and poor measures					■			
	3.3 Ask all teams to select their team performance measures from the finalized database of measures						■		
	3.4 Find the key result indicators (KRIs), and the key performance indicators (KPIs)						■		
	3.5 Design the reporting framework							■	
	3.6 Facilitate the appropriate use of the selected performance measures by all the teams in the organization							■	■
	3.7 Refine CSFs and associated measures after one year of use								■

Exhibit 3.5 The Truncated Three-Stage Process for an SME with Less than 100 FTEs

Notes

1. Elizabeth Haas Edersheim, *The Definitive Drucker: Challengers for Tomorrow's Executives—Final Advice from the Father of Modern Management* (New York: McGraw-Hill, 2006).
2. Dean R. Spitzer, *Transforming Performance Measurement: Rethinking the Way We Measure and Drive Organizational Success* (New York: AMACOM, 2007).
3. Peter Drucker, *Managing the Non-Profit Organization* (New York: Harper Collins, 1992).

Overview

All major project implementations are deeply affected by the success or failure in leading and selling the change. Far too many well-meaning initiatives fail because we have not understood the psychology behind getting change to work. This chapter explores the work of Steve Zaffron and Dave Logan in *The Three Laws of Performance* and John Kotter's *Leading Change*. It covers the importance of Harry Mills' "self-persuasion," emphasizes the importance of selling by emotional drivers of the intended audience, and sets out the steps required in this stage.

This chapter gives instructions on how to access, free of charge, a PDF of the suggested worksheets and checklists to be used by the KPI project team.

The key learning points from this chapter include:

1. How the default future in the organization will always kill change initiatives if it is not appropriately challenged. As Zaffron and Logan point out, "How people perform correlates to how situations occur to them."
2. The key to change is to re-create, in the minds of the organization's staff, a new vision of the future—let's call it a reinvented future.
3. The importance of getting the staff in the organization to have for themselves that *aha!* moment, that "Hell, no! We do not want the default future." When the staff come to this realization, change is inevitable.
4. The importance of having the organization's oracles on the KPI project.
5. John Kotter's eight-step leading change process which is universally accepted as the way to get change across the line.
6. Learn to sell change by appreciating the emotional drivers of the buyer.
7. Ballance Nutrients case study—a blueprint for selling change.
8. Presell the KPI pitch to an influencer in the meeting room before you present.
9. The presentation tips that will help you deliver "killer" presentations to management and staff.

CHAPTER 4

Leading and Selling the Change

Before we venture further into the process of implementation, we need first to address selling the change within our organization. As we well know from past experiences, this sales process is not easy and is prone to failure. I would argue that more than half the initiatives that are declined by the board or senior management were undersold. In other words, given the right approach, the initiative would have gone ahead.

> "How people perform correlates to how situations occur to them."
> —Zaffron and Logan

If you are not prepared to learn the skills to cover the common deficiencies in selling change process, you are better off playing golf or burying yourself in a process rather than commence a KPI initiative. Selling change requires a special set of skills, and we all can, and should, get better at it.

Steve Zaffron and Dave Logan: Why So Many Initiatives Fail

Steve Zaffron and Dave Logan have written a compelling book, *The Three Laws of Performance*,[1] that explains why so many change initiatives have failed. The first law is "How people perform correlates to how situations occur to them." The writers point out that the organization's "default future," which we as individuals just know in our bones will happen—will be made to happen. Thus, in an organization with a systemic problem, the organization's staff will be driven to make initiatives fail so that the default future prevails.

Zaffron and Logan went on to say, "That is why the more you change the more you stay the same." The key to change is to re-create, in the organization's staff's minds, a new vision of the future—let's call it a *reinvented future*.

Zaffron and Logan signal the importance of language (the second law); without language we would not have a past or a future. It is the ability to use language that enables us to categorize thoughts as either the past or the future. Without language we would be like the cat on the mat, sunning itself for yet another afternoon, thinking about the next meal but without the ability to process complex thought.

Zaffron and Logan further add that to make change, we need to use a future-based language (the third law). It is interesting; if you listen to the outstanding orators of the past such as Sir Winston Churchill, you will hear future-based language at work. These great speakers knew, intuitively, about the power of future-based language.

We shall fight on the beaches, we shall fight on the landing grounds, we shall fight in the fields and in the streets, we shall fight in the hills; we shall never surrender.

Harry Mills: The Importance of Self-Persuasion

Harry Mills, a multiple business book author, has written extensively about persuasion.[2] In his recent work, *The Aha! Advantage*,[3] he talks about the significance of self-persuasion.

Self-persuasion is fundamentally more powerful than direct persuasion essentially because of the way it reduces resistance.

Mills talks about the four faces of the *aha!* moment, as shown in Exhibit 4.1, the point when your audience gets the message and now persuades itself to adopt the message as if it were their own. Mills' work is very consistent with Zaffron and Logan. We need to get the staff in the organization to have that *aha!* moment for themselves, that "Hell, no! We do not want the default future." When the staff come to this point, change is inevitable.

This means we need to structure our workshops so there is more involvement, more chance for staff to have that *aha!* moment, and less dogmatic rhetoric about the facts.

64

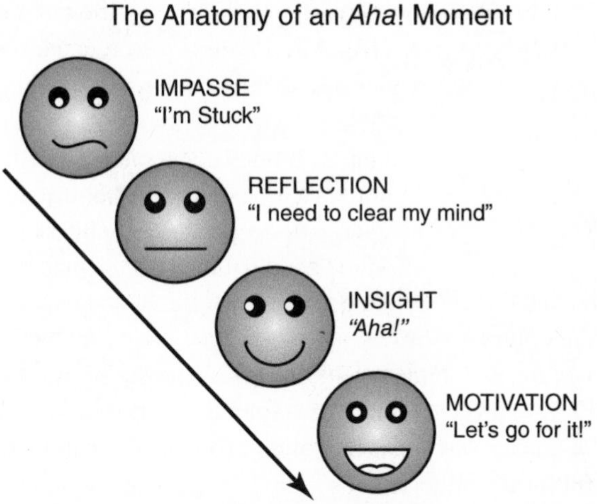

The Anatomy of an *Aha!* Moment

Exhibit 4.1 The Four Faces of the *Aha!* Moment
Source: The Mills Group.

John Kotter: How to Lead Change Successfully

In 1996, John Kotter published *Leading Change*,[4] which quickly became the seminal work in the field of change management. He emphasized that effecting change—real, transformative change—is hard. Kotter proposed an eight-stage process for creating major change, a clear map to follow when persuading an organization to move. I will discuss each Kotter stage while at the same time embedding Zaffron and Logan's and Harry Mills' thinking. If you follow these stages, you will increase the chances of success with change projects.

Establish a sense of urgency. Here we need to appeal both to the intellectual and the emotional sides of the executive team. There are two stages. First, ambush the CEO with a compelling elevator pitch so you get to stage two. Second, deliver a masterful sales presentation of around 15 to 20 minutes, aimed at obtaining permission to run a focus group to assess, validate, and scope the proposed initiative.

No project will ever succeed without a guiding coalition of oracles behind it.

Create a guiding coalition. In every organization you have oracles, those individuals everyone refers you to when you need something answered (e.g., "You need to talk to Pat"). These oracles exist right across the organization and might hold seemingly unimportant positions. Do not be fooled.

An investment at this stage is paramount. In one case study, an organization held three two-week workshops that were designed to progress their planning tool implementation. Yes, that is six weeks of workshops. The CEO was present for part of each of the workshops and the wisdom from the oracles was channeled by an expert facilitator into a successful blueprint for the project.

No project will ever succeed without a guiding coalition of oracles behind it. In *The Three Laws of Performance*, Zaffron and Logan illustrate that when you present the "burning platform" you are aiming for an overwhelming "Hell, no!" response upon asking the question, "Do you want the default future?" The oracles want the reinvented future, which you have also articulated. However, Mills has warned us to be patient and give time for the staff to discuss, think, and mull over the content. In this methodology there is a preference to having two-day workshops thus giving staff more time to let self-persuasion work.

Develop a vision and strategy. In order for the journey to be seen and resources made available, we must master future-based language that is compelling and motivational. As mentioned, Zaffron and Logan have signified the importance of language (the second law) and that it is crucial that you talk using a future-based language (the third law).

Communicate the change vision. Kotter emphasized that it's not likely that you will undercommunicate a little bit; you will probably undercommunicate a lot, by a factor of 10 to 100 times. This will undermine your initiative, no matter how well planned. During a KPI project, the project leader needs to obtain permission from the CEO to gate-crash any gathering in the organization and have a 10-minute slot to outline the project and progress to date. One surefire way to failure is to believe that staff will read your project newsletters and emails.

Empower broad-based action. Early on the need for change and the right to change must be handed over to teams within the organization. Zaffron and Logan concur with this view. Once the invented future is set in the minds of the organization's staff, the staff will march toward this future. All the great writers have emphasized that some chaos is beneficial, so let teams embrace the project in their own way.

Generate quick wins. Obvious to us all but frequently missed. Always remember that senior management is, on occasion, afflicted by attention deficit disorder. Progress in a methodical and introverted way at your peril. We need easy wins, celebrated extrovertly, and we need to ensure we set up the CEO to score the easy goals.

Consolidate gains and produce more change. This is the flywheel effect so well put by Jim Collins in his books *Built to Last*[5] and *Good to Great*.[6] When the staff are working in unison, the flywheel of change will turn quicker and quicker.

Anchor new approaches in the culture. Make heroes of the change agents, make sure their values are embedded in the corporate values, and now ensure you weed out those in management who have not embraced the change and who, over time, will be extinguishing the fire at night when nobody is looking.

Learn to Sell by Appreciating the Emotional Drivers of the Buyer

To sell a product, a service, or a project you need to remember that little was ever sold by logic! You sell through emotional drivers (e.g., remember how the dealer sold you your last car). Thus, we need to radically alter the way we pitch this sale to the senior management team (SMT), to the CEO, and to the board. We have to focus on the emotional drivers that matter to these groups and understand the links between them. Start by asking the management team these questions:

Points of pain/emotional drivers for the senior management team

1. Do we know which of our success factors are critical?

2. Does the lack of alignment of daily activities to strategy concern you?

3. Are you overwhelmed by too many performance measures?

4. Do you enjoy sifting through information overload in your precious family time?

5. Does it concern you that staff are prioritizing based on their view of what is important and not according to the organization's critical success factors?

6. Are the existing performance measures creating positive change and alignment to what is important?

7. Can reporting monthly really be appropriate when the "horse has well and truly bolted"?

8. Is investment of time and money in the current performance measurement system generating enough value?

Also, when you next meet board members, ask these questions:

Points of pain/emotional drivers for the board

1. Are the measures we report to you giving you a clear view of the organization's overall performance?

2. Is the organization making enough progress on the good-to-great journey?

3. Would you benefit from a one-page overview of performance?

4. Are you receiving too much information and thus there is a danger of not seeing the wood for the trees?

Many initiatives fail at this hurdle because we attempt to change the culture through selling logic, writing reports, and issuing commands via e-mail. It does not work. It is important to recognize that maybe the KPI team does not have enough public relations (PR) skills, so PR support will be needed. No presentation, e-mail, memo, or paper should go out unless it has been vetted by your PR expert. All your presentations should be road-tested in front of the PR expert. Your PR strategy should include selling to staff, budget holders, SMT, and the board.

If managed correctly, you will need only four to seven days of PR consultancy time. Once the chosen PR expert has visited the organization and received an adequate brief, keep the PR expert behind the scenes and avoid getting them caught up in lengthy meetings or writing original copy. This expert's role is to rework the output from the KPI team, often advising and amending e-mailed documents. This step should not be underestimated.

Selling by Emotional Drivers: How a Car Sale Is Made

Three customers arrive on the same day to look at a car that has been featured in the local newspaper. The first person is a young IT professional, generation Y, and wearing the latest designer clothing. The salesperson slowly walks up and assesses the emotional drivers of this potential buyer. Having ascertained that the young man is an IT guru, working for a major search engine organization, the salesperson says, "I hope you have some track racing experience. This car has 320 BHP, a twin turbo, and corners like it's on railway tracks. Only a top driver can handle this beast. It's a real driver's car." SOLD.

The second person could be me, with my gray hair visible. The salesperson might say, "This car is five-star rated for safety, with eight air bags, enough power to get you out of trouble, unbelievable braking when you have to avoid the idiots on the road, and tires that will never fail you." SOLD.

The third person is wearing stylish clothing and is impeccably well groomed. The opening sales line might be, "This car has won many awards for its design. Sit in the driver's seat and see the quality of the finish. Everything is in the right place. You look like a million dollars in that outfit you are wearing, and every time you drive this car you will feel like a million dollars!" SOLD.

In each case the salesperson is tailoring the pitch to the buyer. Far too often the sales pitch for a new process is left to a poorly prepared PowerPoint pitch and detailed accompanying report, full of features but signifying nothing.

Selling the KPI Project

The KPI team will need to perform a number of sales pitches to get the go-ahead. The KPI team should incorporate the following tasks within the work it performs to succeed in selling the KPI project as outlined in this book. Please view my webcasts accessed through www.davidparmenter .com, where I have discussed this in more detail and provided you with material to help the sales process.

Task 1. Obtain Public Relations Support for the Project

As mentioned, this project needs a PR machine behind it. Where possible, select a PR expert who already knows the organization. Failing that, seek someone who has helped market a project to an organization's staff. Do check references, and ring a couple of their old assignments asking the Jack Welch question, "Would you have them again?"

Task 2. Prepare Your Elevator Speech

Having now understood why prior initiatives have failed through poor selling, let us now look at how we get the SMT motivated. The key is to have a 30-second elevator speech that is designed to capture their attention. It must be ready so that when we next bump into the decision makers we are practiced and poised, see Exhibit 4.2.

The "elevator speech" term came about in management books describing how you need to be able to get a point across in an elevator ride, around 40 to 60 seconds, as sometimes these are the only chances you may have to get through to a decision maker. The aim is, as they walk away, that they ask you to come to their office in the next few days to discuss this further.

It is important to remember that an elevator pitch is your initiative and there is no time to waste. You have to catch the CEO's attention immediately. It is paramount that you get the wording and emphasis right.

An elevator interaction might go like this:

Hello Jane, I need to tell you that our current KPIs have broken down. We not only have too many, they are costly to report, and they lead to little change. It's like _____ (local analogy).

I have been researching a tried and tested methodology outlined in this book. I would only need 15 minutes of your time to outline a new KPI approach that not only will rectify these issues but also realign our company to our critical success factors.

The key is to fine-tune the elevator speech so that it is compelling. I recommend you practice your elevator speech at least 20 times so that it is focused and completed within 40 to 60 seconds. If time permits, you could talk about how late planes in the sky turned around British Airways. As Kotter said, we need to create a sense of urgency and connect both intellectually and emotionally. See Exhibit 4.3 for an elevator checklist.

Task 3. Selling the Need for a One-Day Focus Group Workshop

Assuming there is a certain level of interest, we now have to prepare a presentation to try to get the SMT to agree to a "tipping point" workshop where

Exhibit 4.2 Never Underestimate the Power of a Good, Well-Practiced Elevator Speech

Read *The Presentation Secrets of Steve Jobs: How to Be Insanely Great in Front of Any Audience* by Carmine Gallo.

all the concepts can be aired, and the experts are asked whether the initiative should proceed to the next stage. This presentation is a game changer and is important to get right. You will not get a second chance.

I would recommend that the KPI team also read *The Presentation Secrets of Steve Jobs: How to Be Insanely Great in Front of Any Audience* by Carmine Gallo.[7] It is a compelling read. I have incorporated his work in creating a list of the better practices around preparing and delivering compelling presentations, which is covered later in this chapter.

To have the required impact in such presentations, I would recommend attending a "train the trainer" session, which will be a more advanced course than the presentations skills course you may have attended some time ago.

Exhibit 4.3 Checklist for Your Next Elevator Speech

Preparation tips	Is it covered?
Use Post-it stickers to brainstorm content, target points of pain. See guidelines in this chapter.	☐ Yes ☐ No
Avoid empty words (common terms that mean nothing; optimize, maximize, best practice etc.).	☐ Yes ☐ No
Practice using good interpersonal skills during the delivery (making eye contact, smiling during pitch, and being engaging).	☐ Yes ☐ No
Connect your sentences so they flow well.	☐ Yes ☐ No
Practice 20 times including in the lift or the car park where the interaction is likely to occur.	☐ Yes ☐ No
Bring personality and passion into your speech.	☐ Yes ☐ No
Aim for a 40- to 60-second pitch.	☐ Yes ☐ No
Be prepared to answer three key questions that may be asked.	☐ Yes ☐ No
Delivery tips	☐ Yes ☐ No
Capture their attention in the first eight seconds with three points of pain.	☐ Yes ☐ No
Use an analogy to sum up the points of pain.	☐ Yes ☐ No
Focus on key benefits that fix the main points of pain.	☐ Yes ☐ No
Where possible, refer to a well-respected case study.	☐ Yes ☐ No
Ask for the chance to deliver a 20-minute presentation and follow the rules described later in this chapter.	☐ Yes ☐ No

Task 4. Hold a Focus Group Workshop

The one-day focus group workshop is important, as we want to create a guiding coalition in Kotter's words. The workshop should be attended by a cross-section of 15 to 30 experienced staff covering the business units, teams, area offices, and head office, and covering the different roles from administrators to senior management team members.

At this workshop, you discuss the existing issues with performance measures, expose them to the new thinking, outline the intended approach, and seek their advice to decide if the CSF and KPI project is viable and, if so, what lessons we should learn from past projects.

As a result of this workshop, the project implementation program will be tailored to cover the main institutional barriers and hot spots, and the SMT should be in a position to select the KPI team and commit to the project.

The aim of this workshop is to be a "tipping point" to get the oracles' green light and their full support, which will be important. The next step is to sell the senior management team the KPI project to revitalize performance measurement.

Task 5. Prepare a Comprehensive CSF and KPI Project Blueprint

From a case study, featured below, I have learned how imperative it is to invest time in developing a robust blueprint, one that sets out the direction and the requirements. One accredited coach, in the winning KPIs methodology, has recommended it could be called "a measures treasure map." In order to achieve this, you will need a series of workshops involving senior management and a cross-section of the oracles where attendance is requested by the CEO and where mobile devices and computers can only be used in the breaks. The output from these workshops is the final blueprint document.

Ballance Nutrients' Case Study: A Blueprint to Selling Change

In a major project to radically change the way Ballance Nutrients forecasted and planned for the future, Ballance Nutrients wanted to develop a blueprint, a vision, and strategy for the new process: just the thing Kotter suggested in his book *Leading Change*.

As an organization with a "thinking approach" to management, they hired an expert to facilitate the blueprint design. They based the blueprint design process around the Toyota principle: "Make decisions slowly by consensus, thoroughly considering all options, and then implement the decisions rapidly."

They held three two-week workshops. Yes, that is six weeks of workshops. This incredible up-front investment ensured that they had a clear understanding of their needs from the model, how the model should work, that every process in the model was using well-thought-out logic, and that wherever possible a "helicopter" big picture view was retained. An important feature of the blueprint process was that it transferred ownership from finance to the organization, once again being consistent with Kotter's suggested approach in his book *Leading Change*.

The Ballance Nutrients approach to building an agreed blueprint should be replicated in the CSF and winning KPIs project, albeit in a quicker time frame, as no software expenditure approval is required.

Task 6. Presell the CSFs and Winning KPIs Project

You need to ascertain who in the meeting is a wise oracle that the CEO will turn to and who is accessible to you. Visit them and ask for their assistance. Sell the project to them: that this could be a great "tipping point" in the development of the organization. Once you have the wise oracle committed ask them for their input into the presentation and particularly for their guidance on how to get a green light for the project. Ask them to attend a couple of practice sessions. Incorporate their feedback and especially their wording into your presentation as this will further enhance their buy-in.

Ask the wise oracle to speak first after your presentation, offering their support and the reasons why the KPI project is such an important initiative right now. I would give the oracle a list of the pointers you would like them to include in their comments.

Task 7. Deliver a Compelling Presentation to the CEO to Seek Project Approval

With a comprehensive blueprint, and with the oracles' support, you are now in a powerful position to seek permission to roll out the KPI project. In many organizations this may require board approval because of its significance. Use the checklist (see Exhibit 4.3) to ensure that nothing is forgotten. Ensure that you remember Kotter's advice: project teams have a tendency to under-communicate.

You will be able to secure more time with this presentation: 30 to 40 minutes is ideal. It needs to cover a summary of the material in this book. I have included some PowerPoint slides in the attached electronic media.

Shortcut for Small to Medium-Sized Enterprises

The following tasks can be eliminated:

Task 1. Obtaining public relations support for the project will not be necessary for organizations with less than 250 FTEs.

Task 3. Selling the need for a one-day focus group workshop will not be necessary for organizations with less than 250 FTEs.

Selling the Winning KPIs to the Organization's Staff

Employees need to be prepared for change; we need to show them that the default future is no longer viable and get them to choose the proposed new future. The project team and the senior management team need to:

- Convey what the organization's CSFs are and why employees need to focus their daily activities around them.
- Convince employees of the need for change by highlighting the performance gap between the organization and best practice.

- Outline what change is required.
- Show how KPIs contribute to the CSFs and the organization's strategy.
- Attract employees' interest so they want to participate by selling the change through their emotional drivers.
- Address employees' resistance to change and performance measurement.

A formal briefing program should be held to outline the changes associated with introducing KPIs into the organization. By its conclusion, all employees should at least believe that they need to do something differently, and a core group should be clear about implementation issues and how performance measures will be used. Those who have shown an interest in the new KPI process should be shortlisted for the team coordinator role, who will support and help the KPI team to develop and implement KPIs.

Task 1. Survey a Cross-Section of Staff

A survey may be useful to find out the current perceptions on existing performance information in the organization, the current concerns about the new project, and what needs to be covered in the employee briefings. This survey should be performed before the performance measures two-day workshops are held in stage three.

With the help of the HR team, make a selection of experienced staff covering all regions, levels of staff, and so forth. This cross-section sample should not be greater than 200, or 10 percent of total staff, and not less than 30 staff. With these numbers, you can close off the survey with a 60 percent return rate and still have a valid survey. Too large a sample will make data mining more difficult and seldom raises any new issues. To assist, I have provided an employee questionnaire in PDF format for you to download.

Task 2. Utilize the Feedback from Employee Survey

The feedback from the employee survey must be incorporated in the workshop design. We need to cover all issues in the opening address by the KPI team presenter. To assist with capturing these issues, I have provided a worksheet in PDF format for you to download.

Task 3. Build a Compelling Case for Change

Demonstrate that KPIs are part of an SMT-agreed package of initiatives to respond to the pressures on the organization. Spell out these pressures in terms that people can understand. Use comparative information from preliminary benchmarking to highlight the performance gap between your organization and best practice.

As already stated, in selling the project to the SMT, nothing was ever sold by logic! You sell through emotional drivers. Thus, you need to radically alter the way you pitch this sale to the staff. You have to focus on the emotional drivers that matter to them:

- The right mix of performance measures will make work more rewarding and enjoyable (e.g., greater staff recognition).
- The focus on the right measures would mean their work would be more effective (e.g., their day-to-day work would be better linked to the organization's strategic objectives).
- In the future they would have more empowerment and autonomy (e.g., staff making more decisions).
- Winning KPIs will enhance profitability and thus offer greater job security and possibly increased remuneration (e.g., through profit-sharing arrangements).

Task 4. Use the Project's Vision Statement to Attract the Staff

Generate interest by painting a picture of how the workplace could look in two to three years once KPIs and other initiatives have taken hold. Over time, empowered staff will begin to generate their own versions of the vision for the workplace. However, in the beginning, it is critical that the KPI project team be passionate about the KPI project vision statement. The PR expert is to ensure that all documentation sells this vision adequately (e.g., memos, presentations, and the KPI team intranet pages).

To assist you with these steps, I have prepared a suggested road show program in PDF format for you to download.

Task 5. "Selling the Concept" Road Show

You may need to have a separate "selling the concept" road show before the series of performance measures workshops are rolled out in stage three. You will need to structure the road show briefings so that all employees hear the message, considering language skills, literacy, and shift work patterns.

It is important to demonstrate the existence of a partnership in change. To this end, employee/union representatives should also address staff attending the road show, outlining their support for winning KPIs. The best workshops seem to be held in informal workplace settings, involving local management known to the audience, which are managed to maximize feedback. In larger groups, the use of written questions submitted by the audience will encourage staff to raise issues.

A formal briefing program should be held to outline the changes associated with introducing KPIs into the organization. By its conclusion, all employees should at least believe that they need to do something differently, and a core group should be clear about implementation issues and how performance measures will be used. Those who have shown an aptitude for the new KPI model should become the team coordinators, who will support and help the KPI team to develop and implement KPIs.

Task 6. Maintain Ongoing Communication

Whatever you have done in the past, it will not have been enough. Follow Kotter's advice and attempt to overcommunicate rather than undercommunicate.

Use the communication mediums that work for your audience. Do not sit behind a vast array of tweets, e-mails, and Facebook entries. You must merge the use of remote communication with "walking the talk."

Most projects make inroads and have quick wins, although few have a project leader that recognizes them, celebrates them, or, worse, communicates with them. Make sure you have an up-to-date elevator pitch on the KPI project's progress, so you can spread the good news and sow the seeds of success to whomever you meet in your daily travels.

Task 7. Empower Broad-Based Action

If the blueprint was successful, you will already have traction in various parts of the organization. At Ballance Nutrients the project was racing ahead on many fronts simultaneously.

Delivering compelling PowerPoint presentations is a skill that the KPI team will have to have mastered before they deliver any presentations or workshops.

Shortcut for Small to Medium-Sized Enterprises

The following tasks can be eliminated:

Task 1. Survey a cross-section of staff—will not be necessary for organizations with less than 250 FTEs. It can be replaced with informal discussions.

Task 5. "Selling the concept" road show—will not be necessary for organizations with less than 250 FTEs. It can be replaced with informal discussions.

Delivering Bulletproof PowerPoint Presentations

Delivering compelling PowerPoint presentations is a skill that the KPI team will have to have mastered before they deliver any presentations or workshops. I will assume that you have attended a presentation skills course, which is a prerequisite to bulletproof PowerPoint presentations. There are some rules for a good PowerPoint presentation.

Prepare a paper to go with the presentation	Always prepare a paper for the audience including large reproductions of any complex diagrams and financial statements so this detail does not need to be in the slides. Understand that the PowerPoint slide is not meant to be a document; if you have more than 35 words per slide, you are creating a report, not a presentation. Each point should be relatively cryptic and be understood only by those who have attended your presentation.
Presentation planning	Last-minute slide presentations are a career-limiting activity. You would not hang your dirty washing in front of an audience, so why would you want to show your audience sloppy slides? Only say "yes" to a presentation if you have the time, resources, and enthusiasm to do the job properly.
	Create time so that you can be in a "thinking space" (e.g., work at home, go to the library, etc.).
	Map the subject area out in a mind map as shown in Exhibit 4.4, and then do a mind dump on Post-it stickers covering all the points, diagrams, pictures you want to cover. Have one sticker for each point. Then you place your stickers where they fit best. Using stickers makes it easy to reorganize your subject matter. This will lead to a better presentation.
	Exhibit 4.4 Using Post-it Stickers to Plan the Content of the Presentation
Presentation content	At least 10 to 20 percent of your slides should be high-quality photographs, some of which will not even require a caption.

	A picture can replace many words; to understand this point you need to read *Presentation Zen: Simple Ideas on Presentation Design and Delivery* by Garr Reynolds,[8] and *Slide:ology: The Art and Science of Creating Great Presentations* by Nancy Duarte.[9]
	Understand what is considered good use of color, photographs, and the "rule of thirds."
	For key points, do not go less than 30-pt-size font. As Nancy Duarte says, "Look at the slides in the slide sorter view at 66% size. If you can read it on your computer, there is a good chance your audience, positioned in the rear seats, will be able to read the slides on the screen."
	Limit animation; it is far better that the audience be able to read all the points on the slide quickly rather than holding them back.
	Use Guy Kawasaki's "10/20/30 rule."[10] A sales-pitch PowerPoint presentation should have 10 slides, last no more than 20 minutes, and contain no font smaller than 30 pt.
	Be aware of being too cute and clever with your slides. The move to creating a lot of whitespace is all very well, provided your labels on the diagram do not have to be very small.
	Never show numbers to a decimal place nor to the dollar if the number is greater than 10,000. If sales are $9,668,943.22, surely it is better to say, "approx. $10 million" or "$9.7 million." The precise number can be in the written document if it is deemed worthwhile.
	Never use clip art; it sends shivers down the spine of the audience and you may lose them before you have a chance to present.
Use technology	Where possible, if you are going to present on a regular basis, make sure you have a tablet PC, which gives you the ability to draw on the slides when you are making points. This makes the presentation more interesting, no matter how bad you are at drawing.
	Have a simple remote mouse so that you can move the slides along independently of your computer.
Practice, practice, practice	Practice your delivery. The shorter the presentation, the more you need to practice. For my father's eulogy, I must have practiced it 20 to 30 times. It remains today the best speech I have ever delivered and the one I prepared the most for.

	If presenting to the senior management team or board, make sure you have presold the concept to the wise oracle in the room who will be first to speak after you finish, outlining their support.
Presentation itself	Bring theatrics into your presentation. Be active as a presenter, walking up the aisle so that those in the back see you close up, vary your voice, get down on one knee to emphasize an important point; have a bit of fun and your audience will as well.
	Always tell stories to relate to the audience, bringing in humor that is relevant to them. A good presenter should be able to find plenty of humor in the subject without having to resort to telling jokes. No doubt, some of the audience will have heard the jokes or would rather hear them from a professional comedian.
	Make sure your opening words grab the audience's attention. Never start with "How pleased you are to present" or an introduction about yourself. These can be included after you have grabbed their attention.
	If using graphs in a presentation, ensure you have referred to Stephen Few's guideline covered in Chapter 10.
	Always remember the audience does not know the whole content of your speech, particularly if you keep the details off the slides. If you do leave some point out, don't worry about it—they don't know or would not realize the error.
	If there has been some issue relating to transportation, technology, and so forth that has delayed the start, avoid starting off with an apology. You can refer to this later. Your first five minutes are the most important for the whole presentation and must, therefore, be strictly on the topic matter.
	Greet as many members of the audience as you can before the presentation, as it will help calm your nerves and will also give you the opportunity to understand their knowledge of and experience with KPIs and CSFs. You can also ask individuals, in advance, for their participation at question time. The other benefit is that it confirms that nobody in the audience would rather be doing your role, so why should you be nervous?
	If you are delivering a workshop, shake hands at the end with as many of the audience as possible by positioning yourself by the door when the audience leaves. This develops further rapport between presenter and audience.
	For each workshop exercise run through an example of the workshop exercise to ensure every workshop group has the correct idea of what is required.

In addition, I have included a checklist that I use for preparing and delivering a presentation; see the PDF supporting this chapter.

PDF Download

To assist the KPI project team on the journey, templates and checklists have been provided. The reader can access, from kpi.davidparmenter.com/fourthedition, free of charge, a PDF of the following chapter templates:

- Draft Employee Questionnaire
- Addressing Staff Concerns and Learning Issues Worksheet
- Draft Agenda for Road Show to Staff
- Checklist for Marketing the KPI System to All Employees
- Half-a-day Workshop for the SMT on Implementing KPIs—and Getting It Right the First Time
- One-day Focus Group on CSFs and Implementing KPIs
- PowerPoint Presentations Checklist

Notes

1. Steve Zaffron and Dave Logan, *The Three Laws of Performance* (San Francisco: Jossey-Bass, 2011).
2. Harry Mills, *Artful Persuasion: How to Command Attention, Change Minds, and Influence People* (New York: AMACOM, 2000).
3. Harry Mills, *The Aha! Advantage* (The Mills Group, 2015).
4. John Kotter, *Leading Change* (Boston: Harvard Business Review Press. 2012).
5. Jim Collins and Jerry Porras, *Built to Last: Successful Habits of Visionary Companies* (New York: Harper Business Essentials, 2004).
6. Jim Collins, *Good to Great: Why Some Companies Make the Leap and Others Don't* (New York: HarperBusiness, 2001).
7. Carmine Gallo, *The Presentation Secrets of Steve Jobs: How to Be Insanely Great in Front of Any Audience* (New York: McGraw-Hill Education, 2009).
8. Garr Reynolds, *Presentation Zen: Simple Ideas on Presentation Design and Delivery* (Berkeley: New Riders, 2008).
9. Nancy Duarte, *Slide:ology: The Art and Science of Creating Great Presentations* (Sebastopol, CA: O'Riley, 2008).
10. Guy Kawasaki, *The only 10 slides you need in your pitch* (guykawasaki.com/the-only-10-slides-you-need-in-your-pitch/).

Overview

The senior management team must be committed to developing the critical success factors and associated measures and driving them through the organization. Thus, the timing of the project is vital. The KPI project must find a suitable window where the senior management team will have time to commit to the change process. The size of the organization will determine which of the approaches outlined here will be chosen.

This chapter outlines the tasks required in this stage and gives instructions on how to access, free of charge, a pdf of the suggested worksheets and checklists to be used by the KPI project team.

Key learning points from this chapter include:

1. The importance of the CEO as the driver for a KPI project.
2. The KPI project proposal presentation will be one of the most important presentations in your working life.
3. Management will need to abandon projects, processes, and reports to make time for the KPI project.
4. The KPI project needs to report its wins to the senior management team each week.
5. The KPI facilitator's role is one of facilitation and mentoring, not project leadership.
6. The importance of the external facilitator's role and how to select them.

CHAPTER 5

Getting the CEO and Senior Management Committed to the Change

Too many projects fail because the senior management team was not committed to the project. It is important that the KPI project not be undertaken in an environment in which they are destined to fail. It is far better to defer the project if there are any doubts about conflicting priorities or adequacy of resources.

CEO and Senior Management Commitment

The senior management team's commitment creates a dynamic environment in which projects can thrive. Before the senior management team can do this, they need to be sold on the concept and fully understand why they should treat monitoring and follow-up on the KPIs as a daily task.

By senior management team commitment, I mean that the senior management will need to set aside time each week to perform exercises that include giving feedback on suggested measures, being available to the winning KPI team for interviews, visiting organizations who have implemented a CSF and KPI project successfully, and approving investment proposals into new executive information systems that will be the main vehicle for reporting KPIs.

Some senior staff can simply view the development of KPIs as an end in itself and go through with it to keep the boss happy. They are not strategic in their perspective, so they don't see the CSFs and the associated performance measures as tools to help them better understand and manage their

The CEO must be the central driver, carrying around the embryonic KPIs all the time, talking about their importance frequently, and so on.

The KPI project proposal presentation will be one of the most important presentations in your working life.

The CEO needs to locate an external facilitator.

organization. This can be reflected in a loss of interest when the process of development gets tough, such as deciding on what KPIs to use and the trade-offs to be made. Although the senior management team is important, the CEO is critical. The CEO must be the central driver, carrying around the embryonic KPIs all the time, talking about their importance frequently, and so on.

Task 1. Prepare and Practice Your Elevator Speech to Get the Senior Management's Attention

As mentioned in Chapter 4, Leading and Selling the Change, it is important to have an elevator speech, a 40 to 60-second sales pitch, ready for the next time we meet the CEO or an influential member of the SMT. By having an elevator speech ready at hand, you can gain their interest in a KPI project and get a 20-minute slot to sell the project to them.

Task 2. Selling the Need for External and Internal Mentor Support for the KPI team

The KPI team will need a couple of mentors to support them. One mentor will need to be someone who has worked on KPI projects and who understands the KPI methodology to be used, most likely an external consultant. Another mentor will be someone who has worked in the organization for at least five years, is well connected to the key players, and knows what needs to be done to get large projects over the line in the organization.

Task 3. Appointment of an External Facilitator

The CEO needs to locate an external facilitator who will work with the senior management team to scope the project, facilitate senior management's commitment, help select the in-house KPI team, and support the

KPI team in their journey of learning, discovery, and achievement. The facilitator needs to be experienced with performance measurement issues as well as with how to develop and implement KPIs. With web-based meetings being a common tool, it is possible to have the facilitators perform their duties from afar. I have achieved this on several projects myself.

It is imperative that you invest as much time as possible in the preselection process, before you are in dialogue with short-listed consulting firms. Your first point of call is to short-list three to five consultants based on reputation. This is easier than you think. It is worth asking consultants who have worked successfully with the organization or whose who have work successfully with you in your previous roles, for referrals. You may even find they put themselves forward for part of the assignment and will work alongside a recommended consultant they have known for years. Just as talented staff know other talented staff great consultants know other great consultants. That is how the business world works.

Having made a shortlist, it is worth contacting a couple of their previous clients to ask, "Would you take Pat Davies on for another consulting assignment?" As Jack Welch pointed out in his book *Winning*,[1] you will be surprised how frank they might be. Assuming a thumbs-up, go on to ask how the consultant works best (consultants may not realize this themselves).

Financial Institution Case Study

The CFO had been exposed to the Winning KPIs methodology ten years ago. The time was right in the organization for the process. The CEO, a very well-read executive, warmed to the idea and emailed me to discuss some KPI training at an executive retreat. Following a series of phone calls and emails it was agreed to turn the training into the two-day CSFs workshop, outlined in Chapter 7. Thus, the executives would receive KPI training and make progress along the CSF and KPI journey.

Task 4. Obtain the Green Light to Run the Critical Success Factors Workshop

The facilitator will need to sell to the CEO the merits of running a two-day CSFs workshop. It will be pointed out that the CEO can then make the second decision, which was to whether, after ascertaining the CSFs, they want to run the KPI project.

This process can happen over a series of phone calls or may already have happened as the CEO has already done their reading. Alternatively, if the CEO wants the SMT to agree, the facilitator can deliver a webinar/workshop to the SMT to kick-start the project. This presentation will, among other things:

- Explain the new thinking on performance measures.
- Explain the differences among key result indicators (KRIs), result indicators (RIs), performance indicators (PIs), and KPIs.
- Emphasize the importance of knowing the organization's CSFs.
- Show that daily activities can be linked to the strategic objectives.
- Convey the importance of monitoring and following up on the KPIs as a daily task.
- Explain the draft project implementation program.
- Emphasize the commitment the SMT needs to make each week. They will need to give feedback on suggested measures, be available to the project team for interviews, and possibly visit other organizations.

Task 5. Agree on the Initial Timing, Resources, and Approach

This involves ensuring that this is the right time for the project to be run in conjunction with concurrent projects within the organization. In addition, it is necessary to consider how best to run the implementation. The most appropriate implementation is influenced by the size of the organization, the diversity of the departments, the organization's locations, and the in-house staff resources available for the project. Each implementation is like a fingerprint that is unique to the organization, and it should be designed in consultation with the stakeholders, the external facilitator, and with consideration of prior experiences that have worked and not worked in past implementation rollouts. There are several questions to answer:

- Is this the right time to embark on this project?
- How big will the KPI team need to be?
- What will we abandon or reassign so that the KPI team can be full time on the KPI project?
- What needs to be abandoned to make room for this project? Do we have a window of opportunity to commit to this project?

- How should we best implement winning KPIs across our organization?
- Have we maximized the fit with the other changes our organization is pursuing to achieve world-class performance?

When you can answer these questions clearly, you will be able to locate winning KPIs in the total performance improvement game plan.

> Management will need to abandon projects, processes, and reports to make time for the project.

> Be aware of the current perception of performance measurement within the organization.

Task 6. Ascertain What Needs to Be Abandoned to Make Room for the KPI Project

Peter Drucker said, "Don't tell me what you're doing, tell me what you've stopped doing."[2] Management will need to abandon projects, performance measures, processes, and reports to make time for the project. Many projects fail because staff and management must carry out all their existing workload as well as the new responsibilities of the new project. In such circumstances, it does not take long before enthusiasm wanes, and the project begins to derail.

The CEO needs to make clear what is to be sacrificed so that that time can be created for the project.

Task 7. Ascertain the Existing Measurement Culture

Be aware of the current perception of performance measurement within the organization. It takes time to adapt new approaches to performance measurement. It is, therefore, important to plan the introduction to KPIs with an appreciation of the organization's existing comfort (or discomfort) levels with performance measurement.

Task 8. Decide How the KPI Project Will Be Rolled Out

For organizations up to 3,000 staff a KPI team of two full-time resources is possible. Over that number you need a team of four so that you can run two performance measures workshops simultaneously. The KPI team, whose members will be trained by the facilitator, will effectively be in-house KPI consultants who travel in pairs to support the KPI coordinators in each main subsidiary.

The KPI team will need to select KPI coordinators in every country/ subsidiary and train them appropriately. A good method is to fly the country coordinators to a Performance Measures Workshop, so they can understand the dynamics and process, and thus, better prepare for the workshop when it is run in their subsidiary.

Financial Institution Case Study

Once trained, the in-house KPI team held the initial two-day performance measures workshop at the head office in Australia. Representatives from the Asian operation attended to experience the training and advise the KPI team on how best to deliver the presentation in their country. Skilled translators were hired so that the workshop had a simultaneous translation.

The two-day workshops, held in Europe, were delivered in a separate trip, using the same training program.

The rollout will also need to consider the current significance of subsidiaries' operations and their long-term future (e.g., there may be no point embarking on a rollout to a foreign subsidiary if it is to be sold).

The rollout success will be dependent on maintaining momentum and energy. Once a subsidiary has been selected, there should be an intensive push to complete. Each rollout phase should not be allowed to take more than 16 weeks, because the groundwork already has been prepared. A subsidiary rollout could take as few as 10 weeks. It is unlikely to be shorter due to the level of consultation and the rollout of the team performance measures workshop.

Task 9. Reporting Progress to Maintain the Senior Management Team's Engagement

The KPI project needs to report its wins to the SMT each week. This report may not necessarily need to be in a formal setting. Having a weekly elevator speech ready each week is the KPI team leader's priority on the Friday. They then need to manufacture situations where they

> **The KPI project needs to report its wins to the SMT each week.**

will bump into SMT members and thus be able to share some wins. As mentioned by John Kotter,[3] project teams have a tendency to undercommunicate by a factor of 10 or more.

During the project, there will be a need to deliver at least two workshops, of about two to three hours in duration, to provide an opportunity for the senior management to give valuable input into the project, launch newly designed reports, and convey progress.

Shortcuts for Small to Medium-Sized Enterprises

The following tasks can be eliminated for organizations with less than 250 FTEs:

Task 2. Selling the need for an external mentor to support the KPI team—can be limited to remote support providing the KPI project lead is an experienced project manager and understands all the concepts in this book.

Task 3. Appointment of an external facilitator—remote support should suffice.

Task 8. Ascertain the size and number of KPI team required—for organizations between 100 and 250 you should have two people on the team. For SMEs with less than 100 FTEs there will be only one person on the project team.

Guidelines for the External KPI Facilitator

If you have been selected as a facilitator to assist in the development of performance measures, you will need to be completely familiar with this book.

The KPI facilitator's role is one of facilitation and mentoring, not project leadership.

This resource kit provides you with three additional components to assist you in executing your role, namely:

1. The Introductory Key Performance Indicator (KPI) presentations on www.kpi .davidparmenter.com. Put "webinars" into the search bar to access a list of KPI webinars I have recorded and are now available via third-party websites.
2. Some checklists in PDF format for you to download.
3. A list of typical questions (and answers) you may expect to confront in your role in PDF format for you to download.

External Facilitator's Involvement in The KPI Project

It is important that the KPI facilitator's role be one of facilitation and mentoring, not project leadership. The facilitator should have little hands-on involvement after the set-up steps have been completed. The message in this KPI book is that project team members, coordinators, and teams should take on significant roles themselves. The facilitator's particular role is to guide the overall process, providing assistance and resources as required.

Each of the three stages contains questions and/or worksheets to be completed as the project team progresses through the implementation. The facilitator should ensure that these questions and worksheets are tailored to the organization and then completed. A rushed and noncollaborative approach to the development and implementation of performance measures, combined with a profound misunderstanding of the differences among key result indicators (KRIs), result indicator (RIs), performance indicators (PIs), and KPIs will result in failure.

Checklist of the External Facilitator's Role

Exhibit 5.1 provides a draft checklist of the main tasks you will need to consider. It is important that the facilitator's role be just that; it should never become the project manager's role.

Exhibit 5.1 Checklist of the Facilitator Role

The facilitator's role is to:	Task completed
1. Help the senior management team (SMT) pick the KPI project team.	☐ Yes ☐ No
2. Convince management that these staff members need to be committed full time.	☐ Yes ☐ No
3. Help select a liaison person for all business units/service teams.	☐ Yes ☐ No
4. Ensure that well meaning senior managers do not end up on the KPI project team.	☐ Yes ☐ No
5. Help sell the concept to the SMT.	☐ Yes ☐ No
6. Access performance measures and reporting templates that have been used successfully in other organizations.	☐ Yes ☐ No
7. Introduce case study material.	☐ Yes ☐ No
8. Obtain a sufficient level of commitment from the SMT.	☐ Yes ☐ No
9. Sell the concept to any new SMT members.	☐ Yes ☐ No
10. Guide the SMT to accept the six balanced scorecard perspectives recommended in this book.	☐ Yes ☐ No
11. Ensure that the KPI project team and SMT refine the hundreds of performance measures to fit the 10/80/10 rule.	☐ Yes ☐ No
12. Help the team differentiate among key result indicators, result indicators, performance indicators, and KPIs.	☐ Yes ☐ No
13. Ensure that the organization does not consolidate business unit performance indicators and end up calling them KPIs.	☐ Yes ☐ No
14. Ensure, with the SMT, that project team members are encouraged, given regular feedback, given recognition when milestones have been achieved, and so forth.	☐ Yes ☐ No
15. Empower and educate the KPI project team members ensuring that the KPI team leader can become the chief measurement officer, the in-house expert on measurement.	☐ Yes ☐ No
16. Utilize the organization's existing software licensees for developing the measures database and reporting requirements.	☐ Yes ☐ No
17. Assist the KPI project team to set up a database, with the recommended fields, recording all designed, tested and approved performance measures.	☐ Yes ☐ No
18. Ensure that work on team performance measures does not divert the project team from ascertaining the organization's KPIs.	☐ Yes ☐ No
19. Help the KPI team make good use of reporting templates outlined in Chapter 10.	☐ Yes ☐ No

PDF Download

To assist the KPI project team on the journey, templates and checklists have been provided. The reader can access, from kpi.davidparmenter.com/fourthedition, free of charge, a PDF of the following chapter templates:

- SMT Commitment Checklist
- Senior Management Team Commitment Questionnaire
- Checklist for Selecting a Facilitator
- Setting Up a Holistic KPI Development Strategy Checklist
- Holistic KPI Development Strategy Worksheet
- Checklist of the External Facilitator's Main Tasks

Notes

1. Jack Welch and Suzy Welch, *Winning* (New York: HarperBusiness, 2005).
2. Peter Drucker, *Management Challenges for the 21st Century* (New York: Harper-Collins, 1999).
3. John Kotter, *Leading Change* (Boston: Harvard Business Review Press, 2012).

Overview

The success of a KPI project rests with trained home-grown staff who have been reassigned so that they are full time on the project. This chapter covers the importance of selecting an in-house person to lead the KPI team, the reasons why choosing an external recruit to run the KPI team is doomed to fail, the training of the KPI team that will be required, and the need for a "just-do-it" KPI team culture.

The KPI project will have a team with the capability to deliver, provided it is supported by a forward-thinking senior management team. This team will need to be supported by both internal and external mentors and receive comprehensive training. Establishing a just-do-it culture and process will enable the project team to cut through red tape and deliver a timely suite of performance measures, recognizing that it will require further tailoring and improvement six to eight months after the commissioning of the CSFs and KPIs.

This chapter also outlines the resources I have provided to help the KPI team and the tasks required in this stage and gives instructions on how to access, free of charge, a PDF of the suggested worksheets and checklists.

Key learning points from this chapter include:

1. The importance of the KPI team working full time on the KPI project
2. The KPI project team should be a mix of oracles and young guns
3. Having a home-grown KPI team leader
4. Linking the KPI team directly to the CEO
5. Research into personnel records is recommended, as many talented in-house staff are found in obscure places
6. Important reference books for the KPI team to read and absorb
7. The extensive training that the KPI team will need especially the exposure to the thinking of the paradigm shifters such as Peter Drucker, Tom Peters, Jim Collins, and Jack Welch
8. The need for the KPI team to have a cluster of mentors supporting them
9. Indicative rollout duration of a KPI project depending on size of organization and size of KPI team
10. Deciding whether to have a big bang or a phased approach
11. The names of the six balanced scorecard perspectives
12. Never straying from the seven foundation stones

CHAPTER 6

Up-Skill In-House Resources to Manage the KPI Project

If a KPI project fails or lacks momentum, one often can look back to this stage and see where it all went wrong. The success of a KPI project rests with trained home-grown staff who have been reassigned so that they are full time on the project. The developing of home-grown resources who have the time to develop into measurement experts is vital. As discussed in Chapter 2, it is a myth that a KPI project can be run by an external consultant.

> The success of a KPI project rests with trained home-grown staff who have been reassigned so that they are full time on the project.

Establishing a Winning KPI Project Team

As mentioned in Chapter 3, there needs to be a new approach to measurement that is done by in-house staff who have been suitably trained: an approach that is consultative, promotes partnership between staff and management, and, finally, achieves behavioral alignment to the organization's critical success factors and strategic direction. I have been working with performance measures for many years and one thing has become abundantly clear: you need measurement expertise in-house.

Task 1. Select the In-House KPI Team

The KPI team should report directly to the CEO.

The KPI project team should be a balanced mix of oracles and young guns.

A small well-trained team will have the best chance of success. A project team of two to four people is recommended, depending on the size of the organization. The KPI team should report directly to the CEO (illustrated in Exhibit 6.1) as they will need frequent access, in any case, to obtain approvals and decisions. Any layer in between the CEO and the team indicates that Stage One has not been successfully achieved.

This point is so important that the project should not proceed if the CEO does not wish to be involved in this way. The senior management will play a supportive role to the project. One senior manager should be the KPI team leader's in-house mentor and assist with advice on all presentations, secure business and unit head's cooperation and provide a positive presence in the difficult times.

The KPI project team should be a balanced mix of oracles and young guns. Oracles are those gray-haired individuals whom you visit if you want to find out about what has happened in the organization in the past.

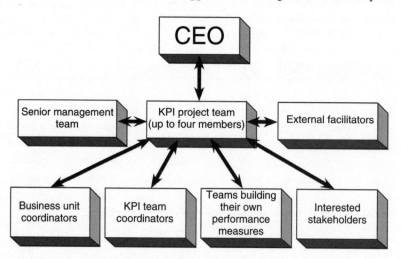

Exhibit 6.1 The KPI Team's Reporting Lines

Young guns are your young, fearless, and pre-cocious leaders of the future who are not afraid to venture into the unknown.

All departments and service teams should appoint a person, as the team KPI coordinator, who is sufficiently knowl-edgeable about their operation to provide information and feedback to liaise with the KPI team. The interested stakeholders consist of those who can add a useful perspective to the project team, such as some members of the board, union representatives, some key supplier representatives, and key customers.

> Research into personnel records is recommended, as many talented in-house staff are found in obscure places, and some may already have some KPI experience.

Do not include senior managers in the KPI team, as they will be unable to meet the required commitment to be full time on this project. The external facilitator should help the senior management team pick a team. Research into personnel records is recommended, as many talented in-house staff are found in obscure places, and some may already have some KPI experience. The facilitator is looking for staff members who have a proven track record of excellent presentation and communication skills, a flair for innovation, the ability to complete what they start, knowledge of both the organization and sector, the aptitude to bring others on board, and the ability to be cheerful under pressure.

The checklists and questionnaire in the PDF download will help with the selection process. It is advisable to run some tests to assess the potential compatibility of prospective team members, such as personality and thinking preference, as it is likely they have never worked together on a large project before. The Human Resources team will be able to organize these psychometric tests and interpret the results thus helping the KPI team members understand how to work more effectively with each other.

Task 2. Full-Time Commitment of KPI Project Team

The facilitator needs to convince management that the KPI team staff members are required to be committed full time. A project office needs to be set up, and the KPI team moved into it. They move their desk photos as well, because their second-in-command will now move into the vacated office and cover their duties. As stated in Chapter 2, it is a myth that this project can be handled while continuing with other duties. If project staff members are still intending to start and finish the day at their desk, this project should be terminated.

Task 3. Facilitator Helps Train the KPI Project Team

The facilitator will need to establish the knowledge gaps and set up training and some team-building exercises for the KPI team. If the team members do not know each other, the facilitator might organize a weekend team-building excursion.

Running good workshops is an acquired skill, and the KPI team should receive specific training in this area. To assist the KPI team I have attached some guidelines to running workshops in the PDF download.

The training exercises might include:

- Preparing a presentation to sell an idea through the audiences' emotional drivers
- Research exercises to find the last five reports done internally on performance measurement issues or articles and whitepapers, written on the topic in major journals and respected websites
- A comprehensive understanding of this KPI book
- How to interview effectively
- How to facilitate workshops that the KPI Project Team will be running
- How to deliver informative presentations
- Better-practice communication techniques
- Maintaining a vibrant project team home page on the intranet

This project is part of a larger topic called revitalizing performance. Fortunately, there have been some paradigm shifters (Drucker,[1] Hamel,[2] Welch,[3] Peters and Waterman,[4] and Hope[5]) who have offered us guidance. The KPI project team need to improve their knowledge in this stage. I have set out some examples of what I have learned from these great masters that are relevant to a KPI project team, as set out in Exhibit 6.2.

Exhibit 6.2 Lessons from the Paradigm Shifters Relevant to a KPI Team

Lesson Implication	KPI Project Team Implication
Do not give new staff new assignments. Peter Drucker referred to these jobs as widow-makers—jobs where the incumbent did not have a chance to succeed.	In this KPI project, it is important to ensure that the project team is made up of experienced staff who know the CSFs and the members of the senior management team. Bringing in consultants to lead the KPI project will doom it to failure.
Recruitment is a life-and-death decision. Peter Drucker was adamant about the significance of recruiting the right staff.	The recruiting of the KPI team should be done very carefully, ensuring they have the right mix of knowledge, experience, and credibility within the organization to be successful.
Abandonment. Peter Drucker said, "The first step in a growth policy is not to decide where and how to grow. It is to decide what to abandon. To grow, an organization must have a systematic policy to get rid of the outgrown, the obsolete, and the unproductive."	Promote Drucker's concept of abandonment. Many existing measures should be abandoned along with processes and reports. The KPI project needs space to work. Other systems need to be abandoned to allow enough time for the KPIs to function properly.
Have three test sites. Peter Drucker pointed out that one pilot site is not enough testing of a new process.	On a KPI project, we should follow the sage's advice and pilot the KPI project in three divisions.
Embrace differences. Gary Hamel is insistent that managers need to: ■ Embrace irregular people; their irregular ideas can be very valuable. ■ Look for positive mavericks.	The KPI team should be selected from all experienced employees. It is important to consider those employees who have always shaken the cart. They may have the X factor to make this project work.
Opt-in commitment. Hamel believes organizations should have an "opt-in" and "self-chosen" commitment.	The KPI team should have an open selection process so that a wide net is cast for the best team members. Passion for performance management will be a very important attribute to look for.

(continued)

Exhibit 6.2 (*Continued*)

Lesson Implication	KPI Project Team Implication
Creative apartheid. Hamel points out that most human beings are creative in some sphere of their lives. The point he makes is that this creativity needs to be embraced at the workplace. He believes that creativity can be strengthened through instruction and practice (e.g., Whirlpool has trained more than 35,000 employees in the principles of business innovation).	The KPI team must be open to new ideas during the project. Be flexible with how workshops are run, ensuring that creativity is given time to flourish.
A cluster of mentors. As Jack Welch says, "There is no right mentor for you; there are many right mentors." He sees mentoring more holistically. A mentor can come from a staff person many levels below who passes on their knowledge to you. In *Winning*, Welch was forever grateful for the young human resources advisor who patiently helped him master e-mail.	Ensure all the KPI team members have appropriate mentor support. The KPI project team leader should ideally have three mentors, each providing support and knowledge in a different area. <ul><li>How to get things done in the organization</li><li>How to implement a KPI project</li><li>How to create and maintain a winning project team</li></ul>
Recognition and celebration. Jack Welch says that eminent leaders celebrate more. As he illustrates, "Work is too much a part of life not to recognize moments of achievement." You can sense from listening to his webcasts that his celebrations would have been fun to attend. Welch was all about making work fun. Realizing that it is not life or death but a game you want to win.	The KPI project team will need to be active with recognition and celebration to assist with buy-in and maintain interest and momentum.

Exhibit 6.2 (*Continued*)

Lesson Implication	KPI Project Team Implication
Productivity through people. Peters and Waterman noted that the following were evident in the best-run organizations: ■ Unabashed hoopla ■ Internal competition ■ Family atmosphere ■ Key data being accessible to all ■ Trust ■ Keeping units small, fast, and flexible	The KPI team will need to apply these techniques to be successful.
Jeremy Hope recommended to always use *tried and tested technologies*.	The KPI team should utilize only tried and tested KPI software.
Cut back on measurement. Jeremy Hope recommended cutting back so there are only six or seven measures that are used at every level.	Follow the 10/80/10 principle and ensure that teams do not have more than six or seven measures.

Task 4. Research for The KPI Team (Key Reference Books and Websites)

The following are required reading for all KPI team members.

■ Paul R. Niven, *Balanced Scorecard: Step-by-Step for Government and Nonprofit Agencies* (Hoboken, NJ: John Wiley & Sons, 2008). My personal copy has earmarked pages, which is a sure sign of how useful I think it is.

■ Robert S. Kaplan and David P. Norton, *The Balanced Scorecard: Translating Strategy into Action* (Boston: Harvard Business Press, 1996). This book is a masterpiece. It is the original book that catapulted the balanced-scorecard journey in the first place. Although I do not agree with all of the content in the book, it should be read by the KPI team so that they can draw their own conclusions. Chapter 12 and the appendix, "Building a Balanced scorecard," in their book should be reread many times. There are also some very useful illustrations throughout the book.

- Stacey Barr, *Practical Performance Measurement Using the PuMP Blueprint for Fast, Easy and Engaging Performance Measures* (PuMP Press, 2014). Stacey has been an active practitioner in the performance measurement field and has developed a methodology that should be understood by the KPI team.
- Stephen Few, *Information Dashboard Design: Displaying Data for At-a-Glance Monitoring* (Burlingame, CA: Analytics Press, 2013). This book will help you make a major step forward in data visualization—the way you report information to management and staff. Everyone involved in the KPI project should have to read the book as a prerequisite to joining the team. It should then be on the project team's bookshelf.
- Elizabeth Haas Edersheim, *The Definitive Drucker: Challenges for Tomorrow's Executives—Final Advice from the Father of Modern Management* (New York: McGraw-Hill, 2006). This book should be on the reading list for any project leader and manager. The KPI team will better understand the significance of abandonment after reading this book.
- John Kotter, *Leading Change* (Boston: Harvard Business Review Press, 2012). A very highly rated book and a major influence in leading and selling change.
- Dean R. Spitzer, *Transforming Performance Measurement: Rethinking the Way We Measure and Drive Organizational Success* (New York: AMACOM, 2007). One of the first books to look into the behavioral aspects of performance measures.

There are a number of useful reference websites that the KPI team should be aware of.

- Stephen Few's Perceptual Edge website, www.perceptualedge.com. A small number of writers can really dominate a space, and Few stands head-and-shoulders above everyone in the data-visualization genre. His three books are masterpieces. His website is full of excellent whitepapers and articles. I would recommend subscribing to his blog and accessing some of his whitepapers, such as "Common Pitfalls of Dashboard Design," "Dashboard Design for Real-Time Situation

Awareness," and "With Dashboards, Formatting and Layout Definitely Matter." Stephen Few conducts workshops around the world. Make sure you view his website to find the workshop nearest to you. You will not regret attending one of his workshops.

- On my website, www.davidparmenter.com, I have placed some complementary electronic resources that will be helpful to readers of this book and my *Key Performance Indicators* book. In addition to these free resources, there are the electronic versions of all the templates from this book and toolkits on a variety of relevant topics available for a fee.

Task 5. Establish a Just-Do-It Culture and Process

"Getting it right the first time" is a rare achievement and ascertaining the organization's winning KPIs and associated reports is no exception. The performance measure framework and associated reporting is just like a piece of sculpture: you can be criticized on taste and content, but you can't be wrong. The

> The external facilitator and the KPI project leader need to instill a "just-do-it" culture.

external facilitator and the KPI project leader need to instill a "just-do-it" culture, not one in which every step and measure is debated as part of an intellectual exercise.

With this "just-do-it" culture comes a belief that we can do it; we do not have to rely on experts to run the project.

Establishing your winning KPIs is not complex, and the process should be carried out in-house, provided the team has the assistance of an experienced facilitator. The facilitator's role is principally that of a mentor to the project team, and thus the facilitator should keep a low profile at KPI team presentations.

There is no need to heavily invest in KPI software during the first 12 months because the team should be utilizing existing spreadsheet, presentation, and database applications. This eliminates the delay caused by having to tender, select, and populate specialized software at this stage. This can be done more efficiently and effectively in the second year of the project when the organization has a better understanding of KPIs.

Applications such as SharePoint Team Services and Microsoft Teams enable the KPI team to set up intranet pages that everyone with an interest in winning KPIs can access:

- Relevant memos and articles (programmed with expiration dates so only current and important pronouncements are available)
- Forums to discuss issues
- KPI documentation that requires collaborative input
- The master performance-measure database

Task 6. The KPI Project Leader Needs a Cluster of Mentors

The KPI team leader will need a mentor, or, as Jack Welch[6] advised, a cluster of mentors. I suggest the following:

- Find a consultant who has credibility within the organization, as they have helped previously in a successful project. Pay for their wisdom and have a series of two- to four-hour sessions with them.
- Find an external facilitator who is experienced in performance measurement and hopefully is aware of this "winning KPIs" methodology. Many of your sessions can be held over video-based tools.
- Find an in-house mentor, an oracle who knows all the key players and how they operate. This mentor may have retired recently and will welcome the odd long lunch as you examine the issues. They may help you solve them yourself or suggest alternative approaches.
- Build a peer group among like-minded KPI experts who are pushing the envelope. It will be comforting to know that someone else is going over the trenches and is still around to share the tales of adventure.

Task 7. Finalize a strategy for the KPI project rollout

As covered in Chapter 4, Leading and Selling the Change, it is important to hold a series of lock-up workshops involving senior management and a cross-section of the oracles to draft the blueprint—a vision and strategy for the new performance measurement process—just the thing Kotter suggested in his book, *Leading Change*.[7]

In a successful project implementation, a company held three two-week workshops for their planning tool implementation. Yes, that is six weeks of workshops. For a KPI project, which is less involved with IT systems, I would suggest this could be completed within a couple of weeks. It would have been started from the first oracles focus group and then continued with a small group of five to eight people.

> For organizations with fewer than 500 staff, a total KPI rollout in 16 weeks is achievable.

An agreed process and plan for introducing KPIs should be developed in consultation with management, local employee representatives, unions representing the organization's employees, employees, major customers, major suppliers, and the board. Many of the concerns held about introducing measurement can be overcome at this stage if these stakeholders validate the process for developing KPIs.

For organizations with fewer than 500 staff, a total KPI rollout in 16 weeks is achievable. Organizations with more than 500 full-time employees will require a phased approach. The larger the organization, the more focused the first phase must be. For an agency with 20,000 or more full-time employees, the first phase would be limited to three subsidiaries (piloting the process in threes as recommended by Drucker) where the benefits are the greatest. Exhibit 6.3 shows the indicative rollout duration for organizations of different sizes.

When a consensus has been reached on the agreed process for developing and using KPIs, a review must take place to ensure that all the steps are consistent with the seven foundation stones:

1. Partner with staff, unions, and third parties
2. Transfer power to the front line
3. Measure and report only what matters
4. Source KPIs from the critical success factors
5. Abandon processes that do not deliver
6. Appoint a home-grown KPI team leader
7. Understanding organization-wide the winning KPIs definition

Exhibit 6.3 Indicative Rollout Duration

Project stages	One-person team	Two-person KPI team			Four-person KPI team	
		Size of organization (FTEs)				
	Less than 100 FTEs	100 to 250	250 to 500	500 to 3,000	3,000 to 10,000	10,000+
1 Getting the enterprise committed to the change and up-skilling an in-house KPI team	1 week	1 week	2–3 weeks	2–3 weeks	2–3 weeks to holding company[a]	
2 Ascertaining the operational critical success factors	2 weeks	2–3 weeks	4–6 weeks	4–6 weeks	4–6 weeks (additional CSF workshops[b] needed where different sectors involved)	
3.1 Run the performance measures workshops	Combined with the CSF workshop	2–3 weeks	4–6 weeks	4–6 weeks[c]	4–6 weeks (for every major subsidiary with smaller subsidiaries attending[d])	
3.2 Refining the measures	2 weeks	2 weeks	2–3 weeks	4–6 weeks[e]	2–3 weeks[f] (for every major subsidiary)	
3.3 to 3.5 Hold performance measures galley; teams select KRIs and KPIs ascertained	Included in the refining process	4–6 weeks (measures will only need to be tested once[g])				

Exhibit 6.3 (Continued)

Project stages	One-person team	Two-person KPI team			Four-person KPI team	
		Size of organization (FTEs)				
	Less than 100 FTEs	100 to 250	250 to 500	500 to 3,000	3,000 to 10,000	10,000+
3.6 Designing reporting process	2 weeks	2–3 weeks		4–6 weeks[h]	4–6 weeks (for every major subsidiary)	
3.7 Facilitate the appropriate use of the selected performance measures by all the teams in the organization	Ongoing	Ongoing				

[a]In a large organization it is imperative that the holding company CEO be behind the KPI project.

[b]Where you have different industries in a group you will need two different sets of CSFs, although the people-related ones will be identical.

[c]Bringing in different groups together creates team building and saves workshop time.

[d]Smaller subsidiaries should attend the workshops run for a simiar larger subsidiary.

[e]Every performance measures workshop will generate duplication in measures. It is tempting to allow attendees to see what other workshops have delivered; however, this will limit learning, possibly leading to a KPI being missed.

[f]With the ongoing rollout, some CSFs will not be reviewed for measures, as the KPI team will be happy with them and simply need to explain them in the workshop.

[g]Once a measure has been tested in a subsidiary, it can be safely used in another subsidiary, without further testing.

[h]With larger organizations the need for more sophisticated and integrated reporting software is paramount.

Task 8. Determining the Perspectives of Measurement

As acknowledgment to the balanced scorecard, we need to determine the perspectives of measurement we will use in the project to help ensure that strategy and the strategic initiatives are balanced. The perspectives I recommend adopting for the first year are:

- Financial Results
- Customer Focus
- Internal Process
- Innovation and Learning
- Staff Satisfaction
- Environment and Community

Task 9. The KPI Project Team Needs to Keep Close to the Fundamentals

Always review the seven foundation stones to check that your efforts and the project do not stray away from these key building blocks.

Sports coaches often talk about doing the fundamental or basic things well to ensure success. This is good advice for the KPI team leader and the external facilitator because, at times the KPI implementation process will appear to be quite involved and complex. As you carry out your role, always review the seven foundation stones to check that your efforts and the project do not stray away from these key building blocks, as illustrated in Exhibit 6.4.

Distribution of This KPI Edition among Your Team

This book is a resource for anyone in the organization involved with the development and use of KPIs. It is desirable that all KPI project team members, the external project facilitator, team coordinators, and local facilitators (if required) have their own book to ensure that all follow the same plan. Team members are expected to take the book with them when meeting staff and management, as they will be able to clarify issues by using examples from the book. (Note that this book is copyrighted, so it is a breach of the copyright to photocopy sections for distribution.)

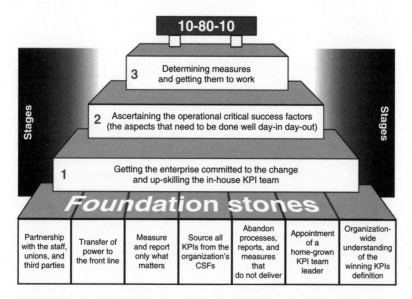

Exhibit 6.4 The Seven Foundation Stones in the Winning KPI Methodology

There is no shortcut for Small to Medium-Sized Enterprises.

All the tasks are required. Many SMEs will think they can perform this exercise with a KPI project manager who has all their other duties as well. This will lead to disappointment.

PDF Download

To assist the KPI project team on the journey, templates and checklists have been provided. The reader can access, from kpi.davidparmenter.com/fourthedition, free of charge, a PDF of the following chapter templates:

- Establishing a Winning KPI Team Checklist
- KPI Team Establishment Questionnaire
- KPI Team 360-Degree Questionnaire

- Establish a "Just-Do-It" Culture and Process Checklist
- Establish a "Just-Do-It" Culture and Process Worksheet
- Job Description for the KPI Team Leader Role
- Workshop Preparation Checklist
- Guidelines to Running Workshops
- Typical KPI Questions and Suggested Answers

Notes

1. Elizabeth Haas Edersheim, *The Definitive Drucker: Challenges for Tomorrow's Executives—Final Advice from the Father of Modern Management* (New York: McGraw-Hill, 2006)
2. Gary Hamel, *The Future of Management* (Cambridge: Harvard Business School Press, 2007).
3. Jack Welch and Suzy Welch, *Winning* (New York: HarperBusiness, 2005).
4. Thomas J. Peters and Robert H. Waterman, *In Search of Excellence: Lessons from America's Best Run Companies* (New York: Harper & Row, 1982).
5. Jeremy Hope, *Reinventing the CFO* (Boston: Harvard Business School Press, 2006).
6. Jack Welch and Suzy Welch, *Winning* (New York: HarperBusiness, 2005).
7. John Kotter, *Leading Change* (Boston: Harvard Business Review Press, 2012).

Overview

Critical success factors (CSFs) are operational issues or aspects that need to be accomplished day-in/day-out by the staff in the organization.
It is imperative that employees and management understand what CSFs are and can therefore focus their attention on finding performance measures in these areas, that will make a real difference.

This chapter looks at the alignment between CSFs and external outcomes and highlights the importance of identifying CSFs—the missing link in management theory. In addition, the chapter points out that an organization has typically five to eight CSFs, and that CSFs should be the source of all the important performance measures—the winning KPIs.

The key learning points from this chapter are:

1. In organizations that do not have clarity and agreement on their operational CSFs, managers will prioritize work based on their view as to what is important.
2. Why critical success factors are the source of all meaningful performance measures.
3. The importance of distinguishing between critical success factors and external outcomes.
4. Common misunderstanding regarding critical success factors
5. To create alignment between teams in an organization, it is important that there be only one set of between five and eight critical success factors (CSFs) for the organization.
6. How to word success factors appropriately.
7. The key tasks for identifying the organization's five to eight critical success factors.
8. The CSF workshop templates to help fast track progress.
9. The only way the operational CSFs will make a change in an organization is when staff live, breathe, and own the operational CSFs.
10. The need to have the critical success factors on the wall in every workplace.

CHAPTER 7

Finding Your Organization's Critical Success Factors

I was first introduced to critical success factors by the talented people who wrote the KPI manual for AusIndustry (an Australian government department). They defined critical success factors as:

> *The list of issues or aspects of organizational performance that determine ongoing health, vitality, and well-being.*[1]

I have always seen these as operational issues or aspects that need to be done well day-in/day-out by the staff. Critical success factors are about what the staff inside the organization can do and should do every day.

> Stephen Covey talked in *First Things First* about putting "the rocks" in first every day, before we work with the pebbles and the sand. We can liken the operational CSFs to the rocks that staff need to focus on every day.

Stephen Covey talked in *First Things First*[2] about putting "the rocks" in first every day, before we work with the pebbles and the sand. We can liken the operational CSFs to the rocks that staff need to focus on every day. They should be the driving force behind prioritization throughout the organization. They are very directional to operational staff who are focused on current demand, current production, and current delivery of products and services.

The term *critical success factor* does not appear to be addressed by some of the leading management performance writers of the past 30 years. Peter Drucker, Jim Collins, Gary Hamel, Tom Peters, Robert Kaplan, and David Norton all appear to ignore the existence of critical success factors.

The critical success factor "Deliver in full on time to key customers" communicates to staff that major orders for our key customers, often the difficult and complex orders, need to be tackled first, whereas if we measure all deliveries to all customers many staff would tackle the smaller orders, putting the easy "runs on the board" thus jeopardizing service to the most profitable customers.

To understand how this stage fits within the KPI methodology, an overview of the important work that needs to be done is set out in Exhibit 7.1.

Exhibit 7.1 An Overview of the Winning KPI Methodology

Task	Description
1.1 Selling the KPI project to the CEO, the senior management team, and the organization's oracles. (See Chapters 4 and 5.)	The project starts off with a well-practiced elevator pitch, followed by a compelling presentation and then a focus group workshop to get the green light from the organization's oracles.
1.2 Locate an external facilitator to mentor the KPI team. (See Chapter 5.)	An external facilitator will help guide the organization with regard to timings, selection, and size of KPI team and with what needs to be abandoned to make room for the KPI project.
1.3 Train a small KPI team. (See Chapter 6.)	The external facilitator helps train a small in-house KPI team and ensures that the KPI team leader has a cluster of mentors supporting them. Working with the organization's oracles, the KPI team develops a blueprint for the implementation, which will cover where the KPI project will be piloted.
1.4 Selling the KPI project to all employees to encourage their participation in the two-day performance measures workshops. (See Chapter 4.)	Employees who are to attend the two-day performance measures workshop need to be convinced that it is an important exercise worthy of their participation.

Exhibit 7.1 (*Continued*)

Task	Description
2.1 Locate the existing success factors and desired external outcomes from documentation and interviews. (Covered in this chapter.)	Determine what your organization's success factors and desired external outcomes are.
2.2 Run the two-day critical success factors workshop to ascertain the critical success factors. (Covered in this chapter.)	Map the sphere of influence each success factor has to ascertain and understand which ones have the most significant impact. These are the critical success factors. Present these to all staff.
3.1 Run the two-day performance measures workshops to train all the remaining relevant staff to develop meaningful measures. (See Chapters 8 and 9.)	Select representatives across the organization to attend a two-day workshop to be trained in the methodology, as well as how and why the organization has chosen its CSFs. Attendees will be shown how to design appropriate measures from the CSFs, how to get a mix of past, current, and future measures.
3.2 Refine the measures after the performance measures workshops. (See Chapter 9.)	KPI team will delete duplicated and inferior indicators, remove those measures where the cost of data extraction is greater than the derived benefit, and reword all indicators to improve their understanding.
3.3 Hold a performance measures gallery to weed out dysfunctional and poor measures. (See Chapter 9.)	Hold a "measures gallery" where staff are invited to share their views on the measures that have been displayed on the walls of the project team's room.
3.4 Ask all teams to select their team performance measures from the finalized database of measures. (See Chapter 9.)	Teams select the relevant measures and indicate their selection in the database.

(*continued*)

Exhibit 7.1 *(Continued)*

Task	Description
3.5 Find the key result indicators (KRIs) and the key performance indicators (KPIs). (See Chapter 9.)	Ascertain the 8–12 KRIs that will be reported to the Board to show how the organization is performing. Ascertain the winning KPIs, ensuring they have the seven characteristics discussed in Chapter 1. Commence the testing of the KPIs in three designated areas.
3.6 Design the reporting framework. (See Chapter 10.)	The intraday, daily, weekly, monthly, and quarterly progress reports are designed utilizing best practice visualization techniques. Utilize existing technology so that the CEO can receive intraday updates on a smartphone or laptop.
3.7 Help facilitate the appropriate use of the selected performance measures by all the teams in the organization. (See Chapter 11.)	For several months, the KPI team will be required to ensure the reporting of measures is prepared on time and correctly, and corrective actions are undertaken where necessary. There will need to be a program to roll out KPI training to existing and new staff.
3.8 Refine CSFs and associated measures after one year of use. (See Chapter 11.)	A review should be undertaken to assess what modifications, if any, are needed to the existing CSFs and measures.

Why Critical Success Factors Are So Important

In Chapter 2, I highlighted the common myth that performance measures are mainly used to help manage the implementation of strategic initiatives. Instead, the main purpose of performance measures is to ensure that staff members spend their working hours focused primarily on the organization's critical success factors. You could be in your tenth year with a balanced scorecard and still not know your organization's critical success factors. It is like going to soccer's World Cup without a goalkeeper or, at best, an incompetent one.

118

Operational Critical Success Factors: The Missing Link

In organizations that do not have clarity and agreement on their operational CSFs, managers will prioritize work based on their view as to what is important. Many counterproductive activities will thus occur based on the premise "What is important to me is important to the organization." For a chief executive officer to steer the ship, everybody needs to know the journey, what makes the ship sail well, and what needs to be done in difficult weather. The term *critical success factors* is a major missing link in balanced scorecard and other methodologies.

> In organizations that do not have clarity and agreement on their operational CSFs, managers will prioritize work based on their view as to what is important.

What Influences the Critical Success Factors?

It is important to understand the relationship between operational CSFs and strategy. An organization's CSFs are impacted by a number of features. Most organizations will have one or two generic CSFs (e.g., "delivery in full, on time, to our key customers"; "Recruit the right people all the time"); but each organization will also have some unique temporary conditions (e.g., a sudden drop in revenue will mean additional CSFs will be introduced until the funding crisis is over). Some CSFs will be determined by strategy, and others will be related to normal business conditions as illustrated in Exhibit 7.2.

Operational Critical Success Factors Are the Source of All Meaningful Performance Measures

The traditional balanced scorecard (BSC) approach uses performance measures to monitor the implementation of the strategic initiatives, and measures are typically cascaded down from a top-level organizational measure, such as return on capital employed. This cascading of measures from one another will often lead to chaos, with hundreds of measures being monitored by staff in some form of BSC reporting application.

119

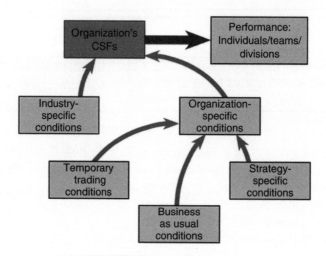

Exhibit 7.2 What Influences the Critical Success Factors

Getting staff to prioritize their daily activities in alignment with the organization's operational CSFs is the "El Dorado" of management, the essence of modern management. Thus, instead of using the strategies as the source of your measures, clarify what your organization's operational CSFs are and then determine what measures would generate alignment to these operational CSFs.

Relationship between Critical Success Factors and Strategy

Although I am aware of the significance of a well-thought-through and -executed strategy, the organization's critical success factors are more fundamental to the business as they focus the staff on what needs to be achieved every day. This aligns their efforts with those "business as usual" strategic initiatives.

Exhibit 7.3 shows that strategic initiatives, although their progress will be monitored, are not as fundamental to the business as monitoring the day-to-day alignment with the organization's CSFs.

It is the operational CSFs, and the performance measures they inherently carry, that link daily activities to the performance of teams, business units, and divisions.

Exhibit 7.3 How Strategy and the Critical Success Factors Work Together

Distinguishing between Critical Success Factors and External Outcomes

I have realized recently the importance of distinguishing operational critical success factors from external outcomes. A member of the Board of a charity rightly pointed out that the CSFs tabled (the operational CSFs) were too internally focused. They wanted to see the external picture: the external outcomes. The Board was naturally looking from outside in. The Board wanted to see the CSFs expressed as the outcomes and impacts they want to see. We want the organization to "deliver this," "deliver that," which will demonstrate that there has been a successful implementation of the organization's strategy.

> External outcomes are a result of the operational CSFs working, day in and day out, for a sustained period of time along with the successful implementation of strategic initiatives.

External outcomes are a result of the operational CSFs working, day in and day out, for a sustained period of time along with the successful implementation of strategic initiatives—such as alliance agreements being signed to obtain operational capacity in a new country. An external outcome such as "Developing and growing the new product x (or market y)" is a result of many different activities happening from secret alliance agreements being successfully signed to new operational capacity being organized in a new

121

country. Once operational, the new plant in a new country will be guided by the operational CSFs already in existence elsewhere in the organization.

To help further clarify, I have separated out the characteristics of operational critical success and external outcomes in the Exhibit 7.4.

Exhibit 7.4 Characteristics of Operational Critical Success Factors and External Outcomes

Characteristics of operational critical success	Characteristics of external outcomes
Are those factors that require a 24/7 focus by all staff in the organization.	A periodic focus on progress at bimonthly/quarterly Board meetings.
Success is a result of operational staff focusing on the CSFs 24/7.	Success is the combination of implementing successful strategic initiatives and the new business opportunities being successfully supported by the existing CSFs.
Worded to be pertinent to the activities staff should focus on in a specific area, avoiding the use of "empty words" like *optimization*, *maximization*. Describe as an activity.	Worded to describe what success will look like for a broad area of the organization, e.g., become an employer of first choice. Described as an external result such as "growth in a new market."
Will not be a surprise to management and the board / government official, as they will have talked about them as success factors.	Wording is generic across many sectors.
Are focused on the organization and thus should not be broken down into department CSFs.	Likewise, will be focused on the organization.
Are few in number; five to eight is sufficient.	Likewise, five to eight is a good number.
Have a considerable positive influence on other success factors.	Do not impact the CSF and SFs as they are a result of the CSF and SFs working for a sustained period of time.

The Benefits of Understanding Your Organization's CSFs

Knowing, communicating, and measuring progress in an organization's CSFs is the El Dorado of management, the Holy Grail. There are some profound benefits of knowing your CSFs, including:

Leads to the KPIs	It leads to the discovery of an organization's "winning KPIs."
Helps eliminate measures	Performance measures that **do not** relate to your CSFs, or impact them, cannot by definition be important and thus can often be eliminated.
Linked daily actions	Staff know what should be done as a priority and thus their daily actions are now linked to the organization's strategies e.g., as they do at Toyota.
Challenge unnecessary meetings, reports and task	Staff meetings, reports, and tasks will be challenged for their validity. All activities that have no direct link to the critical success factors will be seen as noncritical. Over time meetings and reports that occurred because we did it last week/month will disappear.
Leaner reports	Report layout will be more concise as many extraneous issues will be removed.
More CEO walkabout	The CEO's linkage to the workforce will be a daily activity through the phone calls and walkabouts among front-line staff.

The importance of critical success factors on the emergence of KPIs was explained by the British Airways story in Chapter 1.

Relationship between CSFs and KPIs

The relationship between critical success factors and KPIs is vital. If you get the critical success factors right, it is very easy to find your organization's winning KPIs (e.g., once the "timely arrival and departure of planes" was

123

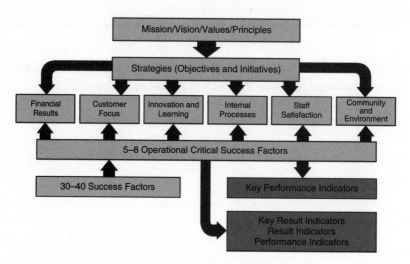

Exhibit 7.5 How Operational Critical Success Factors Drive the
Performance Measures

Critical success factors cut across a number of balanced scorecard perspectives.

identified as being the top critical success factor, it was relatively easy to find the KPI: planes late over a certain time).

As Exhibit 7.5 indicates, critical success factors cut across a number of balanced-scorecard perspectives (e.g., the KPI "timely arrival and departure of planes," featured in Chapter 1, impacts nearly all the balanced scorecard perspectives of the airline).

Common Misunderstandings

It is concerning that many organizations run their enterprise without shared and communicated CSFs. For this to happen there has to be a serious misunderstanding. I have set out in Exhibit 7.6 some common misunderstandings.

To help organizations around the world find their five to eight critical success factors, I have developed a four-task process.

Exhibit 7.6 Common Misunderstandings Regarding Critical Success Factors

Common misunderstandings	Better practice solution
Thinking that "We already know our CSFs"	**It is common for the executive team to believe they and everybody else know the CSFs.** I often joke that I could ask a CEO on consecutive days, "What are your CSFs?" and I would get slightly different answers each day.
	Most organizations know their success factors; however, few organizations have:
	■ Worded their success factors appropriately.
	■ Segregated the success factors from their outcome statements.
	■ Prioritized their success factors to find their critical ones—their operational CSFs.
	■ Communicated the operational CSFs to staff to achieve full understanding and engagement.
Mixing critical success factors and external outcomes	**CSFs and external outcomes are different.** From the previous section you will be aware of the different characteristics.
Too many CSFs	**Limit to Five to Eight Critical Success Factors**
	Better practice suggests that organizational CSFs should be limited to between five and eight, regardless of the organization's size. However, for a conglomerate in the private sector, the CSFs will largely be industry specific (e.g., the CSFs for an airline are different from the CSFs for a retail store). Accordingly, there would be a collection of CSFs in the conglomerate greater than the suggested five to eight.

(continued)

Exhibit 7.6 (*Continued*)

Common misunderstandings	Better practice solution
A set for each division	**Only One Set of Critical Success Factors for the Organization** To create alignment between teams in an organization, it is important that there be only one set of between five and eight critical success factors (CSFs) for the organization. If you allow teams, departments, or divisions to create their own operational CSFs, you will have chaos.
Calling them KRAs	**Critical Success Factors Are Not Key Result Areas** In job descriptions you can often find the words "key result areas" (KRAs), which are often mistaken for CSFs. I believe that job descriptions should have a new section pointing out the organization's CSFs and how the incumbent should maximize alignment of his or her duties with them. This would help to clarify the difference between KRAs and CSFs. The KRAs are those duties and tasks that the incumbent must be able to perform, and the organizational CSFs are the guiding force ensuring that all staff, every day, treat, as a priority, activities that align well with the CSFs.
You can be at peak performance without having a common understanding of your CSFs	**Performance management cannot possibly function optimally without a common understanding of your CSFs.** Without CSFs, performance measurement, monitoring, and reporting will be a series of random processes, creating a small army of measurers producing numerous numbing reports. Very few, if any, of the measures in these reports contain the characteristics of "winning KPIs."

Task 1: Wording the Success Factors and the External Outcomes

The KPI team needs to review the strategic documents in their organization covering the past 10 years and then extract and develop success factors from these documents. You may find an old strategic document written by an executive who has long since moved on, which could prove very helpful because the success factors are still relevant.

> To create alignment between teams in an organization, it is important that there be only one set of between five and eight critical success factors (CSFs) for the organization.

The KPI team should interview as many of the organization's "oracles," the wise men and women whom everybody refers to for advice, as possible, along with the entire senior management team. From this information, you will be able to come up with a list of success factors. To assist, I have provided a checklist in PDF format for you to download.

Gather a selection of experienced managers who will be attending the CSF workshop and train them in how to word success factors. The wording is very important and should meet the SMART criteria attributed to Peter Drucker.[3] While Drucker was addressing goal setting, the same rules apply to success factors. Success factors need to be:

- **Specific**—A statement that avoids using meaningless, empty words, sometimes referred to as "weasel words." Avoiding empty words, which are so common in management terminology, is not as easy as you might think. As we move up the management ladder, we increasingly use empty words having heard them used so often. Common weasel words include:

    Accelerate, adaptive, balanced, barriers, best practice, collaborative, dynamic, effective, efficient, end-user, empowered, holistic, improvements, inclusive, innovative, integrity, optimized, outcomes, outputs, quality, recognition, reliability, renewal, responsibility, significant, solution, special, synergies, targeted, transformation, value-added, well-being, winning, world-class.

    The term "increased profitability from our product range" is an empty statement. There is no guide to how this is to be achieved, whereas "timely departure and arrival of planes 24/7" is clearly specific.

127

- **Measurable**—A statement with words that lend themselves to measurement. If you could not instantly think of a measure or two, then it is odds-on that it does not fit this criterion. "Timely departure and arrival of planes 24/7" is clearly measurable.
- **Achievable**—A statement that talks to the staff in a clear and concise way, making the activity achievable. For example, "timely departure and arrival of planes 24/7" is clearly achievable.
- **Relevant**—Focused enough that it is relevant to staff in the organization. "Timely departure and arrival of planes 24/7" is clearly relevant to many operational teams: flight crew, front desk, baggage handlers, cleaners, fuel and food suppliers.
- **Time sensitive**—Focused on the here and now. "Timely departure and arrival of planes 24/7" is clearly a 24/7 imperative for an airline.

Exhibit 7.7 shows a list of success factor statements that contain empty words. These have been contrasted to SMART success factors and external outcomes.

Exhibit 7.7 Wording Success Factors and External Outcomes

Success factors which are meaningless (empty words signifying nothing)	SMART Operational success factors	External outcomes
Increased profitability	These three statements are a result of more than one operational success factor at work. SMART replacements would be "Delivery in full all the time to key customers," "Fix problems to get quality right the first time," "Seeking excellence in every aspect of our interaction with our key customers."	Increased profitability by selling a higher percentage of higher-margin products.
Retention of customers		Retention of key customers
A say, stay, strive engagement with staff		Maximizing the use of our most important resource—our people.
Optimizing innovation	Innovation is a daily activity.	Growth in sales of new products.
Deliver in full on time	Deliver in full, on time, all the time *to key customers.*	Growing business through our major customers.

A Government Department's Success Factors

A small group of staff met in a CSF workshop and came up with an initial list of outcomes and success factors.

- Increase availability and accessibility of _____'s data and information
- Work with local government and industry to improve our country's infrastructure (outcome statement)
- Help people understand what we do and where we're going (outcome statement)
- Actively promoting our products and services to new customers and partners
- Be the trusted source of expertise and advice (outcome statement)
- Adapt quickly to change
- Develop capable and inspiring leaders (outcome statement)
- In-house training should be prioritized above all other commitments
- Provide easy-to-use products
- Recruit the right people every time

To assist I have provided a list of common success factors, in PDF format, for you to download. However, it is important that these be used after you have performed an exhaustive internal hunt.

Implementation Tips

From my experience this first task is rarely performed with enough intellectual rigor. We are all too busy juggling our priorities. Whenever we have arrived at the two-day workshop, without due preparation, too much time has been spent in the workshop trying to get the success factors sorted.

At this stage it is also worth agreeing on your desired external outcomes. These will be well documented in the current and past strategy documents. To help you with this, I have included some guidelines on drafting outcomes and a checklist of common outcomes in the attached PDF that supports this book.

Task 2: Determining the Critical Success Factors in a Two-Day Workshop

From my experience in this area, most organizations will need to run a two-day workshop attended by experienced staff from around the organization, and with as many of the senior management team as possible. This workshop, if carried out correctly, will provide output that will transform performance through the clarity and alignment critical success factors offer. There are three major outputs from this workshop. A better understanding of measurement and what is a KPI, a clarity of what the CSFs are, and learning how to build robust measures.

Agree on What Approach to Use

From working with clients over the years, I have noted that there are three ways to hold the CSF workshop.

Approach One	Hold a two-day workshop attended by experienced staff from around the organization, as much of the senior management team as possible, as well as the chief executive officer (CEO).
Approach Two	Run the two-day workshop as part of the executive retreat. This means that all the executives are present, albeit without some of the oracles who would have been involved in the first option. One other benefit is that the executive is on hand to agree to the final version.
Approach Three	Run the two-day workshop as a series of three-hour webinars. This means staff can contribute from their locations and the sessions can be run remotely by a skilled presenter, who does not have to travel to the chosen venue.

Forestry Company Using Approach One

A forestry organization held the two-day workshop over a Friday and Saturday to avoid too much disruption to the operation. They had booked a venue in the local hotel and asked all the oracles to attend the two-day course, including foreman, forklift drivers, foresters—all the way through to the senior management team and the CEO. There were close to 50 who attended the two-day session with some staff flying in from an Australian subsidiary to get exposure to the methodology.

Financial Institution Using Approach Two

As this was a global organization, the CSF workshop was run as part of the executive retreat week that is held each year. The CSF workshop was scheduled for the first two days, and the output of the workshops was then worked on and resubmitted for ratification later during the retreat. This saved between two and four weeks of delay that other projects have faced when using the first approach as indicated above.

Food Distributor Case Study Using Approach Three

With plants in many locations, it was decided to run a series of 2.5-hour webinar sessions instead of a two-day CSF workshop for an organization based in the Northeast of England. Senior and experienced staff, from a broad section of their operation, numbering between 5 and 12 in each plant location, were present in their training room. Attendees were paired and sat in front of a laptop so that I could see their level of engagement. I was able to deliver the presentations from my New Zealand office and set up workshop activities using the GoToMeeting application.

Agree on Who Should Attend

It is important to have experienced staff (the oracles) attend this workshop, as you are trying to ascertain the organization's success factors and then determine which ones are critical. It is not a workshop for staff new to the organization. The organization's oracles are the individuals everyone refers you to when you need something answered (e.g., "You need to talk to Pat").

The CEO needs to send out the invite, see a draft in the PDF toolkit, and attend, at the very least, the first half-day and the last session after the

131

afternoon break on the second day. However, in operational CSF workshops I have delivered CEOs who only partially attended have said they regretted not being available for the whole two days. The staff members who are likely to be on the KPI team should also attend.

Agree on Content and Process

After 20 years of work in this area I believe the two-day workshop needs to cover the items in Exhibit 7.8.

An agenda for the two-day workshop that I use has been included in the downloadable PDF.

Exhibit 7.8 Outline of the Content in a Two-Day CSF Workshop

Background	The new thinking of key performance measures.
	The three-stage winning KPI process.
Agree on the success factors	The agreement of the organization's success factors that have been gathered in Task 1: documenting the already identified success factors.
Ascertaining the CSFs	How to perform "Sphere of Influence" mapping to ascertain operational CSFs from the success factors.
	The identification of the organization's operational CSFs through the application of the Sphere of Influence mapping process on the organization's success factors, as outlined later in this chapter.
Deriving measures from the success factors	How to derive performance measures from the organization's CSFs.
	How to report performance measures to staff, management, and the Board, Council, or Minister depending on the sector. The designing of report formats will have commenced during this workshop, and these will need to be finished after the workshop.
Implementation issues	The implementation issues as outlined in Chapter 12 and the myths of performance measurement as outlined in Chapter 2.
Next steps	The next steps where each workgroup delivers a brief presentation covering their next steps to complete their scorecard, some new measures they wish to use, and some existing measures they wish to discard.

Finalize the Wording of the Success Factors and External Outcomes

In one or two breakout sessions the attendees review the operational success factors, tighten up the wording so they are SMART, and separate out the external outcomes (e.g., retention of key customers) and strategic objectives (e.g., product leadership in our sector) into separate lists.

In a recent workshop where we had split the exercise up over six teams, two teams were asked to review the same section (15 of the 45 draft success factors). We created a panel of three comprising the CEO and two GMs. The two teams went to the panel and argued for their proposed changes. The panel had the final decision. The debate created a session that derived a thorough list of approved success factors.

Finding the Operational CSFs through a "Sphere of Influence" Mapping Process

The "sphere of influence" process is a derivative of the BSC cause-and-effect and is a faster process. The aim of the "sphere of influence" process is to understand and document relationships between success factors such as late planes will lead to a loss of customers (both key and non-key customers), late maintenance, low staff satisfaction, poor utilization of planes, and so forth.

To find your five to eight operational CSFs, a good technique is to type all your success factors into numbered boxes on a large sheet of paper (A3/U.S. fanfold), as set out in Exhibit 7.9. Each team of five to seven people is then asked to map the sphere of influence of each success factor. We insert an arrow to reflect the direction of influence.

The mapping process is performed by the team members, starting with one success factor, and then looking at each other success factor and asking, "Does it impact this success factor?" To handle the number of relationships (in most organizations, you will be handling between 30 and 40 success factors), draw truncated arrows. Label these short arrows with the number of the box it is going to, and label the other arrow entering that box with the number of the box it has come from (see Exhibit 7.10). The key point

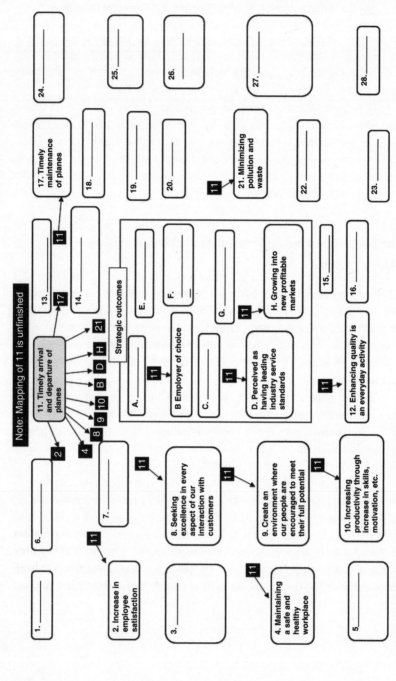

134

Exhibit 7.9 Sphere of Influence Mapping Exercise

Exhibit 7.10 Mapping the Sphere of Influence

to check is the direction. It is understandable that some relationships are two-way. In these cases, we draw another set of arrows, traveling in opposite directions when we are mapping the other success factor.

I always give the following instructions:

- If one member of the team sees a linkage, other members of the team should draw the relationship without debate. This will speed up the process.
- Although the magnitude of the relationships will clearly be different, teams should pretend they are all equal for the time being.
- Each team should mentally jump into one success factor box at a time and look out at the other success factors, drawing the relationships they find.
- As in Exhibit 7.10, there is a two-way relationship. It is important not to get diverted, for when you draw the arrows from "Timely Maintenance of Planes" to "Timely Arrival and Departure of Planes" you have effectively left your success factor and are examining another.
- After a couple of success boxes have been mapped and there is a common understanding of the exercise, each group should split into smaller teams of two or three people, each looking into a designated number of success factors.

There is an alternative method of mapping relationships, shown to me at an in-house workshop I was running. A clever attendee demonstrated how to map the relationships on a spreadsheet matrix (see Exhibit 7.11). This method is preferred by some and also creates easy-to-review documentation of the process. I now ask all workgroups to choose whatever method they prefer. The attendees using sphere-of-influence mapping are asked to have one team member to document their finding on the spreadsheet as well.

Exhibit 7.11 A Spreadsheet Matrix of Success Factor Relationships

#	Success Factor	Count	1	2	3	4	5	6	7	8	9	10	11	12	13	14	15	16	17	18	19	20	21	etc	etc	40
1	Maintaining a healthy and safe workplace	5		X									X					X	X	X	X					
2	We recruit the right people all the time	1	X																					X	X	
3	Delivery in full, on time, all the time to our key customers	12				X																				
4	We finish what we start	2	X																							
5	customers	2	X																							
6		5	X												X			X	X		X					
7		4									X					X	X			X				X		
8		3	X	X													X									
9		2								X	X															
10		10	X										X		X	X	X	X	X	X	X	X		X		
11		3	X	X															X		X					
12		8													X	X	X							X		
etc		3													X		X									
etc		1																								
etc		0																								
40		4										X	X	X		X										

This 'x' represents an arrow from success factor #1 "Maintaining a healthy and safe workplace" to success factor #2 "We recruit the right people all the time".

This 'x' represents an arrow from success factor #7 to success

This shows the total amount of relationships formed between success factors. The higher the number, the greater the likelihood of being a critical success factor.

This exercise is slow to start with and then becomes quicker as teams remember where the success factors are positioned. It is also very subjective, and it is more applicable to participants who know the organization well.

Mapping to the Desired Outcomes Statements

As a recent development to my method, I now like to include the short-term and long-term desired outcomes in the center of the U.S. fanfold (A3) sheet of paper. This will generally give higher scores to the success factors that impact more than one outcome.

When you put an outcome statement on the U.S. fanfold (A3) schedule, you will note that it gathers arrows but does not link the other way. This is to be expected as they are a result of the success factors at work.

The inclusion of the desired outcomes in the U.S. fanfold (A3) schedule also gives management the opportunity to see the connectivity between the positive application of the chosen CSFs and the desired outcomes. In Exhibit 7.9, success factor #11 links to three outcomes (outcomes B, D and H).

Handling the Diversity of the Mapping by the Teams

To handle the diversity of the mapping by the teams—for instance, where one team has 10 arrows out of a success factor and another 16 arrows out for the same success factor—we look at each team's top five operational success factors, the ones with the most arrows out. This way we are gathering what they see as the most important, regardless of the actual count of the number of relationships.

Some of the top five success factors may have the same score, in which case I give them a position of joint second or joint third ranking. Thus, the rankings from one team may be (1st, 2nd, =3rd, =3rd, 4th) and another team may have (=1st, =1st, =2nd, =2nd, 3rd) for their top five success factors. I list their rankings on a summary chart; see Exhibit 7.12 to see which success factors selected are the most significant.

I avoid the temptation to use a weighting as we would be trying to add certainty to a subjective process. It is my belief that the success factors that are rated in the top five by most, or all, of the teams are most likely to be the

Exhibit 7.12 Summarizing the Teams' Top Five Success Factors from the Sphere of Influence Mapping Process

	Team 1	Team 2	Team 3	Team 4	Team 5	# of times selected
1. Be seen in the community as an employer of "first choice"	= 5		= 4		= 2	3
2. Supporting minorities through employment						
3. Environmentally friendly culture and reputation (use of environmentally friendly materials)						
4. Delivery in full, on time, all the time to our key customers	1	= 3	1	1	1	5
5. Finding better ways to do the things we do everyday	= 5					1
6. Optimizing technology that matters			2		4	2
7. Completion of projects on time and to budget						
8. Encouraging innovation that matters		1		4		2
9. Enhancing quality		= 3				1
10. Timely, accurate, decision-based information						
11. We finish what we start	4	2	= 4	2		4
12. Reducing supply chain costs		= 3	= 5		= 2	3
13. Optimize revenue from profitable customers						
14. Increase in employee satisfaction	3					1
15. Appropriate reward and recognition structure for all				5		1
16. Increasing recognition throughout the organization						
17. A pleasant physical work environment for all staff						
Etc.						
Etc.						

organizations' critical success factors. In Exhibit 7.12 success factors 4 and 11 are the more likely critical success factors.

From this exercise you will typically get 10–15 success factors that are ranking well. They will be in two groupings, some clearly CSFs and others competing for the right to be called CSFs. We now need to further fine-tune the result.

Even at this stage you may discover a success factor that is an outcome. This does not affect the scoring, as the outcome will not have any out arrows and thus not be in the top five selection.

Fine-Tuning the First Cut of the Critical Success Factors

During this exercise you will have noted that some attendees have a gift for this mapping process. Identify four to six of these attendees and extract them for a special exercise: the remapping of the 10–15 success factors that have been identified as possible operational CSFs.

The purpose of this exercise is to test the robustness of the 10–15 success factors. The team will

- Look at the spreadsheet matrix of each team for success factors that ranked highly with one team and not the other team. This indicates a scoring issue. In a recent exercise we discovered that one team's scoring could not be relied upon and thus found a critical success factor that they had underscored.
- Rescore the 10–15 success factors—they will use the spreadsheet matrices as reference documents.
- Look for a cut-off point where there is a significant jump in the scoring, leaving you with a shortlist of 6–8 top-scoring CSFs. These will not be ranked, as not all relationships are equal. However, you can safely assume success factors, with say 20 outward arrows, will be more important than success factors with say 8 outward arrows.

Testing the Operational CSFs

When the first cut of the operational CSFs has been ascertained, the KPI project team tests the list of the top five to eight critical success factors against the six perspectives of a balanced scorecard and the organization's strategic objectives, as illustrated in Exhibits 7.13 and 7.14.

Exhibit 7.13 Testing That Your Operational CSFs Link Well to the Six BSC Perspectives

Critical success factor	Perspectives					
	Financial	Customer satisfaction	Staff satisfaction	Innovation and learning	Internal process	Environment and community
e.g., Timely arrival and departure of planes	✓	✓	✓	✓	✓	Possible
_____		✓			✓	✓
_____	✓					
_____	✓			✓		
_____			✓		✓	
_____	✓	✓		✓		✓

Exhibit 7.14 Testing That Your Operational CSFs Link Well to the Organization's Strategic Objectives

Critical success factor	Strategic Objectives (SO)					
	SO#1	SO#2	SO#3	SO#4	SO#5	SO#6
e.g., Timely arrival and departure of planes	✓		✓			possible
_____		✓			✓	✓
_____	✓					
_____			✓			
_____	✓	✓			✓	
_____	✓		✓		✓	

In Exhibit 7.14 the CSFs are not impacting the strategic objective #4, and thus we need to ask whether we have all the CSFs. Could one CSF be reworded, or is the strategic objective #4 correct in the first place?

140

Selection of the Critical Success Factors Is a Very Subjective Exercise

The selection of the operational CSFs is a very subjective exercise, and the effectiveness and usefulness of those CSFs chosen is highly dependent on the degree of analytical skill of those involved. Active leadership by senior management in this step is therefore mandatory.

Implementation Tips

This workshop needs to be facilitated by a skilled workshop presenter familiar with the content in this book. Ideally it would be a member of the KPI team who has been selected because of their ability to deliver workshops. If an in-house resource is not available, you can access accredited coaches who can deliver in person or remotely via web-based training. For accredited coaches, visit www.davidparmenter.com.

Task 3: Presenting the Critical Success Factors to the Staff

Once the CSFs have been ascertained, there is a need to communicate them to those who have not been part of the process.

The senior management team members, managers, and staff who have not attended the CSF workshop will need to understand how the CSFs came about and their significance. The KPI team prepares and delivers a presentation on the organization's CSFs to facilitate discussion and agreement with the senior management team and then to the staff. See accompanying electronic media for the suggested content for this presentation.

The presentation will cover:

- The history of performance measurement within the organization.
- How these CSFs were ascertained and by whom.
- The top five to eight CSFs and their impact on the organization's success factors. One organization showed each CSF on a slide with all the success factors they affected as illustrated in Exhibit 7.15.
- How the CSFs should be used by staff and their anticipated impact.
- How these CSFs will drive the performance measures, which will not be linked to pay or individuals but to processes and teams.

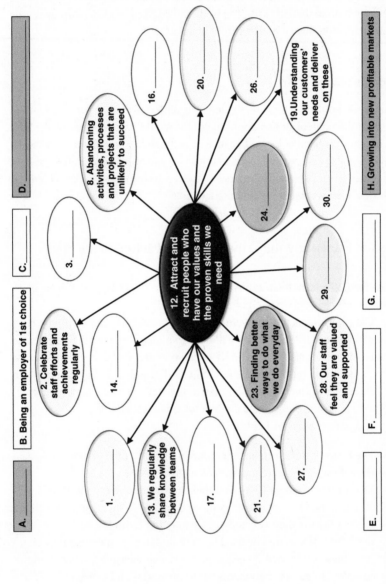

Exhibit 7.15 Showing How the Critical Success Factors Affect Other Success Factors and the Organization's Outcomes

---

Financial institution

Because this was a global organization, the CSF workshop was run as part of the executive retreat week, which is held each year.

The CSF workshop was scheduled for the first two days. On Day 3 the output of the workshop was transferred into a CSF presentation, as shown in Exhibit 7.15. This was delivered in Day 4, discussed and agreed by the executive. Preparing and presenting the final CSFs at the executive retreat fast tracked the process and facilitated a swift agreement.

The CSFs need to be discussed with employee representatives and conveyed to staff to maximize the benefits once the CSFs have been ascertained. If staff members are told what is important, they can align their daily activities to maximize their contribution. This is done in the Performance Measures Workshop outlined in Chapter 9.

> The only way the operational CSFs will make a change in an organization is when staff live, breathe, and own the operational CSFs.

It will be beneficial to brief the board on the KPI project and its effect on the board report. The presentation to the board will need to be different. There will be more of an emphasis on discussing the reasons for the project, the benefits to the board, the difference between external outcomes and operational success factors, and some examples of the reporting they will get on the key result indicators. From prior experiences, you do not need to involve the board in the operational CSFs and the forthcoming KPIs, as these are a management tool.

Task 4: Get the CSFs on the Wall in Every Workplace

This is an important step; however, from my observation it is often overlooked. The only way the operational CSFs will make a change in an organization is when staff live, breathe, and own the operational CSFs. For that to happen, the operational CSFs need to be communicated and agreed upon in a meaningful way rather than just written up as a list.

I came across a brilliant example of how to communicate to staff what is important. In Exhibit 7.16, the company in question prepared a cartoon representation of what it wanted to achieve in the year, and staff pinned it on their office walls. It was printed on U.S. fanfold (A3) paper in full color. I believe this concept is an ideal way to present the CSFs to staff.

Communication of the critical success factors to the workforce has a profound impact on an organization. Maybe, for the first-time, staff and management truly know what is important.

There is no shortcut for Small to Medium-Sized Enterprises.

All the tasks are required. Some SMEs may think they can collapse the two-day workshop into a one-day workshop. This will lead to disappointment.

PDF Download

To assist the KPI project team on the journey, templates and checklists have been provided. The reader can access, from kpi.davidparmenter.com/fourthedition, free of charge, a PDF of the following chapter templates:

- A Suggested Draft of the CEO Invitation to Attend the Two-Day CSF Workshop
- Preparing a List of Draft Operational Success Factors Checklist
- List of Common Operational Success Factors
- A Checklist of Common Outcome Statements
- Critical Success Factor Workshop Timetable
- A Checklist for Planning a Workshop
- Additional Pointers on How to Organize the Critical Success Factor Workshop
- Instructions for Break-out Exercises in the CSF Workshop
- A List of Empty Words to Avoid When Wording Success Factors
- Sphere of Influence Mapping Exercise
- Sphere of Influence Mapping Template

Exhibit 7.16 Communicating Critical Success Factors to Staff

Source: Energy Efficiency Conservation Authority 2009/2010 Plan, www.eeca.govt.nz. Reproduced with permission.

Notes

1. *Key Performance Indicators Manual: A Practical Guide for the Best Practice Development, Implementation and Use of KPIs* (Aus-Industries, 1996). Now out of print.
2. Stephen Covey, A. Roger Merrill, and Rebecca R. Merrill, *First Things First: To Live, to Love, to Learn, to Leave a Legacy* (New York: Simon & Schuster, 1994).
3. Peter F. Drucker, *The Practice of Management* (New York: HarperCollins, 1954).

Overview

Many performance measures are ascertained far too frequently, in a rush, by untrained staff. Seldom will these measures stimulate the desired and appropriate action. This chapter looks at common measurement traps, what we need to measure, and what staff need to understand before they start to look for measures that will work in their organization.

The exercises in this chapter will train the staff, who performed them, to take care when constructing measures. You should expect the outcome of the training to be:

- Fewer measures
- Abandonment of many broken measures
- Introduction of more current- and future-oriented measures that act like a fence at the top of the cliff
- Clarity over the different types of measures, *result indicators* and *performance indicators*
- A recognition that KPIs are unique measures and there will only be a few in the organization

The key learning points from this chapter are:

1. The common measurement traps to avoid
2. Wisdom on measures from other writers e.g., When designing measures begin with the end in mind
3. The rules for designing measures
4. For staff to help the KPI team determine measures, they first need to understand the rules for designing measures
5. Suggested exercises to help staff to design measures
6. The need to abandon measures where the cost of gathering the data is greater than the benefit

CHAPTER 8

Characteristics of Meaningful Measures

I t is very easy for a team in the workshop to come up with poor measures. There needs to be a structured approach following certain rules and avoiding the common measurement traps.

Common Measurement Traps

Numerous performance measures methodologies, including the balanced scorecard, appear to simply say the measures are a by-product of the exercise. Frequently, the task of finding measures is carried out at the last minute by staff members who do not have a clue about what is involved in finding a measure that will create the appropriate behavioral response. There are several common reasons why organizations get their measures radically wrong as set out in Exhibit 8.1.

Wisdom on Measures from Other Authors

There are several writers who have added to our understanding of what are good measures; I have highlighted some of their key contributions in Exhibit 8.2.

Exhibit 8.1 Common Reasons Why Organizations Get Their Measures Radically Wrong

Measuring too much	With so much data available there is the temptation to allow the data to drive the measurement, leading to measuring too much and missing areas where data are not currently available. The cost of measurement often outweighs the benefit of the measurement. Visit any call center and see the myriad performance measures they are measuring.
A lack of connectivity with the organization's critical success factors	Measures are too frequently a by-product of a strategy exercise, project planning, an annual performance pay agreement.
Treating all measures as KPIs	Over the past 25 years I have come to the conclusion that there are four types of performance measures. These four types of measures are in two groups: result indicators and performance indicators, and are discussed in Chapter 1.
KPIs being driven by performance-related pay	If you tie KPIs to performance-related pay, KPI stands for *key political indicator,* rather than *key performance indicator*. Good performance with KPIs should be regarded as a "ticket to the game." Hence a given, the reason why you are employed; thus, there is no need to incentivize them.
A tendency to overrely on financial measures	Financial measures are all *result indicators* and are discussed in Chapter 1.
Driven by the balanced scorecard methodology	Although the balanced scorecard methodology was a breakthrough in helping organizations to have a more holistic and balanced view on strategy it gave birth to a number of problems, such as the lead-lag debate, cascading of organizational measures into myriad meaningless departmental measures, and too simplistic strategy mapping.

150

Exhibit 8.1 (*Continued*)

Relying too much on past measures	It is taking action in the here and now that creates the results of the future. Although we still need to measure the past, we also need to measure current and planned future activities; see Chapter 1.
Confusion over outcome and operational measurement	It is imperative to separate out reporting of progress against outcomes (bi-monthly or quarterly) from reporting operational progress (24/7, daily, weekly). Key result indicators will be your outcome measures, and these will principally be reported by the executive team to the board. Never give the board the operational KPIs.
Random selection from a database of measures	Whether it is using external consultants, relying on industry benchmarks, or accessing one of a number of performance measure databases, the results are the same, chaos.
An initiative is not a measure, e.g., performing a satisfaction survey	A better measure would be the number of implementations made to improve service post-survey.
Mixing measures with targets and milestones	It is very common to see targets, milestones, and measures all mixed up together. "Completing the project by 31 December ____" is a target. "Stage 3 finished by 31 December ____" is a milestone. "List of late projects by manager, reported weekly to the senior management team" is a measure.
Documenting a few vague words does not make a performance measure	Instead of a vague statement such as Maintain a customer loyalty program we could measure month-to-date sales by major customer.
Having a set of measures insisted upon by the governing body or Client e.g., common in Government and large outsourced contracts	Here the tail must wag the dog. Over time you need to educate the requesting body, so they see the absurdity of the measures they are requesting.

(*continued*)

Exhibit 8.1 (*Continued*)

A "SMART" measure is not always the answer	It is a misconception to believe that if a measure is SMART—*specific, measurable, attainable, realistic,* and *time sensitive*—it will do. This, of course, ignores the fact that the measure may not be linked to the critical success factors of the business and that its dark side may be very damaging.
Designed by untrained staff	Giving teams the task of finding measures, without any training, and placing them in the organization's balanced scorecard application is a recipe for disaster. Just as damaging is getting external performance measurement experts to complete this task in the spare moments they have.

Exhibit 8.2 **Key Contributions from Other Authors**

Paul Niven[a]	"Any measure that takes more than 30 seconds to describe probably doesn't belong." "Beware of averages—instead look for performance measures that portray the true picture of the process or event you're attempting to capture."
Dean Spitzer[b]	The balanced scorecard is often manipulated whether it is tied to annual performance bonus or not. As Spitzer says, "The ultimate goal is not the customer—it's often the scorecard." "People will do what management inspects, not necessarily what management expects."
Stacey Barr[c]	"Vague words do not make a performance measure." "When designing measures begin with the end in mind." "Filter your measures by asking two questions: 'How strong an indicator is this measure of the result?'; 'How feasible will it be to measure it?'" "Don't give the team their measures; teach them how to fish."

Exhibit 8.2 (*Continued*)

Tom Peters[d]	"Keep it simple: One or two measures that count." "Our fixation with financial measures leads us to downplay or ignore less tangible nonfinancial measures, such as product quality, customer satisfaction, order lead time, etc. Yet these are increasingly the real drivers of corporate success over middle to long term."
Jeremy Hope[e]	"Many of [the] financial indicators are useful measures that tell how well the organization has performed over a recent period and if their organization is heading in the right direction. They do not, however, tell them what they need to do to improve these results. Nor do they inform users of accounts about many intangible assets (such as R&D, brands, supply chains, etc.) or contingent liabilities (such as financial risks inherent in the use of derivatives and hedge funds) that, for many organizations, have a huge impact on their market value."
Kaplan & Norton[f]	"The balanced Scorecard retains financial measurement as a critical summary of managerial and business performance, but it highlights a more general and integrated set of measurements that link current customer, internal process, employee, and system performance to long-term financial success." "Our experience has shown that an organization's first balanced Scorecard can be created over a 16-week period."

[a]Paul R. Niven, *Balanced Scorecard: Step-by-Step for Government and Nonprofit Agencies* (Hoboken, NJ: John Wiley & Sons, 2008).
[b]Dean R. Spitzer, *Transforming Performance Measurement: Rethinking the Way We Measure and Drive Organizational Success* (New York: AMACOM, 2007).
[c]Stacey Barr, *"Practical Performance Measurement: Using the PuMP Blueprint for Fast, Easy, and Engaging KPIs"* (Pump Press, 2014).
[d]Tom Peters, *Thriving on Chaos—Handbook for a Management Revolution* (New York: Harper Perennial 1988).
[e]Jeremy Hope, *Reinventing the CFO* (Boston: Harvard Business School Press, 2006).
[f]Robert S. Kaplan and David P. Norton, *The Balanced Scorecard: Translating Strategy into Action* (Boston: Harvard Business Press, 1996).

Rules for Designing Measures

"When designing measures begin with the end in mind."
—Stacey Barr

As mentioned in Chapter 2, it is one of the myths of performance measurement that appropriate measures are very obvious. There are a number of rules to follow when designing measures and these are set out in Exhibit 8.3.

Exhibit 8.3 The Rules for Designing Measures

The difference between Result and Performance Indicators	If you can phone managers and they accept the responsibility for a measure, it is a *performance indicator*. Where you have measures that summarize collective action of several teams working together, then a phone call is of no benefit as no one will accept responsibility. These measures I call *result indicators*. Each of these two categories has some exceptional measures, and these are called *key result indicators*, or *key performance indicators*, as appropriate.
Ensure that a measure is designed from or links to one of the organization's CSFs	As mentioned in Chapter 7, I see the CSFs as the source of all performance measures. If you get the critical success factors right, it is very easy to find your winning KPIs. By ascertaining the CSFs first, you have started with the end in mind.
Timely measurement so you are measuring more at the "top of the cliff" rather than at the "bottom of the cliff"	It is clearly better to catch problems early on rather than measure their impact in the monthly report. Where you need change to occur, daily or weekly measurement has a far better chance to prompt corrective action to take place. I do not believe there is a monthly KPI on this planet. If a performance indicator is key to the well-being of an organization, surely you would measure it as frequently as possible.
Focusing measures on the exceptions	Focusing on an exception is better than having to measure everything. It is surely better to measure late planes in the sky over two hours late than the percentage of "on-time" flights in the month.

Exhibit 8.3 *(Continued)*

Remove measures that will lead to damaging or dysfunctional behavior	All measures will have a dark side. The question is, how big is the dark side? Some will lead to damaging dysfunctional behavior; e.g., the measuring of calls made by staff in call centers will lead staff to make more short calls to the same customers, leading to the eventual loss of those customers.
The wording of a measure should leave no doubt what is being measured	Often the initial measure is a statement or even just a clue as to what is to be measured; e.g., "Number of successions plans in place." A better rewording is "Number of key positions with at least two potential replacements," a performance indicator that should be measured quarterly. It will promote managers to recruit and train staff who have the potential to be their successors. It also reminds management that one potential successor is not enough as the odds are that the staff member will leave before the promotion can occur.
Ensure the benefit of measurement is much greater than the cost	Many measures may appear useful but on reflection have a negative cost/benefit relationship, e.g., Number of business opportunities in the pipeline. Although it would be great to have a central database of business opportunities, in reality such lists will be incomplete. Staff will get weary of updating it. The dreaded timesheet should not be introduced to support measurement. It is a far too onerous, error prone, and costly system. Even in some accounting firms the time sheets have been replaced with an agreed high and low fee range with the customer, leaving the eventual fee subject to agreement of the work undertaken.
Design the measure around the action you want to stimulate	When you have the results of a staff or employee satisfaction survey, the net score is interesting but not that important. The key is whether any of the survey recommendations have been implemented. If you do not implement these recommendations, the survey was a total waste of money and respondents' time. Thus, the measure becomes the number of recommendations that have been implemented to date (and this is would need to be reviewed weekly by the executive team).

(continued)

Exhibit 8.3 *(Continued)*

Use your oracles when designing measures	When looking at a CSF, get your wise oracles to ask themselves, **"What has good performance looked like?"** Then ask yourself, **"What has bad performance looked like?"** Both views will shed light as to what should be measured. Then ask yourself, "What 'Top of the Cliff' measures would give advance warnings of this negative performance?"
Prioritize measures that you can compare to other organizations	Relative performance measures are an important addition to KPIs; for example, you may focus 24/7 on all planes in the air that are flying more than two hours late, but in addition compare total late flights, average turnaround times, number of missing passengers, and so forth, to other airlines. Perhaps this could be carried out quarterly, using a benchmarking company. Another benefit of relative measures is that they do not need constant alteration (e.g., if being in the top quartile or 2 percent above the norm is the relative measure, then this benchmark does not need changing).
Have a mix of 60% past, 20% current, and 20% future-oriented measures	Any measures that relate to activities within the last 24 hours are considered *current indicators. Future indicators* are measurements you can do now that will encourage an action to take place, e.g., Number of innovations scheduled to be implemented in the next month. See Chapter 1 for more explanation.

Suggested Exercises to Improve Measure Design

For staff to help the KPI team to determine measures, they first need to understand the rules for designing measures.

For staff to help the KPI team determine measures, they first need to understand the rules for designing measures, as listed in Exhibit 8.3. The best way is through getting the KPI team members and the workshop attendees to undertake the following exercises.

156

Rewording of Measures

Measures need to be reworded to comply with these rules. Here are some examples of how I would have reworded the initial statement.

Original measure: "Number of staff employee suggestions received in month."

The improvement and the reasoning: "Number of employee suggestions implemented by team," a performance indicator measured monthly and "Number of employee suggestions to be implemented, next week/fortnight, by team," a performance indicator measured weekly. Although it is great getting the ideas in, we want to target the change the suggestions have created so we focus on implementing ideas.

Original measure: "Number of employees with no formal systems training."

The improvement and the reasoning: "Number of employees trained on _____ system (advanced technology only)." This is a result indicator as it involves the training department and the cooperation of the teams involved in receiving training. We want to target the important technology. Best to focus on, say, five systems, which should be well understood in the organization.

Original measure: "Percentage of staff attending scheduled training."

The improvement and the reasoning: "List of scheduled training sessions in the next three and six months." A future-based performance indicator that is measured monthly. This future measure will give management a heads-up as to whether there is enough training.

"List of departments who have not registered staff to attend in-house course." This is a current performance indicator that will be measured daily in the three weeks prior to the course. This measure will encourage managers to enroll staff rather than explain to the CEO why their team is too busy to get further training.

Original measure: "Attrition rates in the past six months."

The improvement and the reasoning: "Turnover of experienced staff who have been with the organization for over three years." This is a result indicator measured quarterly to help assess whether the organization is losing experienced staff at an acceptable rate.

"Turnover of new staff who have been with the organization less than one year by department." This is a result indicator, measured monthly, to highlight managers who are creating a dysfunctional work environment.

"List of managers with high turnover of staff." This is a performance indicator, measured quarterly, highlighting problem managers.

Original measure: "Number of weeks each vacancy has been unfilled."

The improvement and the reasoning: "Number of weeks with an unfilled vacancy by key position." This is a result indicator that will be measured weekly. We want to focus on the vacancies for key positions.

Original measure: "Percentage of staff who have scheduled training planned over the next 12 months."

The improvement and the reasoning: "Percentage of staff who have scheduled training planned over the next three to six months." This is a performance indicator measured quarterly. The measure will encourage managers to sit down with staff and plan future training before the quarterly measure highlights their inactivity.

Original measure: "Number of recognitions made last month."

The improvement and the reasoning: "Number of planned recognitions in the next week/two weeks by each manager." This is a performance indicator measured weekly. This would be measured for the CEO and the next two layers of management. Measuring recognition monthly is too late. Whilst there may be times when no recognition has been organized, this weekly measure reminds management to rectify this omission.

Original measure: "Number of succession plans in place."

The improvement and the reasoning: "Number of key positions with at least two potential replacements." This is a performance indicator measured quarterly. It will promote managers to recruit and train staff who have the potential to be their successors. One potential successor is not enough, as the odds are that they will leave before the promotion can occur.

Original measure: "Percentage of team that have completed induction training."

The improvement and the reasoning: "New staff who have not attended an induction program within __ weeks of joining." This performance indicator will be reported weekly to the CEO. The importance of induction programs will be supported by this measure.

Rewording of Measures Exercise

How would you reword the following? There are suggested rewordings in the attached PDF.

Original measure: "Number of staff where a promotion is planned."
Rewording:

Original measure: "Number of late projects."
Rewording:

Original measure: "Number of managers who have been trained in best recruiting practices."
Rewording:

Original measure: "Employee satisfaction percentage derived from the staff opinion survey."

Rewording:

Original measure: "Number of employees on job rotation."

Rewording:

Original measure: "Lead time taken to recruit staff."

Rewording:

Original measure: "Number of staff referrals."

Rewording:

Original measure: "Number of recruitments where checks of authenticity of the qualifications are still outstanding."

Rewording:

| |
| |
| |
| |

Looking for Measures with a Negative Cost-versus-Benefit Relationship

There will be measures that appear reasonable on the face of it, but the cost of gathering the data will outweigh any derived benefit. Set out in Exhibit 8.4 are examples of measures where measurement would not be cost effective.

Exhibit 8.4 Measures Where Measurement Would Not Be Cost Effective

Measure	Reasoning
Number of business opportunities in the pipeline	Although it would be great to have a central database of business opportunities, in reality all lists will be incomplete.
Time spent doing a task	I have seldom found it worth recording time spent as it would involve the introduction of time sheets, a dreaded system that staff hate and is seldom right.
Number of applicants because of our advertisements Number of candidates interviewed	You only need three good candidates for a valid recruitment process.
Number of unsolicited CVs received during a month	Poor quality measure as many CVs may be of no relevance.
Number of leavers during a month	This measure mixes up the data on leavers. We need to look at leavers by experience and by department.
Percentage employees with delegated authority	Difficult and time consuming to gather data accurately.

(continued)

161

Exhibit 8.4 *(Continued)*

Measure	Reasoning
Error rate per IT system	Likely that data will be corrupted.
Number of late reports	Difficult and time consuming to gather data accurately.
Time spent on innovation	Seldom worth having time sheets for measures.
Number of near-miss/risk incidents averted	
Percentage of projects with design documentation	
Hours spent on personal development for leaders and future leaders	
Number of networking and industry events attended	Difficult to measure and likely to have a negative cost-versus-benefit ratio.
Time saved on efficiencies implemented	
Number of projects on budget	
Evaluation of the usefulness of reports	

Exercise to Categorize Measures

At this point it would be worth categorizing the following measures to assess your level of understanding. This exercise should also be done by all attendees at the performance measures workshops. In Exhibit 8.5 I have selected some measures that would be useful in many sectors. For each measure, I need you to decide:

1. Is the measure a **R**esult indicator or **P**erformance indicator? (Read Chapter 1.)
2. Is the measure a "**T**op or **B**ottom" of-the-cliff indicator? (Read this chapter again for clarity.)
3. Is the measure a **P**ast, **C**urrent, or **F**uture indicator? (Read Chapter 1.)
4. Is the measure a **T**argeted indicator, measuring the exception rather than the whole population? (Read this chapter again for clarity.)

Exhibit 8.5 **Categorizing Measures to Assess Your Level of Understanding**

Measure	Result Indicator or Performance Indicators	Measuring at "Top or Bottom" of the Cliff	Past, Current, or Future Indicator	Targeted Indicator
Abandon rate at call center—caller gives up (daily)	P	T	C	T
Number of initiatives planned within next three months to increase sales staff time in front of customers (monthly)				
Number of referrals from key customers (monthly)				
Complaints from our key customers that have not been resolved within ___ hours, reported to the chief executive officer (CEO) and general managers				
Number of initiatives completed from the recent key customer satisfaction survey (weekly)				
Late deliveries/incomplete deliveries to key customers (24/7)				
Number of defective key products returned this week (weekly)				
Health and safety issues raised and not resolved after two weeks (weekly)				
Date of next environmental disaster clean-up practice exercise (quarterly)				

(continued)

Exhibit 8.5 (*Continued*)

Measure	Result Indicator or Performance Indicators	Measuring at "Top or Bottom" of the Cliff	Past, Current, or Future Indicator	Targeted Indicator
Key position job offers that are over 48 hours old and have not yet been accepted by the chosen candidate (daily)				
Number of planned CEO recognitions for next week/two weeks (weekly)				
List of high-performing staff who have been in the same position for over two years (quarterly)				
Number of initiatives implemented after staff satisfaction survey (weekly)				
Number of staff members who have left within three months, six months, 12 months of joining the organization Reported division by division (quarterly)				
Return on capital employed (monthly)				
Number of abandonments to be actioned in the next 30 days, 60 days, and 90 days (monthly)				
Number of key positions with succession plans (quarterly)				
Number of stock-outs in week of major inventory items (weekly)				

Exhibit 8.5 (*Continued*)

Measure	Result Indicator or Performance Indicators	Measuring at "Top or Bottom" of the Cliff	Past, Current, or Future Indicator	Targeted Indicator
Number of manual transactions converted to automated electronic feed in last quarter (quarterly)				
Staff who did not attend a course due to work commitments (weekly)				
List of late projects by manager reported weekly to the senior management team (weekly)				
Number of projects in progress, by project manager, by department (weekly)				

PDF Download

To assist the KPI project team on the journey, templates and checklists have been provided. The reader can access, from kpi.davidparmenter.com/fourthedition, free of charge, a PDF of the following chapter templates:

- Answers to the Rewording of Measures Exercise
- Answers to the Categorize Measures Exercise
- Rewording of Measures Exercise Template
- Categorizing Measures Exercise Template

Overview

We need to understand how to run the performance measures workshops, how to record the performance measures in a database and refine them, and, finally, how to help teams select the appropriate measures.

Determining the measures that will work for the organization will have a profound impact on the organization, stimulating timely action and linking day-to-day activities to the strategic objectives of the organization.

This chapter also outlines the worksheets and checklists that are available, free of charge, to assist the KPI project team.

The key learning points from this chapter are:

1. How to run the two-day performance measures workshop.
2. How to derive a mix of past, current, and future-looking measures from the CSFs.
3. The importance of recording all measures collected from the workshop sessions in a database.
4. How to refine and eliminate performance measures from the database.
5. Holding a performance measures gallery to weed out dysfunctional measures.
6. Ascertaining the 10 KRIs that need to be reported to the board.
7. 10 is the upper limit for performance measures for a team.
8. How to ascertain whether a performance measure is a KPI.

CHAPTER 9

Designing and Refining Measures

Designing and refining measures need a systematic and well-thought-through process to ensure that the measures will promote the desired actions. This exercise will throw up many possible measures; the key to a successful KPI project is being able to sort the wheat from the chaff.

To understand how this stage fits within the KPI methodology, an overview of the important work that needs to be done is set out in Exhibit 9.1. The shaded areas are covered in this chapter.

> Designing and refining measures need a systematic and well-thought-through process to ensure that the measures will promote the desired actions.

Exhibit 9.1 An Overview of the Winning KPI Methodology

Task	Description
1.1 Selling the KPI project to the CEO, the senior management team, and the organization's oracles. (See Chapters 4 and 5.)	The project starts off with a well-practiced elevator pitch, followed by a compelling presentation and then a focus group workshop to get the green light from the organization's oracles.
1.2 Locate an external facilitator to mentor the KPI team. (See Chapter 5.)	An external facilitator will help guide the organization with regard to timings, selection, and size of KPI team and what needs to be abandoned to make room for the KPI project.

(continued)

Exhibit 9.1 *(Continued)*

Task	Description
1.3 Train a small KPI team. (See Chapter 6.)	The external facilitator helps train a small in-house KPI team and ensures that the KPI team leader has a cluster of mentors supporting them. Working with the organization's oracles, the KPI team develops a blueprint for the implementation, which will cover where the KPI project will be piloted.
1.4 Selling the KPI project to all employees to encourage their participation in the two-day performance measures workshops. (See Chapter 4.)	Employees who are to attend the two-day performance measures workshop need to be convinced that it is an important exercise worthy of their participation.
2.1 Locate the existing success factors and desired external outcomes from documentation and interviews. (See Chapter 7.)	Determine what your organization's success factors and desired external outcomes are.
2.2 Run the two-day critical success factor workshop to ascertain the critical success factors. (See Chapter 7.)	Map the sphere of influence each success factor has to ascertain to understand which ones have the most significant impact. These are the critical success factors. Present these to all staff.
3.1 Run the two-day performance measures workshops to train all the remaining relevant staff to develop meaningful measures. (See Chapters 8 and 9.)	Select representatives across the organization to attend a two-day workshop to be trained in the methodology, as well as how and why the organization has chosen its CSFs. Attendees will be shown how to design appropriate measures from the CSFs, how to get a mix of past, current, and future measures.
3.2 Refining the measures after the performance measures workshops. (Covered in this chapter.)	The KPI team will: delete duplicated and inferior indicators; remove measures where the cost of data extraction is greater than the derived benefit; reword indicators to improve their understanding.
3.3 Hold a performance measures gallery to weed out dysfunctional and poor measures. (Covered in this chapter.)	Hold a "measures gallery" where staff are invited to share their views on the measures that have been displayed on the walls of the project team's room.
3.4 Ask all teams to select their team performance measures from the finalized database of measures. (Covered in this chapter.)	Teams select the relevant measures and indicate their selection in the database.

Exhibit 9.1 (*Continued*)

Task	Description
3.5 Find the key result indicators (KRIs) and the key performance indicators (KPIs). (Covered in this chapter.)	Ascertain the 8–12 KRIs that will be reported to the board to show how the organization is performing. Ascertain the winning KPIs, ensuring they have the seven characteristics discussed in Chapter 1. Commence the testing of the KPIs in three designated areas.
3.6 Design the reporting framework. (See Chapter 10.)	The intraday, daily, weekly, monthly, and quarterly progress reports are designed utilizing best practice visualization techniques. Utilize existing technology so that the CEO can receive intraday updates on their smartphone and laptop.
3.7 Help facilitate the appropriate use of the selected performance measures by all the teams in the organization. (See Chapter 11.)	For several months, the KPI team will be required to ensure the reporting of measures is prepared timely and correctly and corrective actions are undertaken, where necessary. There will need to be a program to roll out KPI training to existing and new staff.
3.8 Refine CSFs and associated measures after one year of use. (See Chapter 11.)	A review should be undertaken to assess what modifications, if any, are needed to the existing CSFs and measures.

Running the Two-Day Performance Measures Workshop

Once the critical success factors have been ascertained in the CSF workshop and approved by senior management, you are ready to run the performance measures workshops. In these workshops a much wider group of staff are provided explanations of why and how the CSFs were ascertained. The attendees are also trained on what makes a good indicator and how to derive them from the organization's CSFs.

Staff who attended the CSF would not be required to attend, unless their assistance was required.

Task 1. Workshop Planning

A list of managers, supervisors, and experienced specialists will be drawn up, and the CEO will send out an invitation to them to attend a two-day workshop. The executive and management who attended the CSF workshop will emphasize the importance of the exercise with their presence at workshop sessions.

Decisions will be made regarding the logistics, as well as the locations of workshops and timings. Some performance measures workshop groups can have up to 80 attendees with an experienced trainer.

Representatives across the organization are carefully selected to attend a workshop. Selection criteria include:

- At least two years with the organization
- At least five years working in the sector
- To have demonstrated a full understanding of how their team operates

Before the workshop the attendees are broken into cross-functional workgroups (to increase the level of experiences each group can call upon) of between five and seven staff members (to increase participation). A by-product of this two-day workshop is an enhanced team-building atmosphere.

This two-day workshop requires the following:

- A large room where the workgroups can sit around a table.
- A flipchart, flipchart paper, and whiteboard pens for each table.
- A laptop for each group (for recording measures).

Financial Institution Case Study

As this was a global organization, the CSF workshop was run as part of the executive training week, which is held each year.

At the retreat, The Global CEO made the decision to roll out the CSF and associated measures through the establishment of an in-house KPI team.

Once trained, the in-house team held the initial two-day performance measures workshop at the head office in Australia. Representatives from the Asian operation attended to experience the training and advise the KPI team on how best to deliver the presentation in their country. Skilled translators were hired so that the workshop had a simultaneous translation.

The European two-day workshops were delivered as part of a separate trip, using the same training template.

Food Distributor Case Study

With plants in many locations, it was decided to run a series of 2.5-hour webinar sessions instead of a two-day CSF workshop for an organization based in the Northeast of England. This was followed by further support from the KPI team and a one-day performance measures workshop to compare progress and swap ideas.

Senior and experienced staff, from a broad section of their operation, numbering between 5 and 12 in each plant location were present in their training room. I was able to deliver the presentations from my New Zealand office and set up workshop activities using GoToMeeting. Attendees were paired and sat in front of a laptop so that I could see their level of engagement.

To assist I have provided the proposed agenda for the KPI workshop and the breakout work group sessions in PDF format for you to download.

Task 2. Set Up a Database to Record the Performance Measures

Select a database that is widely available within the organization and is user-friendly. Most organizations operate database applications, which are underutilized. The KPI team needs to design and build a performance-measure database, that is easy to use, in the chosen database application.

The database should include sections where teams:

- Select the critical success factors/success factors that are relevant to them.
- Can interrogate the database using keywords to see if their measure is already included.
- Can add new performance measures (only the KPI team should have power to delete measures).
- Record their selection of all the measures they are proposing to use.

171

Financial Institution Case Study

An Excel database was set up with each workgroup providing their derived measures in the provided Excel template. These templates were then cut and pasted into the database.

To maintain control and traceability, all measures were given a unique number.

The first stage is to train attendees in the new thinking of what are KPIs, why not all measures are KPIs, the four different types of measures, and the importance of an organization knowing their CSFs.

An Access and Excel performance measure database is available from www .davidparmenter.com for a small fee. Open the templates icon, on the website, and search for the "Database of Measures and Associated Success Factors."

Task 3. Outline the Winning KPI Methodology

The first stage is to train attendees in the new thinking of what are KPIs, why many measures are not KPIs, the four different types of indicators, and the importance of an organization knowing their CSFs.

Local senior management who were part of the CSF workshop should welcome the attendees, emphasize the importance to the KPI project and their level of commitment, and be present to explain how the organization chose its CSFs.

In the opening presentation, on the first day, address the issues and perceptions raised in the employee survey run prior to the workshop. Employees often are concerned that performance information will be:

- Collected on individuals and held against them (e.g., for disciplinary purposes)
- Filtered both in content and distribution (e.g., "They only show us information when it suits their purposes.")
- Used to allocate blame for performance problems

Task 4. Train Attendees to Derive Measures from the CSFs

When designing measures, you need a very structured process. You begin with the CSF that will be the easiest to measure, and then you ask the audience, "What results would you expect to see if the critical success factor is working correctly?" You suggest to them to recycle the words used in the critical success factor name. I tend to aim for between four and five results. For example, if we were to ascertain measures for the critical success factor "maintaining a safe, happy, and healthy workplace" (see Exhibit 9.2), the results could be: *staff happy with their work, nice workplace environment, workplace is safe at all times, healthy working conditions at all times, there is a positive "go for it" culture*. Every workgroup will have a slightly different mix of result wording. This does not matter, as it is only the measures that will be recorded.

With each result, you ask the attendees, "What would good performance look like in this area?" Using their answers, ask them, "What measures

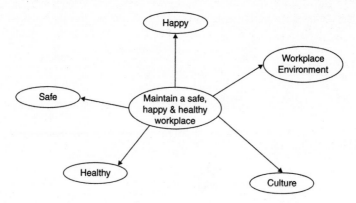

Exhibit 9.2 Ascertaining Measures from a Critical Success Factor

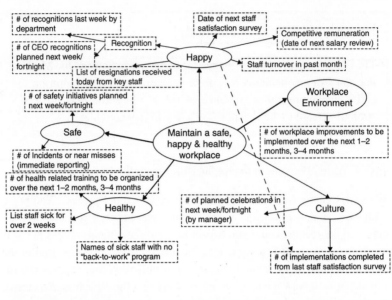

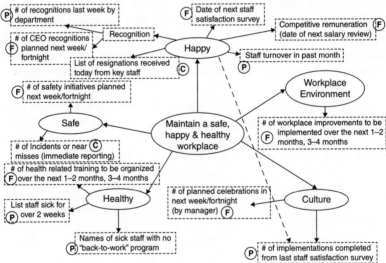

Exhibit 9.2 (*Continued*)

174

would show this good performance best?" Then ask, "What would poor performance look like?" In response to their answers, ask them, "What measures would give advance warnings of this negative performance?"

For *staff happy with their work* we start ascertaining the likely measures. These might include:

1. Number of recognitions given last week by department
2. Number of CEO recognitions planned for next week/next fortnight
3. Number of incidents or near misses (immediate reporting)

The next stage is to mark the measures that are:

1. Past measures with a **P** (1. Number of recognitions given last week by department)
2. Current measures with a **C** (3. Number of incidents or near misses)
3. Future measures with an **F** (2. Number of planned celebrations in next week/next fortnight)

Once you have gone through the worked example allocate the same CSF to at least three groups. First compare their result bubbles, they should be slightly different. Then compare some of their measures. Workgroups will have varying degrees of success with the first exercise. After 20 minutes select the workgroup who has made the best progress and get all the attendees to gather around as they explain what they have done. This highlighting of "better practice" will galvanize the other groups to lift their performance.

In Exhibit 9.3 we are achieving four views of the same CSF. This overlap helps ensure that we see the CSFs from different perspectives and from

Exhibit 9.3 Allocation of CSFs for Workgroups

Critical success factor	Group 1	Group 2	Group 3	Group 4	Group 5	Group 6	Group 7	Group 8
CSF #1_____	x	x					x	x
CSF #2_____	x	x					x	x
CSF #3_____	x	x	x	x				
CSF #4_____	x	x	x	x				
CSF #5_____			x	x	x	x		
CSF #6_____			x	x	x	x		
CSF #7_____					x	x	x	x
CSF #8_____					x	x	x	x

a difference experience viewpoint. You will expect a large overlap of measures. This sorting of measures is carried out later.

Over the course of the remainder of the two days, after every 60–90 minutes of ascertaining measures gather the workgroups back to hear another presentation on related topics (best practice reporting guidelines, project management tips, project's next steps, etc.). Review the accompanying PDF for the draft agenda that I use.

To assist with the designing of measures, here are some useful workshop rules:

- Make sure you have conducted a training session, delivered by the now experienced KPI team, on how to word the performance measures and how to make them measurable, as outlined in Chapter 8.
- The assembled staff will be organized in cross-functional work groups, to increase the level of experiences each group can call upon.
- Everybody is considered an equal during the session; thus, ensure that the most senior member does not act as the facilitator.
- Ensure staff know why measures are designed from the carefully worded critical success factors and are aware of the key lessons from Chapter 7. When you are designing a measure from a well-worded critical success factor, you are already focused like a marksman who is looking through a rifle's telescope.
- Many measures in the workshops will be of little use. The sorting out of wheat from the chaff is carried out by the KPI team.

Task 5. Show How to Word Measures Properly

At this point we need to explain to the attendees what makes a useful measure as outlined in Chapter 8:

- It should be free of abbreviations so that all employees will easily recognize the measure.
- It should describe what is being measured and not be a statement, e.g., customer satisfaction survey (statement), number of initiatives implemented from the customer satisfaction survey (measure).
- There should be a focus on the exception and what is important, e.g., number of *key* customer complaints that have not been resolved within four hours (focusing on key customer complaints).

176

■ It should encourage action in a timely manner (Performance indicator) or report how effectively teams have worked together (Result indicator).

Task 6. Achieve a Mix of Past, Current, and Future-Looking Measures

It is important for staff to learn to restate measures. There will be a tendency to measure in the past, as this is the easiest form of measurement. We now want them to measure also in the current and future time periods.

Current measures are measured 24/7 or daily, and *future measures* are the record of a future date when an action is to take place (e.g., date of next meeting with key customer, date of next product launch, date of next social interaction with key customers). *Key result indicators and result indicators* will all be past measures, whereas *performance indicators and key performance indicators* are now categorized as either past, current, or future measures. You will find that most of the KPIs in your organization will fit into the current or future categories.

See Exhibit 9.4.for an illustration of how you take a past measure and restate it as a current and future measure. The previous debate about lag

Exhibit 9.4 Taking a Past Measure and Restating as a Current and Future Measure

Past measures (last week/fortnight/ month/quarter)	Current measures (24/7 and daily)	Future measures (next day/week/ month/quarter)
e.g., number of late planes last week/ last month	e.g., planes over two hours late (updated continuously)	e.g., number of initiatives to be commenced in the next month, months +2 and +3, to target areas that are causing late planes.
Date of last visit by key customer	Cancellation of order by key customer (today)	Date of next visit to key customer
Sales last month in new products	Quality defects found today in new products	Number of improvements to key products to be implemented in the next month, months +2 and +3

(outcome) and lead (performance driver) indicators is now replaced with an appropriate mix of past, current, and future-looking measures. As pointed out in Chapter 1, defining measures as either lag or lead indicators does not work and serves to confuse.

Task 7. Recording All Measures Collected from the Workshop Sessions in a Database

After ascertaining the relevant measures from a CSF, the workgroups record all measures collected from the workshop sessions in a database, indicating the key features, such as description of measure, suggested measure name, the critical success factor the measure was derived from, and measurement frequency. The suggested fields are set out in Exhibit 9.5.

The database is fed from several sources. The KPI team will have gathered and recorded performance measures from:

- Information gained during discussions held with senior management, revisiting company archives, reviewing monthly reports.
- External research undertaken from the beginning of the KPI project.
- The CSF workshop, which would have been held already.

During all workshops ensure the database is updated before the attendees go to any break. I normally use a simple word table or Excel spreadsheet as the input form, which is updated on an employee's laptop and passed over to the KPI team via a USB stick. At this point we only need to record the source CSF, name of measure, and whether it is a *Past*, *Current*, or *Future* measure. The rest of the detail about the measure can be added once the measure has passed through some editing tests.

You will have gathered some measures from the earlier CSF workshop as you trained the executive and management in the CSF workshop. It is important to record these measures into the database.

Task 8. Removal of Duplicated Measures

Before the workshop ends, all workgroups are asked to review the measures output. The measures are printed out from the database by critical success factor and placed on a wall for review, as shown in Exhibit 9.6. The attendees are asked to view the lists on the wall and delete all duplicated measures and edit any unclear measure names.

178

Name of Performance Measure	Type of Measure (KRI, RI, PI, KPI)	Person Responsible	BSC Perspectives	Time Zone (Past, Current, Future)	Frequency of Measurement (24 by 7, daily, weekly, monthly)	Suggested Target	Origin of Measure (Name of critical success factor)	Team xx	Team xx	Team xx	Team xx	Team xx
Number of initiatives **implemented from** the quarterly rolling key customer survey	PI	John Doe	CF	Past	Weekly after survey (stop after 10 weeks)	All initiatives implemented within 3 months of survey	Retain key customers, Increase repeat business from key customers	✓	✓			
Late planes, more than two hours late	KPI	Susan John	F, CF, E&C IP, SS, I&L	Current	24 by 7	<3 per week	Timely arrival and departure of planes	✓	✓	✓	✓	✓
Number of initiatives **to be implemented** to get planes on time	RI	Basil John	CF, IP, F, E&C	Future	Weekly	>3 per month per team	Timely arrival and departure of planes	✓	✓	✓		
xxxxxxxxxxxxxx xxxxxxxxxxxx	PI	xxxxxxx	xxxx	xxxx	xx	xx	xxx	✓	✓			

F = Financial Results, CF = Customer Focus, E&C = Environment & Community, IP = Internal Process, SS = Staff Satisfaction, I&L = Innovation & Learning

Exhibit 9.5 Performance Measure Database Layout Example

Financial Institution Case Study

In the last session of the two-day workshop, all the measures in the database were printed out, and the attendees were asked to review for duplication and further clarification (filling out any abbreviations). In 20 minutes, by using all the attendees' brains the KPI team was able to save many hours of additional sorting.

Task 9. Introduce a Moratorium on Measures Being Developed Outside the KPI Project

The CEO needs to make it clear that no measures are to be introduced without the KPI team's approval

Every organization is likely to have a number of performance measures in place, even if they are not called KPIs. These existing measures need to be reviewed to fit them within the new four-tiered structure of performance measures (KRIs, RIs, PIs, KPIs). The CEO needs to make it clear that no measures are to be introduced without the KPI team's approval.

Exhibit 9.6 Workshop Attendees Helping With the Removal of Duplicated Measures
Photo Credit: Stephen Robinson

Shortcut for Small To Medium-Sized Enterprises (SMEs)

The performance measures workshop would be integrated with the CSF workshop for SMEs with less than 100 FTEs. No separate workshop would need to be held, as all relevant personnel would have been invited to the two-day combined workshop.

For SMEs between 100 and 250 the workshop could be limited to one day, providing the CSFs have been clearly articulated to staff before the workshop starts.

Refining Performance Measures after the Workshops

After the performance measures workshop there are two quality assurance exercises to perform.

Tidying Up the Performance Measures Post Workshop

Mankind has for thousands of years been able to sort the wheat from the chaff. It is thus in our DNA. We now need to use this ancient practice with all the measures we have designed in the workshop. Leave the sorting of measures until after the KPI staff workshop, and let this exercise be done by the KPI team—the in-house experts on performance measures. I recommend the following sorting techniques:

- Ensure your database has "original measure name" and "revised measure name" fields. This enables you to retain an audit trail back to the workshop output.
- Measures that are merely statements are marked for deletion in the "revised measure name" field.
- Remaining measures are grouped into categories, e.g., training, staff turnover. See Exhibit 9.7 for a suggested list of useful categories.
- Duplicated and inferior measures are marked as "duplicate," "poor measure" in the "revised measure name" field.
- Also recorded in the "Revised measure name" field is where the cost of getting data, for an indicator, is estimated to outweigh the benefit.

Exhibit 9.7 A Suggested List of Useful Performance Measure Categories Index

1	Customer/Key Customer/New Customer/Sales Pipeline/Call Center/ Brand Recognition
2	Quality/On-time Delivery/Order Processing/Pricing
3	Health and Safety/Accidents/Emergency Response
4	Community Involvement/Environmental/Waste/Public Relations
5	Recruiting/Student Internships
6	Employee Satisfaction/Absenteeism/Staff Turnover/Recognition/Leave
7	Capital Expenditure/Cash Flow/Cost Control/Debtors/Financial Reporting/Profitability/Accounts Payable/Payroll
8	Internal Processes/Abandonment/Contractor Management/IT Help Desk/Staff Management
9	Inventory
10	New Products/Research and Development/Patents
11	Innovation/Lean Processes/Training
12	Production/Maintenance/Utilization/Security/Systems/Vehicles
13	Projects
14	Head Office

Alternatively, you may wish to measure only a specified week each month (e.g., Time sales reps were in front of customers in week 4).

- Remaining measures are reworded to make them easier to understand and the alterations are made in the "Revised measure field."
- A member of the KPI team should set about measuring the strength and feasibility of the measure, as recommended by Stacey Barr. It is beneficial to evaluate potential measures by asking two questions:

1. How strong an indicator of performance is this measure (5 = very strong, 1 = very weak)?
2. How feasible will it be to actually measure this (5= very easy as will already be system generated or will be able to be gathered through minimal effort, 3 = special request will be required to gather data, 1 = very difficult to gather data)?

The strength of a measure should be evaluated by the team member with the best understanding of the organization. Avoid gathering multiple scores and then averaging them as it gets too arbitrary.

- Start sorting the measures into the four types of performance measures (KRIs, RIs, PIs, or KPIs). The easiest way to find the possible KPIs is to look for nonfinancial measures, which are reported frequently. These are the first two characteristics of KPIs; mark these as "possible KPIs." Look for measures that summarize progress against the strategic initiatives. These can be classified as "possible KRIs."
- Look for unintended consequences—mentioned in Chapter 1—all measures will have a dark side. Understand what you need to do to minimize the possible dark side to these measures. If this cannot be achieved, the measure should be marked as "PI with a dark side."

Financial Institution Case Study

After five two-day workshops (Australia, Asia, and three in Europe), and with multiple views of the same critical success factors, there were over 1,500 measures. There were a mix of statements and measures.

The deletions were done as follows:

1. Measures that were merely statements were deleted, e.g., customer satisfaction survey.
2. Measures were grouped into categories, e.g., training, staff turnover.
3. Duplicated and inferior measures were marked as such and deleted.
4. Measures were deleted where the cost of measuring outweighed the benefit.

The measures were reworded to improve their understanding and targeting, e.g., "Number of staff employee suggestions received in month" was replaced with "Number of employee suggestions implemented by team."

This procedure reduced the database from 1,700 to around 130.

Holding a Performance Measures Gallery to Weed Out Dysfunctional Measures

At this point in the journey the executive team and management have been involved in the CSF and the performance measures workshops. A selected group of staff have helped designed some measures. How then do we involve all the other staff, and at the same time get their opinion on the shortlisted measures?

> Hold an open session where staff members are invited to share their views on the shortlisted measures displayed on the walls of the KPI project room.

Hold an open session where staff members are invited to share their views on the shortlisted measures displayed on the walls of the KPI project room; this process is called a "Measures Gallery" by Stacey Barr. Visitors are encouraged to give feedback by writing their thoughts on Post-it stickers, which then are placed on the wall by the appropriate measure.

I like the concept as it is a way of accessing the "wisdom of the crowd." James Surowiecki wrote that "a large group of people are often smarter than the smartest people in them."[1] Hence the term "wisdom of the crowd" was born. In other words, a group's aggregated answers to questions that involve quantity estimation have generally been found to be as good as, and often better than, the answer given by any of the individuals in the group.

It also gives another form of testing of the dark side. Staff can put on a sticker, "The last time we used this measure in 20__ the following dysfunctional behavior resulted: _____." I imagine a measures gallery would look something like Exhibit 9.8.

It is important that this process occur before teams select their measures.

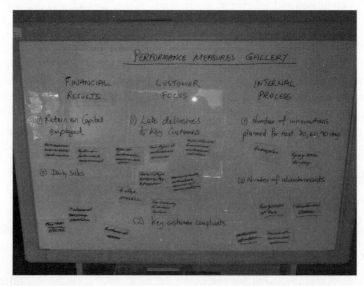

Exhibit 9.8 A Measures Gallery Used to Gather Feedback on Measures

184

Teams Select Their Relevant Performance Measures

The appropriate team performance measures will help teams to align their behavior in a coherent way to the benefit of the entire organization. This is achieved because teams are focusing on those performance measures that are linked to the organization's CSFs. Team performance measures will be comprised mainly of relevant RIs, PIs, and some of the organization's KPIs (e.g., a late plane's measure would have been monitored by the front desk, engineering, catering, cleaning, etc., but not the accounting team).

> **The appropriate team performance measures will help teams to align their behavior in a coherent way to the benefit of the entire organization.**

Although management often tends to become focused on achieving KPI introduction at the global, organization-wide level, in reality the critical issue is getting these KPIs embedded in the teams that need to take corrective action 24/7. Thus, it is at the team level—level 4, as illustrated in Exhibit 9.9—that significant and sustainable performance improvement can be achieved through the use of performance measures.

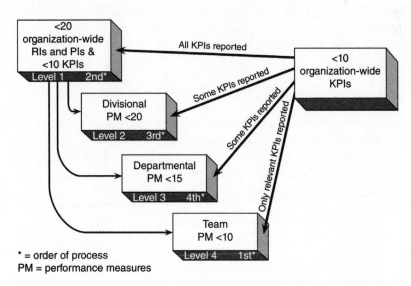

Exhibit 9.9 Interrelated Levels of Performance Measures in an Organization

185

Why Team Performance Measures Are Linked to the CSFs

It would be every CEO's wish that all teams' day-to-day work is aligned with the organization's CSFs and strategic objectives. Yet this is seldom the case. Why does your marketing team measure all customer satisfaction infrequently when the CSF in that area might be "increased repeat business from key customers"? Surely you should be measuring the satisfaction of key customers regularly and ignoring those customers you could do without. Why does dispatch do the same quality control and timely dispatch procedures for all customers, when it is your key customers that should get extra checks at the expense of those customers that you would be better off losing? The answer lies with the fact that we have not communicated the critical success factors to staff, nor have we worked with them to select the measures that stem from these CSFs. Once we have performed this, a magical alignment can occur between effort and effectiveness.

Task 1. Train All Teams to Use the Database

The KPI team needs to train representatives, from all teams throughout the organization, on how to use the database and the significance of each field in the database. This training occurs within the performance measurement workshops. Teams will be trained to review the database to see if any new measure has emerged that is very relevant for their team. This will be performed as part of a later step.

Task 2. Never Lose Sight of Team Ownership

The primary purpose of team performance measures is to assist the teams to focus more on the CSFs and, in doing so, improve their performance. The performance measures will represent what the teams want to monitor in order to improve alignment to the CSFs relevant to their work. The KPI team needs to support this team ownership while steering them gently if they are off course.

Task 3. A Maximum of 10 Performance Measures for a Team

As a guide, 10 is probably the upper limit of performance measures that a team should select for regular use. Some measures will be rotated out once the team have the matter under control and replaced with a new measure relevant to the next issue that needs addressing. These performance measures will include some of the organization's KPIs and some common measures around training, recruiting, and recognition. Some operational teams may have up to three organizational KPIs in their team scorecard whereas many head-office teams will not have any KPIs as the organization's KPIs are not relevant to them (e.g., the British Airways accounting team would not have a late planes measure). Remember that the KPIs affect the entire organization. Thus, there are no KPIs specific to one team.

> There is no shortcut for Small to Medium-Sized Enterprises:
> All the tasks are required albeit they can occur within a week.

Finding the KRIs That Need to Be Reported to the Board

I have already alluded to the fact that the CSFs ascertained in the CSF workshop are the source for all performance measures. I now wish to clarify this. I once thought that the CSFs would also be the source of the key result indicators. However, I now have realized that the critical success factors will not be the sole driver for the KRIs as they focus on inputs and activities; we will also need to review the outcome statements that focus on the external impacts.

In many cases some of the KRIs have already been described in graphs to the board and incorrectly been called KPIs. We need to take these board measures and rebrand them as KRIs. The importance of separating the KRIs from the KPIs should not be underestimated. KRIs will paint the picture of how the organization is performing and help keep the board focused on strategic issues.

An Ocean Liner Analogy

An organization can be likened to an ocean liner. The captain (CEO), officers (senior management team), and crew should be concerned with important daily activities that make the ship function, and the board should be focused on strategic issues. However, far too often, the board members are parked on the bridge wrestling with the captain over control of the helm. We thus need a way to describe to the board that the "liner" is being steered in the right direction at the right speed, giving them confidence that the captain and crew know what they are doing. The board will then be happy to be escorted to the first-class lounge so they can concentrate on what they do best, focusing on the horizon for icebergs and new ports of call.

Task 1. Review Graphs Used in Strategic Documents or Previous Board Papers

Commonly KRIs will have already been graphed in strategic documents or previous board papers, albeit incorrectly named KPIs. Gather these graphs and, now using the Stephen Few guidelines, improve the presentation of the data.

Task 2. Review the Critical Success Factors and Outcome Statements

You need to ensure you have at least one KRI for every CSF and outcome statement. For example, the CSF "Timely departure and arrival of planes" could be represented by a KRI graph showing the timeliness of planes, across the main regions of the world, over the last 15 months.

Task 3. Limit the KRIs to No More Than 10

At first you may have up to 30–40 KRIs. Although there is no magic number, few organizations will need more than 10 KRIs. So, start a process to weed out unnecessary KRIs. This can be done in discussion with the SMT and the board members.

Exhibit 9.10 How Do Your Selected KRIs Cover the Six Perspectives of a Balanced Scorecard?

Key Result Indicator	Perspectives					
	Financial	Customer satis-faction	Staff satis-faction	Innovation and learning	Internal process	Environment and community
Timeliness of planes across the main regions of the world	✓	✓	✓		✓	
Return on capital Employed	✓				✓	
_____	✓					
_____	✓			✓		
_____			✓		✓	
_____	✓	✓		✓		✓

Task 4. Ensure That the KRIs Impact All the Six BSC Perspectives

We need to ensure that the KRIs displayed in the board dashboard are balanced. Thus, the KRIs should be mapped against the six balanced scorecard perspectives, as shown in Exhibit 9.10. We will need at least one KRI impacting each balanced scorecard perspective.

Task 5. Presell the KRIs before Presenting Them to the Board

It is important to presell the KRIs, so select one member of the board who is influential and seek their input before the board meeting. Make sure they understand the purpose of the CSFs, the difference between the four types of performance measures, and why the KRIs were chosen. The aim is to get their buy-in and ensure that they are vocal in the board meeting. Ideally, they should speak immediately after your presentation stating their support.

There is no shortcut for Small to Medium-Sized Enterprises:
    All the tasks are required albeit they can occur within a week.

The KPI Team Ascertaining the Winning KPIs

Team, department, and division performance measures should not be consolidated to become the organization's measures.

It is recommended that the selection of organizational KPIs be started after the two-day performance measures workshops and performance measures gallery have been held.

No matter how complex your organization—whether a public body, a hospital, or a diverse manufacturer—*team, department, and division performance measures should not be consolidated to become the organization's measures.* Doing this creates chaos (e.g., some hospitals have over 200 measures at the organizational level).

Task 1. Ensure That the KPIs Have All of the KPI Characteristics

Ensure that all KPIs selected have these seven characteristics:

- Nonfinancial measure (that is, not expressed in dollars, yen, euros, etc.)
- Measured frequently (e.g., 24/7, daily, or weekly)
- Acted on by CEO and senior management team
- Clearly indicate what action is required by staff (e.g., staff can understand the measures and know what to fix)
- Measure that ties responsibility down to a team or a group of teams that work closely together
- Has a significant impact (e.g., it impacts most of the core CSFs and more than one Balanced Scorecard perspective)
- Encourages appropriate action (e.g., has been tested to ensure they have a positive impact on performance, a minimal dark side)

Task 2. Limit the Organization-Wide KPIs to No More Than 10

I have yet to find an organization that has had more than ten KPIs if they have used the seven KPI characteristics as a filter mechanism.

190

Task 3. Test All the KPIs in Three Divisions

On a KPI project, we should follow Peter Drucker's advice and pilot the KPI project in three divisions. Drucker pointed out that one division will not be enough as other divisions will say "It will not work with us because we are much smaller/larger than them."

Task 4. Communicate the KPIs to All Staff

It is crucial that all staff members fully understand the chosen KPIs. It is important that an announcement be made by the team leaders, department managers, and division general managers. The chosen KPI business unit coordinators can then reinforce the understanding.

> The shortcut for Small to Medium-Sized Enterprises:
> All the tasks are required. The testing should be reduced but not eliminated.

PDF Download

Determining the measures that will work for the organization will have a profound impact on the organization, stimulating timely action and linking day-to-day activities to the strategic objectives of the organization. In addition, this stage will improve job satisfaction (e.g., measures that increase the level of staff recognition), increase job security in the longer term as teams contribute more to the bottom line, and provide a basis for recognizing and celebrating team achievements. Templates and checklists to assist the KPI project team on the journey have been provided. The reader can access, free of charge, a PDF of the suggested worksheets, checklists, and templates from kpi.davidparmenter.com/fourthedition.

The templates include:

- Proposed Agenda for the Performance Measures Workshop
- Exercises in the Performance Measures Workshop
- Assess the Level of Understanding of the Organization's CSFs Worksheet

191

- Checklist to Ensure That You Have a Successful Performance Measures Workshop
- Key Tasks for Recording Performance Measures in a Database
- Selecting Organization-Wide Winning KPIs Worksheet
- Checking KPIs Against the Seven Characteristics
- Design a Dashboard for the Board or Senior Management Team

Note

1. James Surowiecki, *The Wisdom of the Crowds* (New York: Anchor, 2005).

Overview

In order to get measures to drive performance, reports must be designed to accommodate the information requirements of the different levels in the organization (board, senior management team, middle management, and the staff).

KPI reporting needs to be performed 24/7, daily, or weekly, as appropriate to support timely decision making. This chapter displays some better-practice formats that will help speed up this vital step and outlines some advice from the data visualization expert Stephen Few.

The key learning points from this chapter are:

1. The common faults with reporting.
2. KPI team to have sole responsibility for performance report design.
3. For best practice graph design follow Stephen Few's advice.
4. Why Excel is not suitable for a reporting system.
5. Benefits of using 4,4,5-week periods instead of calendar months.
6. Templates for intraday, daily, weekly, and monthly reporting.
7. The importance of a one-page fanfold dashboard for the Board.

CHAPTER 10

Reporting Performance Measures

J ust like the need to follow a structured approach when designing measures, we also
need to do likewise when reporting them.
There are some well-respected rules around
report design and timeliness that should be followed.

At least half of the KPIs
should be reported each
day (electronically) at
9 a.m. or constantly
updated 24 hours a day,
7 days a week.

Develop the Reporting Framework at All Levels

The reporting framework has to accommodate the requirements of different
levels in the organization and the reporting frequency that supports timely
decision making. A suggested framework for reporting performance indicators is set out in Exhibit 10.1. At least half of the KPIs should be reported
each day (electronically) at 9 a.m. or, as in the case of British Airways, constantly updated 24 hours a day, seven days a week.

The other half of KPIs will be reported weekly. Such reports will revolutionize completion in your organization. RIs and PIs will be reported
daily, weekly and monthly using wall mounted flat screens in common walk
through areas covering organization-wide balanced scorecard reporting.

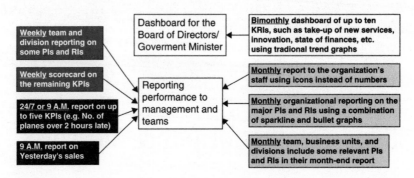

Exhibit 10.1 A Suggested Reporting Framework

> The board should only receive a one-page governance dashboard on the five to eight KRIs.

The board should only receive a one-page governance dashboard on the five to eight KRIs. These KRIs cover the well-being of the organization and are not PIs or KPIs. They should cover progress against the strategic objectives and the six balanced scorecard perspectives, and to do this you may need to track up to 10 KRIs. For every Board meeting, you will only need to report those KRIs that are telling the more important stories. The board should not see the management scorecards because their role is one of governance, not management.

The Common Faults with Reporting

There is a major problem with reporting. The report designers often do not understand enough about the science of reporting. In addition, too many reports have been prepared monthly, which is far too late for prompt action.

Common fault	My recommended solution
Too many poorly constructed measures	As mentioned in Chapter 1, I believe there should be no more than 100 performance measures in the whole organization. In Chapter 8, I have discussed the importance of "exception reporting" and the importance of measuring more at the top of the cliff rather than at the bottom.

Using Excel spreadsheets as a reporting tool	Error-prone, career-limiting, and unprofessional. There is a whole section on this below.
Lack of understanding of data visualization best practice.	Reports are often designed by staff without an understanding of the best practice reporting techniques. The data visualization movement has established rules around making graphics and numbers easier to read.
Lack of distinction between board and management reporting	As mentioned in Chapter 1, KPIs are for management, and KRIs are for the board.
Reporting in calendar months	Monthly trend analysis has been corrupted by the vagaries of the number of working days in a particular month. American manufacturers and retailers have, for some time, reported using four- or five-week periods to get more accurate comparisons. This change also has many other benefits to the finance team.

Designing an Appropriate Reporting Regime

Task 1. KPI Team to Have Sole Responsibility for Performance Report Design

It is recommended that the senior management team leave the design of the reporting templates to the KPI team, trusting their judgment. The KPI team should be up-skilled in data visualization— see the section below—and thus be trusted.

Seek agreement with the senior management team that any of their suggested modifications will be recorded and investigated at the end of the agreed trial period, of say three to four months' duration. It will come as no surprise that many suggested modifications, with hindsight, will not stand the test of time.

Task 2. Get Wide Acceptance of Competent Design Practices

Data visualization is an area that is growing in importance. No longer is it appropriate for well-meaning KPI project team members to dream up report

There is a science behind what makes data displays work. The expert in this field is Stephen Few.

formats based on what looks satisfying to them. There is a science behind what makes data displays work. The expert in this field is Stephen Few, who has written the top three bestselling books[1] on Amazon in this field.

Members of the KPI project team should attend Stephen Few's courses and acquire his books. Then they should train others on how best to report their measures using a combination of the intranet, notice boards, and hardcopy.

Stephen Few has come up with a very useful list of common pitfalls in dashboard design, which include:

Exceeding the boundaries of a single screen	Here Few is warning us to think about the design carefully and avoid giving the reader the choice to access different data. We need to define what should be seen instead of leaving the manager to click on an icon to get additional information.
Introducing meaningless variety	Introducing myriad different graphs just because we can do them.
Arranging the data poorly	Making little attempt to link issues together, as well as not positioning graphs about the same issue, together, on the dashboard.
Using a lot of color to highlight everything	Few points out that many readers cannot distinguish between certain colors, and it is better to be a minimalist with color, only using red to highlight areas of concern.
Cluttering the screen with useless decoration	Managing the whitespace is important. Only things that matter to the reader should be included in the report.

Besides the rules for dashboards, there are additional rules for graphs used in reports. Exhibit 10.2 lists advice with graphs, utilizing Few's wisdom, and some better-practice solutions I have observed over the years.

Exhibit 10.2 Best Practice Graph Design

Common graph problems	Example of a better practice graph
Supply adequate context for the data: Far too often we show dials which do not give enough information as to what is good, satisfactory, or poor performance.	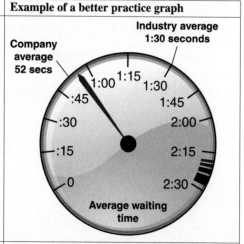
Avoid displaying excessive detail or precision: Graphs should summarize the information and be a big-picture view. The graph should have no more than a five-point scale and be in rounded numbers, e.g., 40 instead of 40,000.	
Always start the scale at zero: Often to emphasize a point, the press will show an exchange rate between a very narrow band, say US$ to euro, within a five-cent range, magnifying the movement. Few is adamant that this may mislead and give rise to a poor decision. Better to express the graph starting the scale from zero.	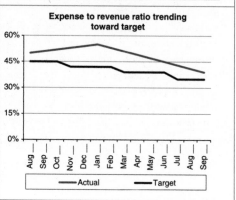

(*continued*)

Exhibit 10.2 (*Continued*)

Common graph problems	Example of a better practice graph
Avoid using these graphs: The following graphs should be banned from use: Pie charts Radar graphs 3D graphs Few points out that it is far better to use a horizontal bar graph instead of a pie chart. In the horizontal bar graph the magnitude between highest and lowest is clearly seen as are the values.	**Good increase with 2 bedroom houses**
Make one data series the baseline: Few also indicates the benefit of making one data series the baseline and showing the other as a variance to it. For example, actual shown against a budget, which is on the baseline.	**Revenue: Actual to Budget variance**
Show a minimum of 15 months' trend analysis: Trend analysis is required, going back at least 15 months to ensure any seasonality in the operations is captured. This gives the ability to compare the performance in last three months against the same period last year.	**Major Costs Are Rising**

Exhibit 10.2 (*Continued*)

Common graph problems	Example of a better practice graph
Avoid using a year-to-date budget line: When showing the annual budget simply show the annual figure. Avoid showing the year-to-date budget line as this is an arbitrary apportionment of the annual planning number that was wrong in any case.	 **NPBT Falling Just Short of Budget**
Explain turning points: Key turning points on graphs should be explained by a note on the graph.	 **Revenue: Actual to Budget Variance**
Use up to five gridlines: The gridlines on the graph should be limited to around five lines. I always make these a medium tone of gray. Black on yellow is the best combination for clarity, so when using color graphs, make the graph background a light yellow.	 **Income Forecast Based on a Slight Decline**
Use the graph title to say something important: Like a journalist, you need to treat the graph title as an important headline. If you cannot think of a good headline maybe, you should use a different graph.	 **NPBT Falling Just Short of Budget**

Spreadsheets have no place in performance measure reporting.

Stephen Few has set out clear guidelines for graph design in his whitepapers on the topic such as, "Common Pitfalls in Dashboard Design," available on www.perceptual edge.com/articles. This chapter should be read in conjunction with the whitepapers and books written by Stephen Few (see www.perpetualedge.com).

Task 3. Designing Reports Using Reporting Software

There is a whole raft of software applications that can revolutionize your reporting. Some of the current solutions, at the time of writing, are:

- Tableau
- Targit
- Dundas BI
- QlikView
- Board
- Cognos BI
- Crystal reports
- Proclarity

It is highly likely that your organization has licenses in one or more reporting softwares. At first instance, review these options, as it will cut costs, save time, and lastly offer a vastly better option than the common default, an Excel-based reporting system.

There are many reporting solutions available. It is a good place to start by seeking out advanced users of the key systems that will be proving performance measure data. Contact them and organize a benchmarking visit. During the discussions ask them, "What reporting tool do you use?" "Why did you choose it?" How does it link with the base systems?"

Spreadsheets have no place in performance measure reporting. Spreadsheets were not designed for many of the tasks they are currently used. In fact, I often remark, in jest, at workshops that many people, if they worked at NASA, would try to use Microsoft Excel for the U.S. space program, and many would believe that it would be appropriate to do so. A spreadsheet is a great tool for designing and testing a reporting template. It is not and never should have been a building block for your company's reporting systems.

The high level of errors in spreadsheets is the main reason why. A major accounting firm has pointed out that there is a 90 percent chance of a logic error for every 150 rows in an Excel workbook.[2]

Common Problems with Spreadsheets

Senior management are often blissfully unaware of the risks they take every time they rely on a report derived from large spreadsheets.

Some of the common problems with spreadsheets are:

Broken links or formulas	An individual might add or eliminate a row or column so that, when a group of spreadsheets is rolled up, the master spreadsheet is taking the wrong number from the spreadsheet that was modified.
Consolidation errors	Often, a spreadsheet will lock up or show a screen full of "REF" "REF" "REF" errors, because it was not designed to be a tool for handling a rollup of dozens of different worksheets.
Input of the wrong numbers	Entering the wrong number can happen in any process, but spreadsheet-based systems often require rekeying of information, which can produce data inconsistencies. A spreadsheet might use a look-up table that is out of date, or have entries in cells that might have been inadvertently entered over formulas.
Incorrect formulas	A subtotal might omit one or more rows, columns, or both. An individual might overwrite a formula because they believe theirs is more accurate.
No proper version control	Using an outdated version of a spreadsheet is very common.
Lack of robustness	You can never have complete confidence in the final numbers a spreadsheet generates as you seldom have the time to check all the formulas that can reside in any of the thousands of cells in a spreadsheet.

KPI reporting should be almost instantaneous, and once appropriate systems are in place, weekly and monthly reporting should also be quick routines. As a guide, the monthly reports should take no more than half a day's preparation and be delivered to the relevant team by the close of the first working day of the new month. Late reporting has no place in performance measurement.

Task 4. Design Reports That Can Work on a Tablet or Smartphone

It is important to design your reports based on the user's technology. Many 24/7, daily, or weekly reports will now be read via the user's phones and tablets. See Exhibit 10.3 for an example from Stephen Few.[3]

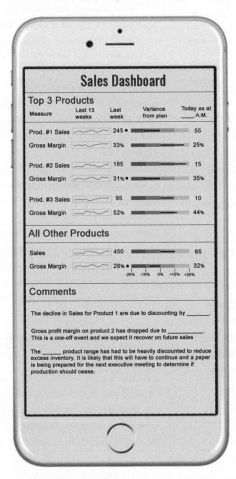

Exhibit 10.3 A Smartphone Dashboard

Task 5. Consider Using 4,4,5-Week Reporting Periods for Each Quarter of a Year

Julius Caesar gave us the calendar we use today. It is a major hindrance to reporting. With the weekdays and number of weekend days in any given month being different from the next month it is no wonder reporting is unnecessarily compromised.

Reporting performance would be improved if all organizations made periods of four or five weeks with two four-week periods and one five-week period in each quarter. There would be a much more precise comparison. The eight four-week periods could be accurately compared, as could the four five-week month periods.

To make progress in this area I would recommend that the KPI team hold discussions with the finance team. The finance team may well be thinking about this change as well. The best way forward is to contact your general ledger supplier and ask, "Who is a very sophisticated user of this general ledger, and who uses 4,4,5-week reporting periods?" Arrange to visit them and see how 4,4,5-week periods work in their organization. Ask them, "Would you go back to regular calendar reporting?" Most are likely to give you a look that says, "Are you crazy?"

There is a well-trodden path to converting from calendar months to 4,4,5-week reporting periods. Why not walk along it!

Task 6. Develop a Hierarchy of Reports to Staff, Management, and the Board

If KPI reporting is not available 24/7 and it is not the focus of action and discussed at performance improvement meetings, attention will wane, and the graphs will become symbols of frustration rather than the focus for continuous improvement. Make sure you never give KPI reports to the board. They should receive more summarized information, as shown in the board dashboard below.

There is no shortcut for Small to Medium-Sized Enterprises (SMEs).

All the tasks are required. One of the hardest things to change in SMEs will be the reliance on Excel spreadsheets. Although Excel can be used by SMEs for reporting, in the short term, a replacement application will be necessary for the reasons stated above.

To the report designer, I point out that being an expert in Excel is career-limiting in the twenty-first century.

Reporting the KPIs to Management and Staff

Reporting measures to management needs to be timely. As mentioned previously, KPIs need to be reported 24/7, daily, or, at the outside, weekly; other performance measures can be reported less frequently (monthly and quarterly).

Intraday/Daily Reporting on KPIs

At least half of the KPIs will be reported 24/7 or daily. Exhibit 10.4 shows how KPIs should be reported on the intranet. Some form of table giving the contact details, the problem, and some history of performance is required. Another benefit of providing senior management with daily/ weekly information on the key performance areas is that the month-end becomes less important. One government department had a 9 o'clock news report every morning covering the processing of benefit payments by each office around the country. Regional management teams were able to compare their service levels and achievements daily. In other words, if organizations report their KPIs on a 24/7 or daily basis, management knows intuitively whether the organization is having a good or bad month.

Exhibit 10.4 Example of a Daily KPI Report

Planes more than two hours late

Time: 4.30pm 12 Sept 201X

Flight number	Statistics of last stop			Region manager's name	Current time at location	Contact details			Number of planes over one hour late		
	Arrival late by	Departure late by	Time added			Work	Mobile	Home	Past 30 days	30-day average of past three months	30-day average of past six months
BA123	1:40	2:33	0:53	Pat Carruthers	18:45	xxxxx	xxxx	xxxx	4	4	2
BA158	1:45	2:30	0:45	Basil John	10:48	xxxxx	xxxx	xxxx	2	3	1
BA120	1:15	2:27	1:12	xxxxxxx	20:45	xxxxx	xxxx	xxxx	4	4	7
BA146	1:25	2:24	0:59	xxxxxxx	21:45	xxxxx	xxxx	xxxx	5	4	4
BA177	1:15	2:21	1:06	xxxxxxx	22:45	xxxxx	xxxx	xxxx	1	4	2
BA 256	1:35	2:18	0:43	xxxxxxx	23:45	xxxxx	xxxx	xxxx	5	4	5
BA124	1:45	2:15	0:30	xxxxxxx	0:45	xxxxx	xxxx	xxxx	2	4	6
Total	7 planes										

Intraday Exception Reporting to the Chief Executive Officer on Human Resources Issues

> It is vital that certain human resources issues be reported to the chief executive officer immediately when they occur.

It is vital that certain human resources issues be reported to the chief executive officer immediately when they occur. The following issues need to be addressed in private and public organizations:

- All job offers that are more than three days outstanding should be personally followed up by the CEO. The lack of acceptance means, in most cases, that the candidate is still looking around. A personal call from the CEO saying, "I understand, Pat, that we have offered you the position of _____. I believe you will succeed well in this role, and I will take a personal interest in your career. What do we need to do to get your acceptance today?" could help convince the candidate to accept. This 10-minute call could well save over $20,000 of recruiting costs, a return of $120,000 per hour!
- In-house courses with low registrations because staff and their managers think that daily firefighting is more important than training. Here the CEO makes a phone call to the manager emphasizing that training is and should be the most important priority. Managers will know to expect a call whenever they get this priority wrong.
- Staff members who have been ill for over two weeks who do not have an activated back-to-work program—the CEO should phone the HR advisers responsible for setting up the back-to-work program that might include a visit to the organization's doctor and a phased back to work schedule.
- Most CEOs treat accidents or safety breaches seriously, and, therefore, these are reported—an acceptable report-back time would be within an hour of the incident.
- The CEO should follow up on all key staff members who have handed in their notice. This would be reported within an hour of resignation. A personal phone call may be enough to turn around the situation or, at the very least, open the door for a return in the future.

These issues can be reported, by HR staff, in a simple intranet-based report, as illustrated in Exhibit 10.5, to the senior management team and the CEO.

Exhibit 10.5 Example of a Daily Human Resources KPI Report

		Contact details		Details	
		Work	Mobile		
Position offers still outstanding	Candidate			Recruiting manager	Days outstanding
Financial Controller	Pat Toms	——	——	Jim Curruthers	3
Stores Manager, Brisbane	Basil John	——	——	Sally Smith	3

		Contact details			
		Work	Mobile		
Key recruitments in progress for which the last interview was over two weeks ago	Manager				
Sales representative (Northern region)	Jim Curruthers	——	——		
CFO	Sally Shell	——	——		

		Contact details			
		Work	Mobile	Expected numbers from team	Average training days of team in past six months
Teams not represented in the in-house courses to be held in next two weeks	Manager				
Team xx	Jim Curruthers	——	——	3	1
Team yy	Sally Shell	——	——	4	1.25
Team zz	Bob Helm	——	——	2	1.5
Team ss	Ted Smith	——	——	1	0

		Contact details			
		Work	Mobile	Remedial action	
Accidents and breaches of safety	Manager				
Pat Gow was in a car crash, unhurt but needs two weeks' recovery time	Jim Curruthers	——	——	Increase participation in advanced driving courses paid by company	

		Contact details			
		Work	Mobile	Length of service	Importance
Key staff who have handed in their notice today	Job Title				
Susan George	Financial Controller	——	——	3 years	Considered next CFO
John Doe	HR Manager, ___	——	——	10 months	Managed the ___ project
Jenny Gilchrist	Systems Coordinator ___	——	——	15 years	Expert in ___ system

Weekly KPI Reporting to the CEO

Some KPIs need only be reported weekly. Set out in Exhibit 10.6 is an example of a weekly KPI report.

Reporting RIs and PIs to Management

Management will need some weekly reports covering *result indicators* and *performance indicators*.

Weekly Human Resources Update to CEO

There are some HR issues that the CEO needs to focus on weekly. They are not as critical as the intraday or daily HR exceptions, and thus are not considered KPIs. The following HR issues need to be addressed in most organizations:

- It is not uncommon for new staff to miss out on the planned induction program. This can have a negative impact on their performance over the short-to-medium term. The CEO should make it known that there is an expectation that staff will attend induction programs and that phone calls will be made to follow-up on exceptions.
- In-house courses to be held within the next two months should be highlighted weekly where there are low registrations.
- Higher-than-average sick leave in a team may indicate a problem with leadership. The CEO should follow up when next in the area.
- The CEO needs to keep a weekly focus on the recognitions planned for the next week or two weeks. Peters and Waterman[4] and Collins[5] have emphasized the importance of celebration as a communication tool and a way of inspiring staff to exceed normal performance benchmarks.

The report could look like the one shown in Exhibit 10.7. It would be prepared by the HR staff for the senior management team.

Exhibit 10.6 Weekly KPI Report

Status of initiatives completed from the recent key customer satisfaction survey

	Status	Mobile	Manager assigned responsibility
Improve order entry system	No action		Jim Curruthers
Improve tracking of deliveries	No action		Sally Smith
Improve accuracy of pricing and discounts	Extra check in place for key clients		Not assigned

Date of next visit to key customers

	Sales representative	Date of visit	Mobile	Date of last order	Working days lapsed between visits
ABC Limited	Jim Curruthers	12/11/_		1/11/_	15
	Sally Shell	5/11/_		12/10/_	10
	Bob Helm	14/11/_		12/09/_	30
	Unassigned				60

List of key projects that are running late

	Manager	Weeks late	Mobile	Remedial action
KPI project	Jim Curruthers	6		Increase participation in advanced driving courses
New sales ordering system	Bob Helm	10		

List of project managers with late projects

	Number of late projects	Late projects last month	Mobile	Recommended action
Susan George	6	4		Abandon ____, reassign ____ and ____.
John Doe	5	7		Phone call as progress being made
Jenny Gilchrist	4	2		Phone call as problem brewing

Innovations planned for implementation

	Within 30 days	30–60 days	60–90 days	Details
Team ____	0	0	1	
Team ____	2	2	2	
Etc	1	2	1	

Abandonments planned

	Within 30 days	30–60 days	60–90 days	Details
Team ____	2	1	1	
Team ____	2	2	2	
Etc	1	2	1	

Exhibit 10.7 Example of the Weekly Human Resources KPI Report

Number of planned CEO recognitions for next week/two weeks

	Reason	Work	Mobile	Suggested recognition
Jim Curruthers	Led project	___	___	Meeting in CEO's office
Sally Shell	Led project	___	___	Meeting in CEO's office
Susan George	KPI project manager	___	___	Meeting plus CEO newsletter feature

In house training courses due in next two months

	Enrollments	Expected numbers	Date of course	Days left
First Aid	5	20	___	25
Supervisors Part 1	3	45	___	18
Leadership part 2	40	60	___	14
Presenting	6	20	___	15

Staff who have been ill for over two weeks

Manager	Work	Mobile	Length of illness	Back-to-work program started
Jim Curruthers	___	___	10	Yes
Sally Shell	___	___	15	Yes
Ted Smith	___	___	25	No

Teams with above average sick leave

Manager	Last 30 days	Days per employee	Average per month for past three months
Jim Curruthers	5	1.5	4
Sally Shell	8	2	7
Ted Smith	3	1	12

New staff who have not attended an induction program within ____ weeks of joining

Manager	Work	Mobile	Mitigating circumstances
Jim Curruthers	___	___	
Sally Shell	___	___	
Ted Smith	___	___	

Weekly/Monthly Updates to Management and CEO

There are endless ways these can be shown—see Exhibit 10.8—through icons, gauges, traffic lights, and so on. Stephen Few has introduced a new concept called "bullet" graphs. These are particularly powerful when combined with Edward Tufte's[6] "sparkline" graphs; see Exhibit 10.9. A sparkline graph looks like a line graph without the axes. Even with this truncated diagram, you can still see the trend. The bullet graph shows different details about current performance. The shades used range from dark gray (to indicate poor performance) through to lightest gray (to indicate good performance). The dark vertical line indicates a comparative measure such as a target or last year's result. Stephen Few is very cautious about the use of color. He draws attention to the fact that many readers will have some form of color blindness. In Exhibit 10.10, the only use of color would be red bullet points indicating the exceptions that need investigation and follow up.

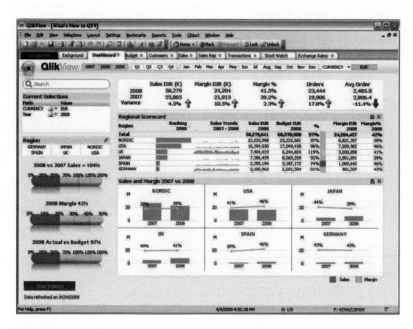

Exhibit 10.8 Examples of a Monthly Report to Management
Source: Used with the permission of Inside Info, www.insideinfo.com.au.

213

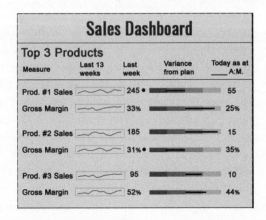

Exhibit 10.9 Combination of "Sparklines" and "Bullet" Graphs

	Performance measure	Last 13 weeks	Last week	Weekly target	Today as at ___A.M.
Top three products	Sales revenue _____		245 ●	275	55
	Gross profit margin _____		33%	28%	25%
	Sales revenue _____		185	155	15
	Gross profit margin _____		31% ●	32%	35%
	Sales revenue _____		95	87	10
	Gross profit margin _____		52%	45%	44%
All other products					
	Sales revenue all other products		450	410	65
	Gross profit margin		28% ●	30%	32%
Commissions	Amount of sales commission		120	135	20
Bad debts	Amounts written off as uncollectable		0	0	0
Staff	Sales made by top three sales staff				
	_____		55	40	12
	_____		49	40	15
	_____		41	40	2
	Sales by remaining sales staff		29	32	9

		Date of next training	Annual training target	Date of last training
Training				
	Pat Carruthers	15-Sept-__	8 days	26 months
	Sam cane	15-Sept-__	8 days	8 months
	Juliet Smith	15-Sept-__	8 days	26 months
	Tom Peterson	Non scheduled	5 days	4 months
	Sam Drucker	Non scheduled	5 days	1 month

The decline in sales for product 1 are due to discounting by _____.

Gross profit margin on product 2 has dropped due to _____. This is a one-off event and we expect it recover on future sales.

The _____ product range has had to be heavily discounted to reduce excess inventory. It is likely that this will have to continue and a paper is being prepared for the next executive meeting to determine if production should cease.

Exhibit 10.10 Examples of a Monthly Report to Management

Reporting Performance Measures to Staff

Using a monthly icon-based report for staff is a good idea because they tell staff what is good, what is adequate, and what needs to be improved without giving away confidential data. If this icon report happens to be left on a bus, it would not be damaging to the organization if it found its way to a competitor. Exhibit 10.11 is an example of an icon staff report that covers the critical success factors and reminds staff about the strategies.

> Using a monthly icon-based report for staff is a good idea because they tell staff what is good, what is adequate, and what needs to be improved without giving away confidential data.

Progress Report for July xxxx

Our Mission	To provide our customers energy at the right price at the right time
Our Vision for next five years	To be the preferred energy provider in the xxx
Our Strategies	1. Acquiring profitable customers 2. Increase cost efficiencies 3. Innovation through our people 4. Using best business practices

Our progress against our critical success factors

Delivery in full on time to key customers		We are a learning organization		Innovation is a daily activity	
On time deliveries to key clients	☺	Staff training this month	☹	Ideas adopted last month	😐
Goods rejected due to quality defects	😐	Staff with mentors	☺	Paperless transactions with key suppliers/customers	☺
We are warriors against waste		**We grow leaders**		**We are respected in the communities we work in**	
Wastage reduction programs started in month	☹	Leaders appointed from within last month	☺	Community participation by employees in month	😐
Waste reduced from existing programs	☺	Managers in leadership programs	☺	New initiatives planned for community, next 3 months	☺
We finish what we start		**Attracting new profitable customers**		**Increase in repeat business from key customers**	
Number of late projects	😐	New customer orders	☺	Order book from key customers	☺
Number of project finishes in month	☹	Feedback from new customers	😐	Number of product developments in progress	😐
Points to note:					
xxxxxxxxxxxx xxxx xxxx xxxxx xxxxxxx xxxxx xxxxxx xxxxx xx x x xxxxx xxxxx xxxxx xxxxx xxxx xxxxx xxxx xxxx xxxxx xxxx xxxx xxxxx xxxxx xxxxxxx xxxxxx xxxxxx xxxxx xx x x xxxxx xxxxx xxxxx xxxxx xxxxx xxxxx xxxx xxxx					

Exhibit 10.11 Example of a Monthly Icon-Based Report to Staff

215

Reporting Performance Measures to the Board

Because the board's role is clearly one of governance and not of management, it is totally inappropriate to be providing the board with KPIs.

Typically, a board would need to see between 9 and 12 graphs covering the critical success factors and outcome statements.

Entities in the private and public sectors need to report to a board, a council, or an elected government official. To simplify, let's call the reporting body a board.

In most organizations that have boards, there is a major conflict of interest over what information is appropriate for the board to receive. Because the board's role is clearly one of governance and not of management, it is totally inappropriate to be providing the board with KPIs. As mentioned in Chapter 2, it is a myth that a balanced scorecard can report progress to both management and the board.

To me, KPIs are the very heart of management. Used properly, many of them are monitored 24/7 or at least weekly; they are certainly not performance measures to be reported monthly or bimonthly to the board.

We need indicators of overall performance that need only be reviewed on a monthly or bimonthly basis. These measures need to tell the story about whether the organization is being steered in the right direction at the right speed, whether the customers and staff are happy, and whether we are acting in a responsible way by being environmentally friendly.

These measures are the key result indicators (KRIs), which you were introduced to in Chapter 1. Typically, a board would need to see between 9 and 12 graphs covering the critical success factors and outcome statements. These measures work particularly well in helping the board focus on strategic, rather than management issues, and they will support management in their thrust to move board meetings away from the monthly cycle. These KRIs are best reported in a dashboard. A dashboard should be a one-page display, as illustrated in Exhibit 10.12 with the graphs, summary financials, and commentary all appearing on the page.

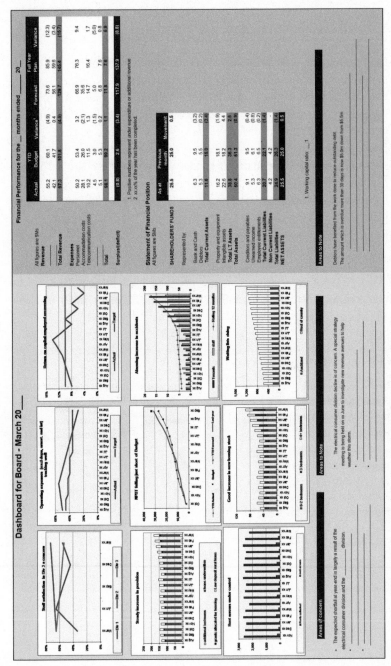

Exhibit 10.12 A Board Dashboard on a Fanfold (A3) Page

A Board Dashboard Completed Overnight

One accountant, after attending a KPI workshop, went home and prepared a board dashboard for the board meeting the following day. It was not hard as most of the graphs required had been prepared for previous papers. He simply updated and repositioned them. He arrived early to meet the chairman and said, "I know you do not like surprises, but I have just prepared a one-page summary of the organization, I think you will find it useful." The chairman agreed and opened the board meeting explaining the origins of this new one-pager. It was such a success that the accountant was instructed to make it the first page of all future board papers.

Suggested Graphs for the Board Dashboard

To help teams, there are 10 good KRIs graphs in Exhibit 10.13 that you might want to use.

Exhibit 10.13 Key Result Indicators for a Board

Staff satisfaction:	
As one person said, "Happy staff make happy customers, which make happy shareholders." A staff satisfaction survey should never be sent out to all staff; instead a survey should be sent to a statistical sample run three to four times a year. This will give more useful and timely information	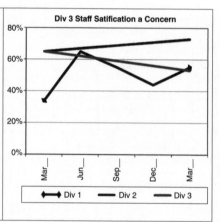

Exhibit 10.13 *(Continued)*

Expenses as a ratio to revenue: The Board should be interested in how effective the organization has been in utilizing technology and continuous improvement. This graph clearly shows if the cost of operations is tracking down as a percentage of revenue.	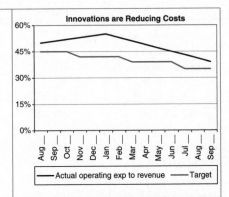
Customer satisfaction: In every organization, your customers should be set out in groups as to their importance to you. Airlines have between four and five different categories for their registered frequent flyers. Satisfaction needs to be measured at least every three months for your key customers and for the next level down. I believe the lowest group of customers should not be surveyed as they contain the disgruntled and price driven customers that are often not profitable and thus can be abandoned.	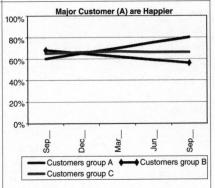
Value of new business: All businesses in the private sector need to focus on the growth of their new offerings, their rising stars. In the government and nonprofit sectors, this graph would look at the take-up of new services.	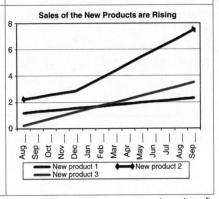

(continued)

219

Exhibit 10.13 *(Continued)*

Net profit before tax (NPBT): Since the board will always have a focus on the year-end, it is worthwhile showing the cumulative NPBT. This graph will include the most recent forecast, which should be updated on a quarterly basis bottom-up. Note that the year-to-date budget line is not included. Instead we show last year's actual progression which is a more valid comparison.	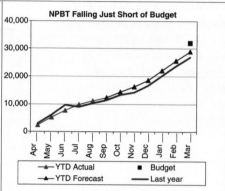
Health & Safety: The well-being of staff is a major focus of responsible management, and boards are interested in the status. For manufacturing, accident rate, including near misses, should be the focus. In the service and nonprofit sectors, we might look at staff turnover rate.	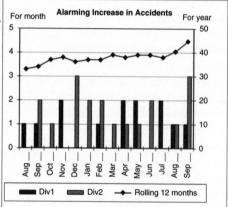
Return on capital employed (ROCE): ROCE has always been an important KRI and should not ever be called a KPI. It is a result of all the actions of management and staff over a period of time.	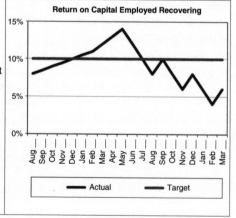

220

Exhibit 10.13 *(Continued)*

Cashflow: This cashflow graph should look 15 months back and 6 months forward.	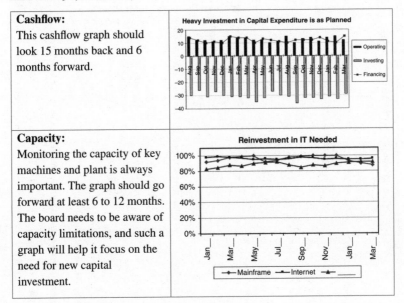
Capacity: Monitoring the capacity of key machines and plant is always important. The graph should go forward at least 6 to 12 months. The board needs to be aware of capacity limitations, and such a graph will help it focus on the need for new capital investment.	

Reporting Team Performance Measures

For a number of years I illustrated a busy team scorecard that I was shown over 25 years ago. It had around 20 measures and was a monthly report which would have taken time to prepare and in reality the report had been covering the past rather than helping ensure that the current week was better than last week. I now believe that team reporting should be about what happened yesterday and last week and these results should be shown on a flat screen mounted on a wall in a common walk-through area for the team in question. See Exhibit 10.14 for a simple example. The criteria for reporting are now changed to:

- Selecting up to ten measures that are a mix of 24/7, daily and week updated measures
- Replacing measures when the team have locked-in the desired change with a new issue that requires attention
- The organization-wide KPIs are reported in a separate system which the team will, like other teams be also monitoring if relevant to them

	Performance measure	Last 13 weeks	Yesterday	Today	
Bags	No. of unsuitable bags allowed by front desk		6	3	
	No. of bags that missed connected flights		10	0	
	% of late planes where baggage handler ready to unload as plane is parked		75%	100%	●
	No. of bags that did not make the flight		3	0	
	Lost bags still unresolved		5	5	
	No. of uncollected bags over 2 hours old		4	1	
	No. of planes made late by the loading of late bags		2	0	
Equipment	Breakdowns with baggage equipment		0	0	
Staff	No. of days since request for maintenance on key baggage equipment	n/a	n/a	56	●
	Average time it took to off load planes (by plane type)				
	_____ (plane type)		12 mins	15 mins	
	_____ (plane type)		10 mins	12 mins	
	_____ (plane type)		8 mins	12 mins	
	_____ (plane type)		7 mins	4 mins	

	Date of next training / Months since last training by team member	Date of next training	Months since last training	
Training	Pat Carruthers		26 months	●
	Sam cane	15-Sept-___	8 months	
	Juliet Smith	15-Sept-___	12 months	
	Tom Peterson	15-Sept-___	4 months	
	Sam Drucker	15-Sept-___	1 month	

Comments

The lost bags are a main focus and believe this number will be down to 2 by the end of the week.

Due to shortage of equipment the off loading of _____ have been slower. New equipment arrives within 10 days to resolve the matter.

I am meeting with Pat Carruthers on Friday to resolve training shortfall. Pat is on holiday on 15 Sept.

Exhibit 10.14 Example of a Weekly Team Progress Update (Baggage Handling)

- Each team will have a flat screen, in their work area, which is updated in real time from a dedicated laptop
- Using sparklines and associated bullet graphs to convey information concisely

The Performance Reporting Portfolio

Exhibit 10.15 shows how the reporting of performance measures should work in a private, public, or not-for-profit organization. The daily and weekly KPI reports, shown in the left-hand column, are the most important. These are seen by the senior management team and the relevant operational staff. Some of these KPIs would be intranet-based, being updated 24/7 (e.g., late planes in the sky).

Teams and business units would be monitoring their performance through their wall mounted screen. Some measures would be updated in real time and others overnight or at the longest, weekly. Divisions would be monitoring progress halfway through the month and at month-end.

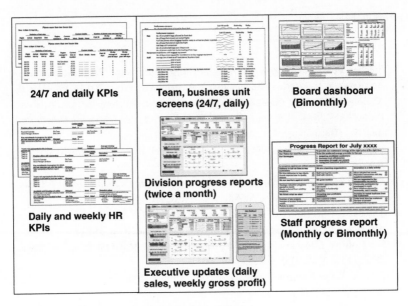

Exhibit 10.15 Performance Reporting Portfolio

The executive would get daily sales numbers, weekly gross margin and personnel costs, and two updates a month on non-financial data.

The board, who should be meeting, four to six times a year, will receive the dashboard as the leading document.

The staff might receive a bimonthly or monthly update giving them feedback on their alignment with the organization's critical success factors.

PDF Download

To assist the KPI project team on the journey, templates and checklists have been provided. The reader can access, from kpi.davidparmenter.com/fourthedition, free of charge, a PDF of the following chapter templates:

- Developing the Reporting Frameworks at All Levels Checklist
- Developing Display, Reporting, and Review Frameworks at All Levels—Worksheet for Completion

Notes

1. Stephen Few's three books, *Information Dashboard Design: Displaying Data for At-a-Glance Monitoring* (Burlingame, CA: Analytics Press, 2013); *Show Me the Numbers: Designing Tables and Graphs to Enlighten* (Burlingame, CA: Analytics Press, 2004); *Now You See It: Simple Visualization Techniques for Quantitative Analysis* (Burlingame, CA: Analytics Press, 2009).
2. Rickard Warnelid, Reducing the Risk in Excel Risk Modelling (CompAct, January 2011).
3. Stephen Few, *Information Dashboard Design: Displaying Data for At-a-Glance Monitoring* (Burlingame, CA: Analytics Press, 2013).
4. Thomas J. Peters and Robert H. Waterman, *In Search of Excellence: Lessons from America's Best Run Companies* (New York: Harper & Row, 1982).
5. Jim Collins, *Good to Great: Why Some Companies Make the Leap and Others Don't* (New York: HarperBusiness, 2001).
6. Edward Tufte, *Beautiful Evidence* (Graphics Press, 2006).

Overview

Although most KPIs should always be maintained because of their relevance to the organization-wide CSFs, there will be some changes through constant improvement, refinement, and the introduction of a new CSF.

There needs to be a careful process before there are any changes to the suite of CSFs and their associated measures.

It is essential that the use and effectiveness of KPIs be maintained. Teams will need to modify and change some of their KPIs and PIs as priorities change during their journey of process improvement.

The key learning points from this chapter are:

1. The need for continuous improvement in the use of KRIs, RIs, PIs, and KPIs.
2. The need to constantly support empowerment of the frontline to correct deficient performance.
3. The importance of the rollout KPI training to existing and new staff.
4. Maintaining a constant focus on John Kotter's eight-stage selling change process and Peter Drucker's abandonment rule.
5. The need to review the organization's CSFs annually.
6. The need for an annual one-day focus group to revisit the performance measures.

CHAPTER 11

Ongoing Support and Refinement of KPIs and CSFs

Many organizations have performed worthwhile KPI groundwork, only to have it fail or become buried when the originator leaves the organization. It is, therefore, important that the use of KPIs become widespread in an organization and that it be incorporated into its culture.

To understand how this stage fits within the KPI methodology, an overview of the important work that needs to be done is set out in Exhibit 11.1.

Exhibit 11.1 An Overview of the Winning KPI Methodology

Task	Description
1.1 Selling the KPI project to the CEO, the senior management team, and the organization's oracles. (See Chapters 4 and 5.)	The project starts off with a well-practiced elevator pitch, followed by a compelling presentation and then a focus group workshop to get the green light from the organization's oracles.
1.2 Locate an external facilitator to mentor the KPI team. (See Chapter 5.)	An external facilitator will help guide the organization with regard to timings, selection, and size of KPI team and what needs to be abandoned to make room for the KPI project.
1.3 Train a small KPI team. (See Chapter 6.)	The external facilitator helps train a small in-house KPI team and ensures that the KPI team leader has a cluster of mentors supporting them. Working with the organization's oracles, the KPI team develops a blueprint for the implementation that will cover where the KPI project will be piloted.

(continued)

Exhibit 11.1 *(Continued)*

Task	Description
1.4 Sell the KPI project to all employees to encourage their participation in the two-day performance measures workshops. (See Chapter 4.)	Employees who are to attend the two-day performance measures workshop need to be convinced that it is an important exercise worthy of their participation.
2.1 Locate the existing success factors and desired external outcomes from documentation and interviews. (See Chapter 7.)	Determine what your organization's success factors and desired external outcomes are.
2.2 Run the two-day critical success factor workshop to ascertain the critical success factors. (See Chapter 7.)	Map the sphere of influence each success factor has to ascertain to understand which ones have the most significant impact. These are the critical success factors. Present these to all staff.
3.1 Run the two-day performance measures workshops to train all the remaining relevant staff to develop meaningful measures. (See Chapters 8 and 9.)	Select representatives across the organization to attend a two-day workshop to be trained in the methodology, as well as how and why the organization has chosen its CSFs. Attendees will be shown how to design appropriate measures from the CSFs and how to get a mix of past, current, and future measures.
3.2 Refining the measures after the performance measures workshops. (See Chapter 9.)	KPI team will delete duplicated and inferior measures and remove measures where the cost of measuring will outweigh the reworded measures to improve understanding.
3.3 Hold a performance measures gallery to weed out dysfunctional and poor measures. (See Chapter 9.)	Hold a "measures gallery" where staff are invited to share their views on the measures that have been displayed on the walls of the project team's room.
3.4 Ask all teams to select their team performance measures from the finalized database of measures. (See Chapter 9.)	Teams select the relevant measures and indicate their selection in the database.
3.5 Find the key result indicators (KRIs) and the key performance indicators. (KPIs). (See Chapter 9.)	Ascertain the 8–12 KRIs that will be reported to the Board to show how the organization is performing. Ascertain the winning KPIs ensuring they have the seven characteristics discussed in Chapter 1. Commence the testing of the KPIs in three designated areas.

Exhibit 11.1 (*Continued*)

Task	Description
3.6 Design the reporting framework. (See Chapter 10.)	The intraday, daily, weekly, monthly, and quarterly progress reports are designed utilizing best practice visualization techniques. Utilize existing technology so that the CEO can receive intraday updates on a smartphone and laptop.
3.7 Help facilitate the appropriate use of the selected performance measures by all the teams in the organization. (Covered in this chapter.)	For several months, the KPI team will be required to ensure that the reporting of measures is prepared on time and correctly and that corrective actions are undertaken, where necessary. There will need to be a program to roll out KPI training to existing and new staff.
3.8 Refine CSFs and associated measures after one year of use. (Covered in this chapter.)	A review should be undertaken to assess what modifications, if any, are needed to the existing CSFs and measures.

Facilitate the Ongoing Support and Refinement of KPIs and CSFs

If the CEO, members of the senior management team, and management focus on the KPIs every day, staff will naturally follow suit. When a CEO spends about 30 minutes a day asking for explanations from managers and staff about a wayward KPI, this will soon create focus. It certainly will be seen that receiving two phone calls from the CEO is not a good career move! In other words, the CEO should walk the talk and always know where the KPIs are heading at any point during the day from the exception reports sent directly to their smartphone.

> If the CEO, members of the senior management team, and management focus on the KPIs every day, staff will naturally follow suit.

In turn, the senior management team needs to be committed to empowering staff to take immediate action where a KPI highlights a problem. This empowerment should match what happens at Toyota, where staff working in the car plant are empowered to stop the production line if they find any defect in a car on which they are working.

> **The KPI team will need to develop training programs so new staff can be educated in CSFs, the four types of measures, and how measures are reported.**

> **The KPI reporting system will fail if the review process relies on structured, monthly meetings because KPIs are indicators that need monitoring, reporting, and action 24/7.**

The KPI team will need to develop training programs so that new staff can be educated in CSFs, the four types of measures, and how measures are reported. The ongoing delivery of the material should be the responsibility of the team delivering in-house courses.

The KPI reporting system will fail if the review process relies on structured, monthly meetings because KPIs are indicators that need monitoring, reporting, and action 24/7.

Teams will need to modify and change some of their KPIs and PIs as priorities change during their journey of process improvement. This review should be on a periodic basis, certainly not more frequently than every six months.

It is simply a case of moving on to the next priority area for improvement as the previous ones have been mastered and behavior alignment has been locked in.

Some KPIs should always be maintained because of their relevance to the organization-wide CSFs; for example, the late-plane KPI will always be used by an airline. In addition, it is likely that KPIs relating to customer focus and workplace culture will always remain in place. Teams will also need to amend and build new measures to respond to the emergence of new CSFs.

Task 1. Constantly Support Empowerment of the Frontline Staff

It is essential that the members of the senior management team learn to relax their control and empower their frontline staff to act to correct deficient performance. Delays created through seeking permission are too costly and unnecessary.

Task 2. Roll Out KPI Training to Existing and New Staff

At this point some staff will have been involved in the project ascertaining the CSFs and/or by attending the two-day performance measures workshop.

This, however, will seldom represent more than 20 percent of the staff and in larger organizations less than 5 percent.

In a recent CSF project one of the project team members was a skilled trainer who showed me the importance of developing a training program so that all staff are up-skilled.

The training program should be delivered in person by a skilled presenter from the project team accompanied by someone from the senior management team. The workshop should start with an introduction from the CEO or member of the senior management team. The trainer will now deliver a presentation on the new thinking on key performance indicators explaining to staff:

- The importance of the CSFs
- How the KPIs were chosen
- Why these KPIs are so important
- The monitoring and action that will be taken by the senior management team
- The delegated empowerment that allows employees to correct situations as they arise on a 24/7 basis

Task 3. Maintain a Constant Focus on John Kotter's Eight-Stage Selling Change Process

John Kotter's eight-stage process, discussed in Chapter 4, should be your constant guide, in particular his last four stages:

- Stage 5: Empower broad-based action
- Stage 6: Generate quick wins
- Stage 7: Consolidate gains and produce more change
- Stage 8: Anchor new approaches in the culture

Stage 5: Empower Broad-Based Action

The KPI team needs to ensure that the rollout progresses through all plans and subsidiaries and in all countries. Allowing one or two operations to maintain the old view on KPIs could end up being a disease that will spread, in time, through the organization as individuals from that entity start getting promoted and moved to other entities within the group.

231

Stage 6: Generate Quick Wins

To avoid the impact of attention deficit disorder, it is important to have 40–60-second elevator success stories about the project, every week. The project must be perceived as one that is making progress; otherwise it will be assigned to the ever-growing bucket of "disappointing projects." Once the senior management team loses interest in the KPI project, the death knell is being sounded.

Stage 7: Consolidate Gains and Produce More Change

As the project progresses, certain adaptations will work and others will fail. It is important to embrace Kaizen and further modify the process. At this point, the project team should consider spreading the word outside the organization by speaking at conferences about their case study. From the CEO's perspective, nothing develops a sense of pride so much as hearing from a third party how impressed they are with the organization's achievements.

In addition, some of the process should be written up and included in the staff induction program so you catch new staff early on. The KPI team leader and the chief measurement officer should consider having a slot in any such programs to outline how CSFs and KPIs work.

Stage 8: Anchor New Approaches in the Culture

We need to make heroes of the departments that are using the new KPI methodology best. During the project some teams will make great strides. It is important that the KPI team impart to the CEO the need to publicly recognize their endeavors. Recognitions will encourage others to lift their game.

Task 4. Maintain a Constant Focus on Peter Drucker's Abandonment Rule

There will need to be a constantly culling of measures so you keep within the 10/80/10 rule. For every new measure, you will need to remove one or two that are not delivering change. As you work more with the measures you will find similar indicators that are, in fact, a duplication. Select the one that has the best wording and delete the other.

As discussed in Chapter 1, you will need no more than:

- 10 key result indicators, with only 6 to 9 shown to the board at any one time.
- 80 performance indicators and result indicators used across all teams.
- 10 KPIs. It is unlikely that an organization will have more than 10 KPIs that fit the seven KPI characteristics.

Maintaining the team's sense of ownership of performance measures is critical and will be achieved only if employees view performance-measure information as valuable, useful, and worthwhile. As teams complete the process-improvement cycle, KPI usefulness will be tested against new challenges to the team. Team performance measures must be adapted, as required, to maintain their relevance and use.

Task 5. Review the Organization's CSFs Annually

It is essential that the use and effectiveness of the CSFs be reviewed annually. Many of the CSFs will stay consistent for years; for instance, timely arrival and departure of planes will be a CSF as long as we fly in planes.

The KPI team should hold discussions with the senior management team to ascertain whether a new CSF has emerged. If so, the KPI team with at least two people from the previous CSF exercise should remap the relationships of the existing and proposed new CSFs. A hierarchy will emerge, and the new CSF may usurp an existing one.

Before any change to the CSFs occurs, we need to recognize that it will mean reprinting documents, posters, and rewriting training materials.

- Ascertain the measures from the new CSF. What measures does it throw up? If all measures seem to already exist, maybe you have incorporated the CSF in existing ones so a rewording of them may suffice.
- Test the wording with some experienced teams. Ask what they understand by the new CSF. And ask, "What actions will you take following this new CSF?"

Task 6. Hold an Annual One-Day Focus Group to Revisit the Performance Measures

The objectives of the workshop are to revisit the performance measures with a key group of staff and management. Staff and management also need to learn from experience and enhance the value gained from using performance measures. A focus group needs to be selected consisting of 15 to 30 experienced staff members from the departments, teams, area offices, and the head office. The staff members should include the different roles, from administrators to senior management team members.

It is desirable that any new CSFs be introduced to the attendees and that they break up into smaller groups to ascertain new measures, using the techniques outlined in Chapter 9.

Task 7. Revisiting the KPIs

At least annually, the KPI team should road test the KPIs by:

- Ensuring that they are still measured 24/7, daily, or weekly. If any have slipped back to a fortnightly or monthly measure, they are no longer operating as KPIs.
- Through discussion and observation ascertain whether the KPIs are directing action to take place. If not, they are no longer KPIs.
- Look for a new KPI among existing PIs that are successful in creating action to take place.

The Shortcut for Short to Medium-Sized Enterprises

Task 6. Hold an annual one-day focus group to revisit the performance measures—this can be reduced to a two- to three-hour session.

Task 7. Revisiting the KPIs. It is important that the KPI team leaders not be tempted to perform this exercise on their own, thus alienating staff and limiting the future use of KPIs in the organization.

PDF Download

To assist the KPI project team on the journey, templates and checklists have been provided. The reader can access, from kpi.davidparmenter.com/fourthedition, free of charge, a PDF of the following chapter templates:

- Facilitating the Use of KPIs Checklist
- Draft Agenda for a Staff Workshop
- Refining KPIs to Maintain Their Relevance Checklist
- Refining KPIs to Maintain Their Relevance—Worksheet for Completion
- Draft Agenda for a One-Day Focus Group Meeting to Revisit the Performance Measures
- Draft Agenda for a Two-Hour Team Workshop to Revisit a Team's Scorecard

Overview

This chapter covers case studies from private, nonprofit, and public sector organizations, implementation lessons, and comparisons to other methodologies (Kaplan and Norton's Balanced Scorecard and Stacey Barr's PuMP).

The chapter also outlines the suggested worksheets and checklists, which can be accessed from the accompanying PDF, free of charge.

The key learning points from this chapter are:

1. The importance of a well-read and enthusiastic CEO to the successful outcome of the KPI project.
2. The significance of the KPI team leader selection process.
3. Differences between external outcomes and success factors are not always immediately obvious.
4. How lack of compliance to the seven KPI project foundation stones has led to project failure.
5. Each project is different, and the KPI team leader will be modifying the approach to best suit the organization.
6. The 10 key implementation lessons.
7. The four foundation stones the balanced scorecard methodology needs.

CHAPTER 12

Implementation Case Studies and Lessons

This chapter contains an overview of some of the implementations of the winning KPI methodology. This chapter will be of use to all those talented in-house staff members who have been asked to run the KPI project.

Recent Case Studies

I have been involved in two major implementations since writing the third edition. The case studies set out the observations I have made, the lessons learned, and the changes to the winning KPIs methodology that have evolved from them.

Private Sector Case Study: Financial Institution

This organization was led by a visionary CEO, who recognized the importance of constantly learning. The CEO organized an annual retreat where the international executives got together to review the past, make plans for the future, and learn something new.

The CFO, who had attended a workshop of mine over five years earlier, was aware that the organization was ready to do something positive with their measures and exposed the CEO to the winning KPI methodology. The CEO made a personal approach to me about a training session for their annual retreat.

I sold the concept that instead of learning about the methodology we could actually start the process by using the two allotted days, in the executive retreat, as the CSF workshop providing that some prework could be performed with a chosen number of the executive.

The prework involved training six of the attendees about performance measures and how to word success factors so they are SMART and to learn how to separate out the external outcomes (e.g., retention of key customers, be an Employer of choice, product leadership in our sector) into separate list. The importance of this separation is explained in Chapter 7. The chosen six then were the workgroup leaders of the six groups.

We split the list of 45 draft success factors (SFs) into three lists of 15 SFs. With six work groups, we were able to give two teams the same 15 success factors to edit. We then created a panel of three comprising the CEO and two general managers. A representative of each of the two teams went to the panel and argued for their proposed wording changes. The panel had the final decision. The debate created a session that derived a list of approved success factors and a reinforced understanding of the success factors among all participants.

Success factors included:

- Make major decisions after obtaining consensus, using data-driven insights and well-thought-through project plans so the decisions can be implemented rapidly.
- Celebrate staff efforts and achievements regularly.
- Willingness to "fail fast" by abandoning activities, processes, and projects that are unlikely to succeed.
- Starting projects that we can complete as planned.
- Fixing problems correctly the first time.
- Attract and recruit people who have our values and the proven skills we need.
- Maintaining a flexible, healthy, and supportive workplace.

The outcome statements included:

- Skilled and "can do" workforce.
- Employer of choice.
- Delivering market-leading innovative solutions so we are one or two in the chosen markets.
- Turn customers into advocates by exceeding their expectations.
- Our staff feel they are valued and supported.

238

In day three of the retreat, the output of the workshop was transferred into a CSF presentation, as shown in Exhibit 12.1. The slides were designed so that the area of influence of the proposed CSF was clearly shown with the desired outcomes (shown in shaded boxes, around the top and bottom of the slide), with other CSFs (shaded circles) and with other success factors (unshaded circles). During the preparation of the presentation, more outcome statements were identified which up until then had been considered success factors.

The proposed CSFs were presented on day four of the retreat and the final wording was signed off by the executive. This sped up the process and ensured all the executives understood how the CSFs were arrived at and why. This fast-track process saved weeks of delay that other projects have faced when the executives are not all in attendance at the critical success factors two-day workshop.

At the retreat, the global CEO made the decision to roll out the CSF and to ascertain the associated measures through the establishment of an in-house KPI team.

The CFO, who is the KPI project sponsor, looked for some time for suitable staff for the in-house KPI team. One was a trainer from the HR team who had been in the organization for over four years. The KPI team leader, had been with the organization for less than a year, had much sector experience as a consultant for a major international firm and had exceptional people skills.

Once trained, the in-house team held the initial two-day performance measures workshop at the head office in Australia. The CEO opened the performance measures workshop, and the marketing and communications executive delivered the presentation on the CSFs, explaining the importance of the wording and how the CSFs strongly related to the organization's day-to-day activities.

Attendees were chosen by the executives who had been exposed to the process during the executive retreat.

The subsequent two-day performance measures workshops, were run in six countries, following the agenda set out in Chapter 9. All the measures derived by workgroups in their sessions were recorded in an Excel template, using the headings set out in Exhibit 12.2.

In the last session of the two-day performance measures workshops, all the measures gathered were displayed on a wall, and the attendees were asked to review for duplication and further clarification (filling out any

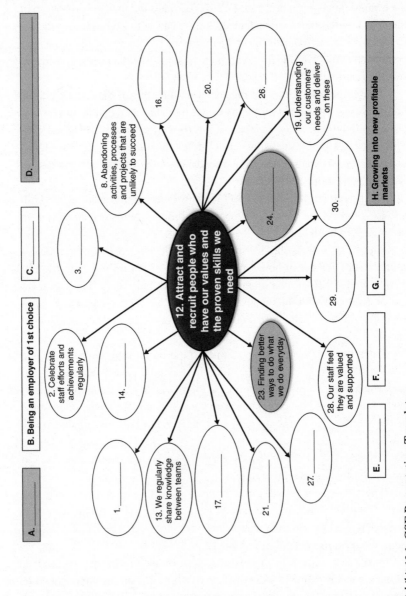

Exhibit 12.1 CSF Presentation Template

Note: Boxes are the outcomes that are impacted; shaded circles are links to other CSFs.

240

Exhibit 12.2 Database Headings Used by the KPI Project Team

Original measure number	Name of measure	Suggested treatment of measure	David Parmenter's feedback	Result/Key performance indicators	Critical success factor

abbreviations). In 20 minutes, by using all the attendees the KPI team was able to save many hours of additional sorting.

Representatives from the Asian operation attended the Sydney session to experience the training and advise the KPI team on how best to deliver the presentation in their country. Skilled translators were hired so that the workshop had a simultaneous translation during all times of the presentation.

The European two-day workshops were delivered as part of a separate trip, using the same timetable and exercises as set out in Chapter 7.

A groupwide performance measure database was set up where all measures were given a unique number to maintain control and traceability. The original number of measures was over 500, and the culling process was time consuming. The KPI project team had resisted the temptation of sharing previous measures with the new workgroups as it would have reduced the learning component of "How to ascertain measures."

The key steps for reducing the number to less than 100 measures included:

- Sorting all measures by their source critical success factor.
- Marking all obvious duplications—no deletions were done so traceability could be maintained.
- Marking those that were not measures but merely statements.
- Adding a column where the KPI team added their comments or a suggested rewording.
- I was asked to also review the measures, and pass comment in a column set aside for my review. My comments ranged from good PI, good RI, negative cost vs. benefit, to a suggested rewording of measure, delete measure, this will be difficult to measure.

Private Sector Case Study: Food Distributor

A well-read CEO had come across my work and had assigned a manager, with over five years of experience in operations with the organization, the task of being the KPI project team leader.

> It was decided to run a series of 2.5-hour webinar sessions covering the content in the two-day CSF workshop set out in Chapter 7.

The KPI team leader was selected because of his excellent communication style, success in other projects, and because he was widely respected in the organization.

The KPI team leader met up with me during a United Kingdom visit, and a plan was hatched. Because of a likely delay waiting for me to next be in the UK and with plants in many locations, it was decided to run a series of 2.5-hour webinar sessions covering the content in the two-day CSF workshop set out in Chapter 7.

Senior and experienced staff, from a broad section of their operation, numbering between 5 and 12 in each plant location were present in the training room at their location. I was able to deliver the webinar from my New Zealand office using GoToMeeting. Attendees were paired and sat in front of a laptop so that I could see their level of engagement in the presentations and the workgroup activities. Between the webinars the teams made progress with wording the organization's success factors, which included:

- Deliver to _____ on time, in full, always.
- We make complex things simple.
- A culture of stopping to fix problems at source, to get everything right the first time.
- We attract, engage, and develop the right colleagues.
- Training always comes first.
- Make the right decisions and ruthlessly prioritize.
- We take time to consult and consider the impact of change, agree, then implement with pace.
- Reduce red tape to free people to deliver.

After the webinars the KPI team completed the finalization of the critical success factors and a cartoon representation of the CSFs for distribution around the workforce.

The KPI team trained all teams not present in the webinars on how to ascertain measures from the critical success factors. All measures were recorded in a database, using the headings in Exhibit 12.3. This was followed by further support from the KPI team and a one-day performance measures workshop to compare progress and swap ideas.

Exhibit 12.3 Database Headings Used by the KPI Project Team

Name of measure	Team using measure	Key word (for sorting)	Frequency of measurement (24/7, daily, weekly, monthly)	Time zone (past, current, future)	Related to which critical success factor	Suggested target (if applicable)

Three months into the project, it was time to evaluate progress and a one-day workshop was proposed. On the day, each team were allocated a specific table and had been asked to prepare a short presentation to explain their measures and raise any issues.

The executive, the KPI team, and I were split across the ten tables to hear their short presentation. After each 15-minute interval, we moved to a different team table to hear another presentation. My role was to present a refresher on the four types of indicators and to comment on the completeness of each team's measures.

Previously Reported Case Studies

Here are the case studies reported in the third edition. I have made further refinements to the case study documentation.

Private Sector Case Study #1: An Asian Conglomerate

An Asian conglomerate principally in the construction and design sector with around 600 staff wanted to improve its use of KPIs. A member of their team had attended a two-day KPI workshop I had presented earlier that year. The HR manager was responsible for a company-wide KPI program and implementation to align and consolidate further their current performance management system. A two-day workshop was organized, which was attended by a cross-section of the company. Attendees from the company ranged from the CEO down to the staff in the operational areas. The vast bulk of the attendees were the company oracles, and there were over 700 years of corporate knowledge in the room. The two-day CSF workshop, as set out in this book, was followed. From the first day workshop the success factors they came up with included:

- Delivery in full, on time all the time, for our key customers (building projects)
- _____ as a brand with new and innovative product/services of a global standard that add value to our customers
- Delivering design, innovation, and quality that matter
- Get the right project team for the job
- Get the right contractor for the job
- Explore opportunities to increase the size and quality of our land bank
- Obtaining timely approvals from relevant authorities for development of new projects
- Getting the right product in the right place at the right time

Outcomes identified include:

- Reducing supply chain costs
- Being a preferred supplier for key customers and their business associates
- Increased business from new and repeat customers
- Identify and capture the potential of new and emerging markets

The conglomerate had at least three distinct business entities that warranted having some different critical success factors. The people orientated CSFs were replicated across all businesses. The teams shared their measures with the other businesses during the workshops which led to some cross fertilization of indicators.

Private Sector Case Study #2: Medical Company

The financial planning and analysis managers of a medical company were charged with updating the KPIs. They contacted me to run a series of web-based workshops using GoToMeeting technology. It required laptops and fast Internet connections at both ends. These workshops were run by having a laptop between two people and a laptop connected to a data show to project the slides on the screen in the workshop room. I could see all attendees and they could see me. We ran three workshops (2.5 hours long) to kick-start the process of ascertaining the success factors and then short-listing those success factors that could be deemed critical.

The success factors were developed from my generic list, provided in the PDF that accompanies Chapter 7, and from their understanding of their business. With hindsight the teams adopted too much of the wording from my list without the necessary editing to reflect words and phrases commonly used within the organization. The list of success factors included:

- Develop exceptional people and teams who follow our organization's philosophy
- Finding better ways to do the things we do every day
- Be seen in the community as an employer of "first choice"
- Encouraging voluntary assistance by staff in the local community
- Safety always comes first

The critical success factors that emerged included:

- Expand sales force with high-performing staff who are profitable within six months of start
- Timely logging of, reporting of, and responding to customer feedback

External outcomes that were also identified included:

- Create an environment where our people are encouraged to meet their full potential
- Increased repeat business from key customers
- Reduce patient deaths during operations
- Acquisition of profitable customers
- Retention of key customers
- Execute successful marketing campaigns

Private Sector Case Study #3: Forestry Company

The accountant of a forestry company, who was well respected in the organization and had excellent communication skills, had been assigned the job to rationalize the KPIs in the organization. The CEO was a well-informed, contemporary thinker who was very supportive of undertaking the KPI project.

To ensure that staff live and breathe them, a poster of the CSFs was issued and is widely seen around the work environment.

It was agreed, because I was only based an hour away, for me to run the two-day CSF workshop. They had booked a venue in the local hotel and had asked all the oracles to attend the two-day course, including foremen, forklift drivers, foresters, all the way through to the senior management team and the CEO.

There were close to 50 people who attended the two-day session with some staff flying in from an Australian subsidiary, to get exposure to the methodology.

The two days followed the outline of the two-day critical success factors workshops featured in Chapter 7. Throughout the two days, we broke the workshops up into groups no larger than seven and ensured that they were

Exhibit 12.4 Poster and Water Bottle Used to Promote the CSFs

made up from at least two different teams. The project manager had prepared two lists for cross-functional workshops and one for team workshops.

They came up with 65 success factors, which created more work in the relationship-mapping process. The attendees were able to narrow down the 65 success factors to eight critical success factors that included:

1. Every day we innovate and continuously improve.
2. We select and work closely with the right customers and suppliers.
3. We attract, develop, and retain the right people.

As with other case studies the project team had difficulties in separating external outcomes from success factors.

Following the workshop, staff members who had excelled in the exercises were further employed in the KPI project. The finalization of the CSFs took a number of months; all were nonfinancial. To ensure that staff live and breathe them, a poster of the CSFs was issued and is widely seen around the work environment. One month they issued a new water bottle with a critical success factor printed on it, as shown in Exhibit 12.4.

The project is now over four years old and has made a substantial change to the organization.

Private Sector Case Study #4: Car Manufacturer

I was asked to run a two-day CSF workshop for a major car manufacturer, based in the Persia. Due to the language barrier, a bilingual consultancy firm that worked closely with management organized the arrangements with me. The two-day workshop had simultaneous translation.

I spent time with the translators to ensure they understood the slide deck and that they were familiar with the meanings of all the keywords. I also had a factory walk-about, so I could relate back to the organization's operations.

We broke the 120 attendees into cross-functional work groups of no more than seven people. This breakout had already been organized before the workshop started, so a seating plan was organized.

Randomly selected work groups were asked to share their progress with me with the help of the translator. I was able to highlight teams that were progressing well and thus "raising the bar" for the other teams.

Private Sector Case Study #5: Timber Merchant

An Australian timber merchant company approached me to deliver a two-day workshop. They had booked a venue in the local hotel and asked 60 of their knowledgeable and experienced staff to attend the two-day CSF course, which included foreman, store men, all the way through to the senior management team and CEO. There was over 1,000 years of company knowledge in the room.

A clever accountant set out the success factors in an Excel matrix, shown in Exhibit 12.5, so the connections could be counted automatically. I now give teams the option to either map by arrows or by the Excel matrix. Each team being required to record their finished work in the audit friendly Excel matrix.

Nonprofit Membership Organization Case Study #1: Golf Club

A small golf club, located in a seaside hamlet, had a membership of no more than 350 playing members. Despite the relatively small membership, this club has produced two successful professional golfers. The chairman of the golf club asked me to help the club management committee look at their operations. A two-hour workshop was scheduled for the committee members.

The draft success factors were drafted before the workshop, based on a review of the strategic documents over the past 10 years, onto a fanfold piece of paper.

The workshop was held in the boardroom where one of the committee members worked as the CEO. The CEO's personal assistant was on hand to record the workshop output. The workshop included the following activities:

1. Quick agreement on the wording of the balanced scorecard perspectives:
   - Satisfaction of members and visitors
   - Satisfaction of paid and voluntary staff
   - Finance
   - Internal processes
   - Learning and growth of paid and voluntary staff
   - Environment and community

#	Success Factor	Count	1	2	3	4	5	6	7	8	9	10	11	12
1	Positive public perception of ___	2		X									X	
2	Be seen in the community as an employer of first choice	1	X											
3	Minimizing pollution and waste	2	X							X				
4	Encouraging voluntary assistance by staff to the local community	2	X				X							
5	Supporting local businesses (___ % of purchases to have local content)	1	X											
6	Delivery in full on time, all the time, to our key customers	2	X	X										
7	Finding better ways to do the things we do every day	4	X	X				X			X			
8	Maintaining a safe and healthy workplace	2	X	X										
9		2								X		X		
10		2	X										X	
11		2	X	X										
12		4							X	X	X	X		

Exhibit 12.5 Mapping of Relationships Using the Excel Matrix

249

2. The attendees reviewed the wording of the success factors, and some changes were made. The PA updated the success factor fanfold sheet, while the committee members practiced the mapping of an airline's success factors, an exercise that is included in the PDF supporting Chapter 7.
3. The committee members were formed into three teams and were given a section of the success factors to map against all the success factors and the desired outcomes, as shown in Exhibit 12.6.
4. The number of arrows out from each success factor was counted, and the higher-scoring success factors were identified. At a subsequent meeting, three committee members, with a good aptitude for this exercise, were selected to reconsider the influence the top success factors had on the entire list of success factors on the sheet. The sphere of influence mapping exercise highlighted eight critical success factors including:

- Capture the potential of the _____ connection
- Timely maintenance of course equipment
- Finish activities we start

The identified external outcomes included:

- Family-friendly club
- Increase in members' satisfaction through programs and activities
- Growth in revenue from alternative sources
- Optimize revenue from profitable members

The exercise gave a better understanding of what should be the main focus. However, in a club that is run by volunteer leaders who are often active in other institutions, momentum is quickly lost. The most beneficial gain was derived from the knowledge of the critical success factors rather than from the resultant measures, which were never embedded. A KPI project would be more beneficial with clubs who employ at least more than ten paid staff.

Nonprofit Membership Organization Case Study #2: Surf Life Saving

The beaches around the world are often manned by nonprofit organizations that undertake rescues, train children about water safety, offer sporting activities for their members, and patrol dangerous surf breaks in the summer months.

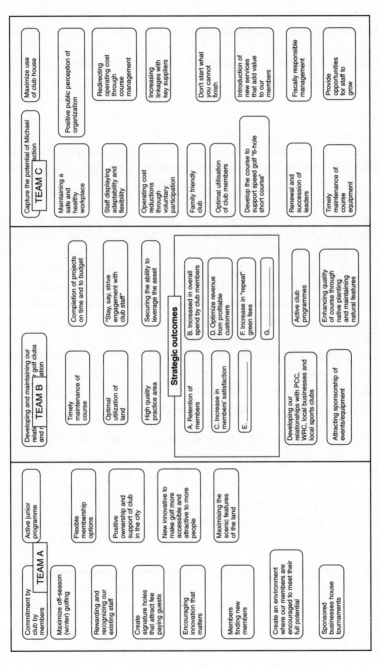

Exhibit 12.6 Mapping the Success Factor Relationships for a Golf Club

251

A two-day workshop was sponsored by a national sports body that wanted to pilot the winning KPI methodology. The two-day CSF/KPI workshop was arranged based on the workshop set out in this book. Staff members were requested to attend the workshop from around the country, including many experienced staff members who were knowledgeable about the organization's success factors. Over half of those attending were volunteers.

Although representatives from the national sports body attended the full two-day session, the CEO from Surf Life Saving did not attend any sessions, even though a strong recommendation was made to the CEO to attend the first session of day one and the last session of day two.

The key stages of the process included:

1. The relationship-mapping process was carried out by four teams of between four and five attendees.
2. To ensure that the critical success factors were balanced, they were mapped against the organization's balanced scorecard perspectives: Financial results; Satisfaction of district offices and clubs; Learning and growing full-time staff members; Internal processes; Staff and member satisfaction; and Community and environment.
3. The performance measures were ascertained for each of these critical success factors. These were recorded on an Excel spreadsheet.
4. The critical success factors were ratified at a board meeting, thus permanently locking them into the organization.

Head-office teams after the workshop commenced the drafting of their team scorecards; however, as weeks passed, a number of things happened:

- The CEO, who had never bought into the process, was still very distant.
- The key sponsor was headhunted to another organization.
- Daily firefighting diverted the energy elsewhere, and the project lost momentum.

The exercise gave a better understanding of what should be focused on. However, the lack of adherence to the foundation stones outlined in Chapter 3 was the main reason for the project's lack of progress.

Government Department Case Study #1

A government department in an Asian country, involved in community projects to integrate the feeling of togetherness in the country's population, had for some time realized the importance of performance management and had embarked on a balanced scorecard approach.

After the balanced scorecard was found to be floundering, they wanted to hold a two-day CSF workshop to restart the balanced scorecard project.

Right from the start the CEO was totally behind the project. The project leader had excellent communication skills and was well connected to the CEO.

A two-day CSF and KPI workshop was arranged around the workshop discussed in Chapter 7 with the aim not only to find the critical success factors, but also to show the team leaders how to ascertain appropriate performance measures from the critical success factors.

All departmental staff members were requested to attend, with all the senior management team present. The venue was a local hotel, which ensured far greater commitment from the attendees. The CEO attended the first and the last sessions and later admitted to regretting that he had not attended for the whole two days.

The attendees in the workshop carried out the sphere of influence mapping process as set out in Chapter 7. There was a confusion between CSFs and external outcomes with the following outcomes being mistaken for CSFs:

- Effective community outreach and engagement
- Effective grass-roots leaders/volunteers/staff
- Enhanced partnerships with groups and organizations with common interests
- An environment that encourages innovation and creativity

The performance measures were ascertained for each of the critical success factors and were recorded on an Excel spreadsheet. Teams now have their own scorecards and performance measures, and the accompanying critical success factors are driving performance. The lack of adherence to the foundation stones outlined in Chapter 3 was the main reason for the project's lack of progress, as illustrated in Exhibit 12.7.

Exhibit 12.7 Lack of Adherence to the KPI Foundation Stones

Recommended Foundation Stones	Level of Adherence
1. Partnership with the staff, unions, and third parties	While the organization has very good communication channels, it had not invited any community leaders it worked with to the workshop.
2. Transfer of power to the front line	This delegated authority had already been established.
3. Measure and report only what matters	There was a tendency to report everything. The lesson that less is better than more was not practiced.
4. Source all KPIs from the organization's critical success factors	Never occurred.
5. Abandon processes that do not deliver	There were many activities that could have been culled that would have freed up time for this project.
6. Appointment of a home-grown KPI team leader	Never occurred.
7. Organization-wide understanding of the winning KPIs definition	Never occurred.

Government Department Case Study #2

A key government department in a small Pacific country wanted to utilize the KPI methodology. To finance the workshop, they asked other organizations from the public and private sectors whether they wished to attend. Thirty staff members from the government department attended with another 70 from over 10 other organizations. Organizations with over seven attending were broken into smaller workgroups.

It was interesting to see the public and private organizations learn from each other. Feedback from the workshop exercises created an environment where teams that excelled raised the bar for the others. Once a couple of teams had impressed the attendees with the quality of their workshop output, the remaining teams work rate lifted remarkably.

Professional Accounting Body Case Study

A professional accounting body in Asia had a CEO who had been exposed to the winning KPI methodology and who was the active sponsor of the project. A two-day CSF/KPI workshop was held in its head office, attended by all members of the senior management team. The agenda and processes were the same as the workshop in Chapter 7.

At the time of the workshop the professional body was awaiting a KPI team leader to implement the project. The recruitment process had been delayed because of workload and the CEO's moving on.

On reflection, the timing of the workshop was not right. The manager for the project should have been identified and should have attended the two-day workshop.

While the attendees understood the seven foundation stones and responded particularly well to Peter Drucker's abandonment rule, they could not put it into practice. The attendees did not take the vital step of removing the procedures and processes they had identified to abandon and, therefore, they were too tied up in the existing workflow to implement the KPI project.

Charity Case Study

A charity based in Europe, whose main mission was to fight key diseases, wanted to revisit the use of its KPIs. It used both external key result indicators, which were in a published document, and operational KPIs.

The project manager, who was very experienced both with the organization and with performance management issues, arranged for me to deliver the two-day CSF and KPI workshop.

It was decided to commence with a series of web-based workshops prior to the visit to fine-tune the likely success factors. Progress was made with success factors, and the two-day workshop did succeed in achieving this result: to ascertain the critical success factors.

The charity was to report back to the board. As none of the board had attended the two-day workshop there was a huge knowledge gap. Even though the board attended a brief presentation using videoconferencing, the concept of the critical success factors being operational, and thus internal, was never understood.

The board was naturally looking from the outside in. The board wanted to see the CSFs expressed as naturally as outcomes and impacts they wanted to see. The board wanted the organization to "deliver this," "deliver that," which would demonstrate that there had been a successful implementation of the organization's strategy. The board members thus made changes to the CSFs so that they became external outcomes, completely nullifying the exercise.

Due to the small size of the charity, they were unable to assign a staff member full time to this project, nor were they able to establish a full-time in-house KPI team leader as recommended in Chapter 3. This coupled with the frequent movement of staff left the project largely uncompleted.

Implementation Lessons

Kaplan and Norton, in their ground-breaking book *The Balanced Scorecard: Translating Strategy into Action*,[1] indicated that 16 weeks is sufficient time to establish a working balanced scorecard with key performance indicators (KPIs). However, organizations of all sizes and complexity stumble with this process, and 16 weeks easily turns into 16 months. The key to success is to learn from these 10 implementation lessons:

1. Select a small KPI team to be full time on the KPI project.
2. Leading change the John Kotter way.
3. Start off with a six-perspective balanced scorecard (BSC).
4. Focus on the critical success factors.
5. Follow the 10/80/10 rule.
6. "Just do it."
7. Use existing systems for the first 12 months.
8. Trap all performance measures in a database and make them available to all teams.
9. KPI reporting formats should follow the guidelines of the data visualization experts.
10. Embracing Peter Drucker's abandonment rule.

Lesson 1: Select a Small KPI Team to Be Full Time on the KPI Project

With the exception of small organizations, with fewer than 250 staff, a small team with two full-time staff members is recommended, for organizations up to 3,000 staff. If larger, a team of four is recommended, so that the KPI team can run two workshops simultaneously at different locations. The external project facilitator, if involved right at the beginning, should help the senior management team (SMT) pick a team. Research into personnel records is recommended, as many talented staff members who may already have some KPI experience are found in obscure places.

You need to look for staff who have excellent presentation skills, knowledge of the organization and its market, a track record of innovation and completion, sound communication skills, and the ability to be cheerful under pressure. The KPI team leader will also need to be part trainer, part salesperson, and part project manager. They will need to be respected in the organization so that they can challenge the executive when necessary.

The SMT needs to have the selected staff committed *full time* to the KPI project. By that I mean the family photos are removed from their desks and taken to the project team location. Their second-in-command will move into their office and undertake their duties, a succession-planning bonus.

Reporting Line

Once selected, this team must have a direct reporting line to the CEO, as shown in Exhibit 12.8. Any layer in between means that the SMT and CEO have not understood just what SMT commitment means.

Besides the KPI project team, the organization also needs to identify a liaison person (a coordinator) for each business unit and team. This liaison person needs to be knowledgeable about the operation and to be available to provide detailed knowledge and feedback to project team members.

Senior managers should exclude themselves from the project team. An SMT member in the team will lead to a string of canceled meetings as the senior manager is caught in the firefighting activities that make up much of their working days. Even SMT members with the best willpower in the world can never be fully focused on just one project.

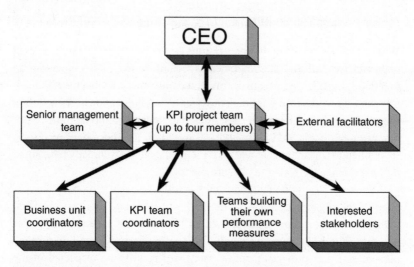

Exhibit 12.8 KPI Team Reporting Directly to the CEO

In-House or External Appointment

Peter Drucker said, "Never give a new job to a new person"—he called it a widowmaker. When an organization wants a new system implemented, it is very tempting to hire someone who has expertise, as a consultant or a permanent appointment. Drucker pointed out that they do not stand a chance, as staff members who are concerned about the change will do their utmost to destabilize the project. Instead you need to appoint an in-house person best suited for the role, someone who is well respected in the organization, who can call on favors when required. Staff will support the CSF and KPI initiative when it is led by such an appointee.

Benefit of This Action

This action will lead to a carefully picked project team who, along with the KPI team coordinators, will have a good chance of success.

Lesson 2: Leading Change the John Kotter Way

I would argue that more than half the new initiatives that are declined were undersold. In other words, given the right approach the initiative would have gone ahead.

258

If you are not prepared to learn the skills to cover the common deficiencies in leading change you may as well cancel the KPI project as it does not have a chance to succeed. Selling change requires a special set of skills, and we all can and should get better at it. In Chapter 4 on leading and selling change, I point out:

- Nothing was ever sold by logic! You sell through emotional drivers. Thus, we need to radically alter the way we pitch this sale to the senior management team (SMT), to the CEO, and to the board. We have to focus on the emotional drivers that matter to these groups.
- In 1996, John Kotter published *Leading Change*,[2] which quickly became the seminal work in the change management space. He pointed out, as we already know, that effecting change—real change, trans-formative change—is hard. In his work he had an eight-stage process of creating major change, a clear map to follow when faced with influencing an organization to move.
- In 2009 Zaffron and Logan published *The Three Laws of Perfor-mance*.[3] They pointed out that staff will always march toward their default future, the one they believe will happen, the one they see as the prescribed future. The key to change is therefore to make it very clear that there is a burning platform by painting the absurdity of the default future, ending up by asking them, Is that what you are voting for? When the default future is challenged in this way, a new future can be put in its place and, as Zaffron and Logan argue, the staff will willingly march toward to the new future.
- The importance of having an elevator speech to start the sale process off for the KPI project and, when it is in progress, a weekly updated elevator speech.
- When you are presenting, it is best to be both well prepared and practiced. See the checklist in Chapter 4 on delivering bulletproof PowerPoint presentations.
- The importance of getting the oracles involved in the project. You can do this by holding a one-day focus group, as described in Chapter 4, as their approval and support should be sought before you propose the project to the SMT. You can bypass that step if the CEO is driving the project and involve them in the two-day CSF workshop as out-lined in Chapter 7. As John Kotter advises, you need to create a guiding coalition.

- The need to establish a comprehensive blueprint, mimicking Toyota's management principle, "Slow with consensus, fast with implementation."
- The importance of generating quick wins—obvious to us all but frequently missed. Remember that senior management is, on occasion, inflicted with attention deficit disorder. Progress in a methodical and introverted way at your peril. We need easy wins, celebrated extrovertly, and we need to ensure that we set up the CEO to score the easy goals.

The SMT attitude is crucial—any lack of understanding, commitment, or prioritizing of this important process will prevent success. It is common for the project team and the SMT to fit a KPI project around other competing, less important firefighting activities.

The SMT must be committed to the KPI project and to driving it down through the organization. Properly implemented, the KPI project will create a dynamic environment. Before it can do this, the SMT must be sold on the concept. This will lead to the KPI project's being treated as the top priority, which may mean that the SMT allows some of those distracting fires to burn themselves out.

Consider this quote from a senior consultant:

Senior staff view the development of the BSC as an end in itself and go through the motions to keep the boss happy. If the SMT is not strategic in its perspective and consequently does not see the BSC as a tool to help it better understand and manage the organization, this will be reflected in a loss of interest when the process of development gets tough, for example, when deciding on which KPIs to use and the trade-offs to be made. While the role of the SMT is important, the role of the CEO is critical. The CEO must be the central driver carrying the embryo BSC with him all the time, talking about it frequently, and so on.

It is common for BSC and KPI projects to flounder when a new chief executive takes the helm. Sadly, not all CEOs are equal and thus it is important that the Board, when recruiting the new CEO, ensure that the new appointee is conversant with modern performance measurement.

Benefit of This Action

The SMT will get a buzz from being involved in a dynamic project, and there will be wider ownership as the oracles put their full weight behind the cause.

Lesson 3: Start Off with a Six-Perspective Balanced Scorecard (BSC)

Although I believe the BSC is a flawed model, the overall message of having both a balanced strategy and balanced performance measures is very important. I therefore support the need to work with BSC perspectives, six of them.

Too often, time is spent debating the perspectives, their names, and the design of the scorecard. The SMT loves this time of intellectualizing; however, it does not create much value. It is easy to get carried away with the debate. I came across one team, in a government department, that had spent months determining the names of the perspectives while making little progress on defining the CSFs. Let me save you some trouble. You will need:

1. One on the financials performance—call it *financial results*
2. One on innovation and the development of the staff—call it *innovation and learning*
3. One on customer satisfaction—call it *customer focus*
4. One on internal business processes—call it *internal process*
5. One on staff satisfaction—call it *staff satisfaction*
6. One on relationship with the environment and the community—call it *environment/community*

Using the suggested six perspective names will mean that you are using a better-practice perspective template for the first 6 to 12 months. After 12 months, the SMT and staff will have enough experience, knowledge, and understanding to fine-tune the perspective names to better suit the organization's needs.

Benefit of This Action

The SMT members will invest the scarce time they have available for this project in more important areas.

Lesson 4: Focus on the Critical Success Factors

The critical success factors, as the name suggests, are the aspects the organization's staff need to perform well in day-in and day-out. Key result indicators (KRIs), result indicators (RIs), performance indicators (PIs), and KPIs are the actual performance measures, which naturally cascade from these CSFs. It is crucial that the SMT focus on providing the KPI project team with CSFs. If this is done well, winning KPIs are much easier to find.

Most organizations know their success factors (SFs). However, few organizations have:

- Worded their SFs appropriately
- Segregated out SFs from desired external outcomes
- Sifted through the SFs to find their critical ones—their *critical* success factors
- Communicated the CSFs to staff

If your organization has not completed a thorough exercise to know its CSFs, performance measurement will be a random process. It will create an army of measurers producing numerous numbing reports, measurers who often "measure" progress in a direction very remote from the strategic direction of the organization.

CSFs identify the issues that determine an organization's health and vitality. When you first investigate CSFs, you may come up with 10–15 issues that can be argued as being critical for the continued health of the organization. The second phase of thinning them down is relatively easy, as the more important CSFs have a broader influence, impacting many success factors. Better practice suggests that there should be only between five and eight critical success factors.

Once you have the right CSFs, finding the KPIs is much easier, as they will reside within these CSF factors. This process is explained in detail in Chapter 7.

Benefit of This Action

Ascertaining the organization's CSFs is the El Dorado of management. It will have a profound impact on staff members, as for the first time they will know what their focus should be on a daily basis. It will also help link daily activities to strategy and improve all forms of performance reporting.

Lesson 5: Follow the 10/80/10 Rule

Many balanced scorecards fail because the wrong measures are used. In such exercises, all their measures are called KPIs. I argue that many organizations are not working with their true KPIs, measures with special characteristics that were discussed in Chapter 1.

Kaplan and Norton[4] recommend no more than 20 KPIs. Hope and Fraser[5] suggest fewer than 10 KPIs. The 10/80/10 rule is a good guide: 10 KRIs, up to 80 RIs and PIs, and 10 KPIs.

The KPI project team need to have a good understanding of the characteristics of KRIs, RIs, PIs, and KPIs and be able to distinguish between them. One important role for the KPI project team is to educate all relevant staff on these differences.

Many organizations call every measure a KPI and end up with over 200, which will create confusion rather than clarity. All leading writers are saying the same thing: "Less is better."

Many consultants, authors, and managers confuse result indicators with KPIs. Sales, net profit, customer satisfaction, and return on capital employed are not KPIs, as they are a result of many events occurring. These examples are *KRIs*, as they are measures that give a clear picture of whether you are traveling in the right direction. If a problem exists, they show it, but they will not tell you what you need to do to correct it. KRIs provide useful information to the board of directors, which should not be involved in day-to-day management.

The KPIs lie several layers beneath the KRIs. The KPIs connect the "workface" to the chief executive officer (CEO). During the day or every morning, CEOs working with KPIs are contacting people directly, asking for explanations or giving recognition of their success. Not all teams will have KPIs, as they cannot influence them. These teams will have RIs and PIs. It is important to note that the 10/80/10 is for the whole organization and is repeated if you have totally separate, unrelated businesses (e.g., manufacturing umbrellas and ice cream).

Benefit of This Action

The KPI team will immediately focus on the end product (the 10/80/10) and not try to identify 80 KPIs in 200-odd performance measures.

Lesson 6: "Just Do It"

The exact structure of the KRIs, RIs, PIs, and KPIs is rarely right the first time. Kaplan and Norton agree with Nike and say, "Just do it." The SMT and KPI project team need to ensure that the project culture is a "just do it" culture. It is important to ensure that the project team first reads the key reference books set out in Chapter 6.

A "just do it" culture means that the team will not have to rely on external experts to run the project. Progressive CEOs are wary of large projects managed by staff sourced from expensive international consulting firms. The past decades are littered with six- or seven-figure consulting assignments that have not delivered on the value expectations. A "just do it" culture brings the belief that the KPI project team can do it. The external project facilitator's role is to ensure that the project team members remain confident (but not overconfident) and have picked up all the required skills they will need (e.g., delivering persuasive KPI presentations) and understand all the templates available with this KPI book.

Benefit of This Action

The project will be protected against procrastination and have a good chance of implementing the KPIs within a 16–20-week period.

Lesson 7: Use Existing Systems for the First 12 Months

The project team should promote the use of existing in-house applications, such as Microsoft's Excel, PowerPoint, Teams, Access, and OneNote for the collection and reporting of the performance measures for at least the first 12 months.

The reason for the delay is because all the balanced scorecard–based applications will be inconsistent with this methodology and it will take the KPI team time to understand the differences.

The organization's intranet software will be of great assistance as these applications will help the team set up its intranet website so that anyone interested in the development of performance measures can obtain access and contribute. Such applications can provide preformatted lists with expiration dates to keep announcements current and a place to collaborate on the development of KPI documentation and reports in real time.

The team will need to update the KPI intranet site frequently themselves. Updating is too important to be left to a systems administrator who is not part of the KPI project.

Benefit of This Action

Focusing on an immediate solution using existing in-house software will avoid compromising the KPI project time scales by delays in pre-purchase assessments, purchasing, and implementing a new system.

Lesson 8: Trap All Performance Measures, Both Existing and New, in a Database and Make Them Available to All Teams

During the 16 weeks, a number of performance measures will be found that, while not in the top 10 KPIs, still are highly relevant to business unit and service teams. The project team needs to establish a database to record these measures and communicate them through a KPI intranet home page. The fields for the database are discussed in Chapter 9.

The database should show not only all the current teams' measures but also any discarded measures. The project team can then help the teams, business units, and divisions with consistency and completeness (e.g., one measure devised by one team can and should be used by others, where appropriate).

During the project, it is important that the project team purge the database on a regular basis to eliminate duplication and ensure consistency (e.g., the KPI team can suggest to one team, "You might like to look at measure Y as teams A, B, and C are choosing to use it").

Benefit of This Action

This action will create a comprehensive and user-friendly resource for all.

Lesson 9: KPI Reporting Formats Should Follow the Guidelines of the Data Visualization Experts

Data visualization is an area that is growing in importance. No longer is it appropriate for us to dream up report formats based on what looks good to our eyes. There is a science behind what makes data displays work. The expert in this field is Stephen Few.

Stephen Few has written the top three best-selling books on Amazon in this field. I recommend that the SMT leave the design of the reporting formats (24/7, daily, weekly, and monthly reports) to the KPI team, trusting in their judgment. The SMT should tell the KPI project team that they will be happy to live with their formats. The key is to seek agreement that suggested modifications to the new formats will be recorded and looked into at the end of the agreed review period. It will come as no surprise that many suggested modifications will not stand the test of time.

The KPI project team should make good use of the reporting templates provided in Chapter 10 before attempting to develop any of their own.

Benefit of This Action

Understand Stephen Few's views and you will improve your reporting of information, its attractiveness, and its ability to stimulate action.

Lesson 10: Embracing Peter Drucker's Abandonment Rule

Of all Peter Drucker's legendary insights, "abandonment" stands head and shoulders above them all. Drucker saw abandonment as the vital source, the fountain of innovation. Abandonment is a sign that management is recognizing that some initiatives will never work as intended and it is better to face this reality sooner rather than later. It is essential that the organization have freed up enough time to give the KPI project the time and commitment it deserves.

I believe that this is so important that it has become one of the seven foundation stones of the winning KPI methodology. Organizations need to:

1. Create an abandonment day each month during which teams report on what they intend to abandon. Other teams have 24 hours to appeal the abandonment.
2. Make heroes of the teams who embrace abandonment the most.
3. Trap all existing measures in the performance measures database so that broken and out-of-date measures can be disbanded.
4. Abandon performance reports that are completed the same way they were last month and the month before, with nobody reading them.
5. Abandon performance review meetings that have become a ritual, held because they were held last week and last month, and yet the action points are never cleared.
6. Abandon the existing balanced scorecard if it is not working.
7. Abandon linking KPIs to performance-related pay, as discussed in the Introduction and Chapter 2.

Benefit of This Action

This action makes more room for the innovations coming from this project.

Comparison to Other KPI Methodologies

Robert Kaplan and David Norton's *The Balanced Scorecard: Translating Strategy into Action*[6] was a game changer. It should be read by the KPI team and the external facilitator. My personal copy has many highlighted sections, which indicates how useful I think Kaplan and Norton's book is. I have given a chapter by chapter summary of their book in the pdf download that accompanies this chapter.

There are a number of methodologies that I should address. I am a firm believer that the in-house project team, having researched the methodologies, will follow the one that is best for them. At times it will be necessary to cut an exercise from one methodology and use it with an exercise from another methodology. That is both understandable and desirable.

The Balanced Scorecard

Nobody has done more than Kaplan and Norton to ensure that strategy is balanced and well thought through and that its implementation is monitored and managed.

The Harvard Business School paper was a masterpiece, and the follow-on book *Translating Strategy into Action: The Balanced Scorecard* a classic from inception. As a writer I can appreciate the herculean effort Kaplan and Norton undertook to amass so much case study material in such a short time. However, I have been concerned for over twenty years now as to why so many balanced scorecard implementations fail to deliver when the concept of implementing strategy and having a balanced performance is surely a given with most of us.

I believe the failure stems from the balanced scorecard being a table without any legs. You can use it for a while until it becomes impracticable. The four foundation stones, as shown in Exhibit 12.9, are (1) that KPIs are special and have seven characteristics (see Chapter 1), (2) ensuring that the measures used have a minimal dark side (see the Introduction), (3) The KPI project is led and managed in-house (see Chapter 3), and (4) all measures are sourced from the organization's ascertained CSFs (see Chapter 7).

Exhibit 12.9 The Four Foundation Stones the Balanced Scorecard Methodology Needs

The Difference between the Balanced Scorecard and Winning KPIs Methodologies

The more I read their book, the more questions I had about; the purpose and characteristics of KPIs; how were measures reliably derived; and why was the lead or lag decision so difficult.

The differences between the two approaches are summarized in Exhibit 12.10.

Exhibit 12.10 The Difference between the Balanced Scorecard and Winning KPIs

Winning KPIs Methodology	BSC Methodology
The primary role of performance measures is to help the workforce focus on the *critical success factors* of the business, day-in and day-out.	Kaplan and Norton see the primary purpose of performance measures as the need to monitor the implementation of strategic initiatives.
All KPIs are entirely nonfinancial, measured frequently, and have five other characteristics, and, thus, are rare, with fewer than 10 in a business. Measures that are not KPIs are either result indicators, key result indicators, or performance indicators.	Kaplan and Norton see all measures as KPIs.

Exhibit 12.10 *(Continued)*

Winning KPIs Methodology	BSC Methodology
You find your critical success factors through mapping the relationships of the organization's success factors and ignoring any attempt to place these success factors into balanced scorecard perspectives.	Kaplan and Norton focus on a strategic mapping process where strategic objectives and success factors neatly fit into a balanced scorecard perspective. It seems to argue that every action or decision has an effect elsewhere in the organization and that you can boil down cause-and-effect to one or two relationships.
The critical success factors and KPIs are seen as transcending more than one balanced scorecard perspective. In fact, the "timely arrival and departure of planes" critical success factor featured in this book, impacts all six perspectives.	Kaplan and Norton see the perspectives as firm boundaries into which you can slot strategic objectives neatly. Strategic objectives are seen as a succinct statement describing what an organization needs to do well (success factors) in each of the four perspectives in order to implement the strategy.
"Sphere of influence" mapping of success factors often has multiple relationships.	Strategy mapping where there are only one or two cause-and-effect relationships.
You need to know your organization's critical success factors because these are the crux of finding the KPIs.	Critical success factors not addressed in Kaplan and Norton's work.
Performance measures are determined from the CSFs.	Performance measures are determined from strategic initiatives.
An organization needs to look at six perspectives, adding "environment and community" and "employee satisfaction" and changing the "Learning and Growth" perspective back to its original name, "Innovation and Learning."	Kaplan and Norton came up with four balanced scorecard perspectives, "Financial," "Customer Focus," "Internal Process," and "Learning and Growth."
Measures seen as either looking at the past, the here and now, or the future.	Performance measures are either lead / lag indicators.

(continued)

Exhibit 12.10 (*Continued*)

Winning KPIs Methodology	BSC Methodology
A methodology that says that the KPI project has to be implemented by an in-house team following Peter Drucker's advice of "Never giving a new job to a new person."	The balanced-scorecard approach, due to its complexity, is frequently led by balanced-scorecard consultants.
No software applications required. At some stage a reporting tool will be needed to monitor and report on measures.	Myriad BSC applications that support the strategy mapping and cascading performance measures leading to hundreds of performance measures without any linkage to the organizations' CSFs.
The KPI book is a toolkit for implementation, containing checklists, agendas for workshops, a framework for a database, report formats, and guidance notes on all steps.	The BSC book is largely an academic-based approach with limited implementation guidelines provided. There is an implicit suggestion that you will need a consultant to implement.

Have a Balanced Strategy

One of the greatest gifts given by Kaplan and Norton (K&N) has been high-lighting the need to have a balanced strategy, no matter how small your organization is. They pointed out that strategy has to be balanced and the

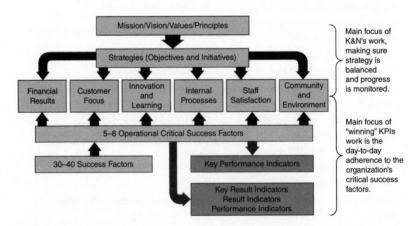

Exhibit 12.11 Main Focus Areas of the Two Methodologies

strategic initiatives reflect this balance. It has always been important that an organization's strategy could be conveyed to those who were to implement it, and the tools and diagrams in their book were an attempt to make this more transparent.

In Exhibit 12.11, I set out the main focus areas of the two different approaches.

Stacey Barr's PuMP Methodology

Stacey Barr has spent the past 20 years or so helping organizations world-wide find measures that drive performance. She has developed a methodology to fill in the gap that the balanced scorecard and other methodologies have left. Barr believes that many organizations have an ad hoc approach to measuring performance and underestimate the effort and rigor needed to produce meaningful measures.

Stacey Barr's *Practical Performance Measurement: Using the PuMP Blueprint for Fast, Easy, and Engaging KPIs*[7] is also a game changer. It should be read by the KPI team and the external facilitator.

Barr has developed a successful methodology that is a step-by-step process of simple techniques and templates that create meaningful measures that drive strategic improvement.

The eight steps of this methodology are:

STEP 1: Understanding Measurement's Purpose

STEP 2: Mapping Measurable Results

STEP 3: Designing Meaningful Measures

STEP 4: Building Buy-In to Measures

STEP 5: Implementing Measures

STEP 6: Reporting Performance Measures

STEP 7: Interpreting Signals from Measures

STEP 8: Reaching Performance Targets

Stacey Barr has called this methodology PuMP (Performance Measurement Process) and shares the same vision: namely, organizations finding and using the measures that will make a difference when monitored by staff management and the senior management team. Visit www.staceybarr.com for more information.

The differences between the winning KPIs and Stacey Barr's PuMP methodology are summarized in Exhibit 12.12.

Exhibit 12.12 The Difference between the PuMP and Winning KPIs

Winning KPIs Methodology	PuMP Methodology
The primary role of performance measures is to help the workforce focus on the *critical success factors* of the business, day-in and day-out.	Barr implies that their function is more to support the implementation of strategic initiatives.
I believe that nonfinancial measures will be the main drivers of performance, and thus the important measures, the KPIs, are all nonfinancial.	Barr has a looser definition on KPIs and thus permits the user to have financial KPIs.
Critical success factors (CSFs) are seen as more fundamental to an organization than its strategy. CSFs are the issues or aspects of organizational performance that determine ongoing health, vitality, and well-being.	Barr sees CSFs as the "overarching themes or headings under which related goals or objectives are clustered."
"Sphere of influence" mapping of success factors often shows multiple relationships.	Barr's result mapping process is a welcomed development and will replace, in time, strategy mapping.
When ensuring a balanced strategy, CSFs, and measures, an organization needs to refer back to these six perspectives: 1. Financial results 2. Innovation and learning (replacing "learning and growth" 3. Customer focus 4. Internal process 5. Staff satisfaction 6. Environment/community	Barr sees the balanced scorecard as a powerful strategy tool, not a measurement tool. Barr is rightly critical of the scant regard the BSC has for the science behind performance measure design. PuMP does not use the BSC perspectives as a checking device.

272

Exhibit 12.12 *(Continued)*

Winning KPIs Methodology	PuMP Methodology
There are two groups of measures: **Result indicators:** the measures that are a summation of more than one team's input. These measures are useful in looking at the combined teamwork, but unfortunately do not help management fix a problem, as it is difficult to pinpoint which teams were responsible for the performance or nonperformance. **Performance indicators:** These are measures that can be tied to a team or a cluster of teams working closely together for a common purpose. Good or bad performance is now the responsibility of a team, and a phone call can be made. These measures thus give clarity and ownership.	Barr calls all measures "performance measures" and thus does not distinguish between result and performance indicators.

PDF Download

To assist the KPI project team on the journey, templates and checklists have been provided. The reader can access, from kpi.davidparmenter.com/fourthedition, free of charge, a PDF of the following chapter templates:

- Chapter-by-chapter outline of Robert Kaplan and David Norton's *The Balanced Scorecard: Translating Strategy into Action*
- Chapter-by-chapter outline of Stacey Barr's *Practical Performance Measurement: Using the PuMP Blueprint for Fast, Easy, and Engaging KPIs*

Notes

1. Robert S. Kaplan and David P. Norton, *The Balanced Scorecard: Translating Strategy into Action* (Boston: Harvard Business Press, 1996).
2. John Kotter, *Leading Change* (Boston: Harvard Business Review Press, November, 2012).
3. Steve Zaffron and Dave Logan, *The Three Laws of Performance* (San Francisco: Jossey-Bass, 2011).
4. Robert S. Kaplan and David P. Norton, *The Balanced Scorecard: Translating Strategy into Action* (Boston: Harvard Business Press, 1996).
5. Jeremy Hope and Robin Fraser, *Beyond Budgeting: How Managers Can Break Free from the Annual Performance Trap* (Cambridge: Harvard Business School Press, 2003).
6. Robert S. Kaplan and David P. Norton, *The Balanced Scorecard: Translating Strategy into Action* (Boston: Harvard Business Press, 1996).
7. Stacey Barr, *Practical Performance Measurement: Using the PuMP Blueprint for Fast, Easy, and Engaging KPIs* (The PuMP Press, 2014).

Performance Measures Database

The KPI team will have gathered and recorded performance measures from their research undertaken prior to the workshops including; discussions held with senior management; investigating company archives; reviewing existing monthly reports; and from communicating with other enterprises.

During the CSF and Performance measures workshops measures will be recorded, collated, and modified in a database that is available to all staff. This database will have a read-only facility for all employees. Amendment to the database measures only being permitted by the KPI team.

The following performance measures are provided to help start this process off. They will be a valuable resource to the KPI team when reviewing the workshop output for completeness. You can acquire this database electronically from www.davidparmenter.com (for a small fee).

I have been influenced by Stacey Barr's work and agree that it is beneficial to evaluate potential measures by asking two questions for each potential measure:

1. How strong an indicator of performance is this measure (5 = very strong, 1 = very weak)?
2. How feasible will it be to measure this (5 = very easy to measure as the data is already available, 3 = some data extraction and manipulation will be required, 1 = very difficult to gather data)?

The strength of measure should be evaluated with regard to the critical success factor you are working with. However, with this list I am giving weightings based on their likelihood as an indicator of performance.

It is advisable not to provide attendees with this list of performance measures until they have reviewed the relevant critical success factors and spent time ascertaining measures themselves. Introducing this list too early will lead to a narrowing of potential performance measures. The measures in this appendix are separated into result and performance indicators. Some of them will be key performance indicators (KPIs) and some key result indicators (KRIs). It is up to the KPI project team to ascertain their appropriate grouping for relevant measures.

Key for Database

Past All measures measuring past activity (Note: Yesterday's activity is considered a current measure.)

Current Yesterday's or today's activity

Future Measuring an event that is to occur in the future (date of next meeting with key client, date of next promotion, etc.)

Performance measure category index

1 Customer/Key Customer/New Customer/Sales Pipeline/Call Center/Brand Recognition

2 Quality/On-time Delivery/Order Processing/Pricing

3 Health and Safety/Accidents/Emergency Response

4 Community Involvement/Environmental/Waste/Public Relations

5 Recruiting/Student Internships

6 Employee Satisfaction/Absenteeism/Staff Turnover/Recognition/Leave /Communication

7 Capital Expenditure/Cashflow/Cost Control/Debtors/Financial Reporting/Profitability/Accounts Payable/Payroll

8 Internal Processes/Abandonment/Contractor Management/IT Help Desk/Staff Management

9 Inventory

10 New Products/Research and Development/Patents

11 Innovation/Lean Processes/Training

12 Production/Maintenance/Utilization/Security/Systems/Vehicles

13 Projects

14 Head Office

Measure	Frequency of measurement	Time zone (past, current, future)	Result/ performance indicator	Strength/feasibility		Keyword	Performance measure category
Search engine ranking for website	Monthly	Past	R	3	3	Brand recognition	1
Market share of key brands	Quarterly	Past	R	5	2	Brand recognition	1
Market share of major product lines	Quarterly	Past	R	3	3	Brand recognition	1
Abandon rate at **call center**—caller gives up	Daily	Current	P	5	5	Call center	1
Calls on hold longer than _____ seconds	Daily and in some cases 24/7	Current	P	5	5	Call center	1
Calls answered first time by call center (not having to be transferred to another party)	Daily and in some cases 24/7	Current	R	5	5	Call center	1
Training hours in systems and protocols to **call center staff** in last quarter	Monthly	Past	R	3	3	Call center	1
Average queue time of **incoming calls**	Monthly	Past	R	3	2	Call center	1
Peak queue time of **incoming calls**	Monthly	Past	R	3	2	Call center	1

(continued)

Measure	Frequency of measurement	Time zone (past, current, future)	Result/ performance indicator	Strength/feasibility	Keyword	Performance measure category
Number of initiatives planned within next three months to **increase sales staff time in front of customers**	Monthly	Future	R	5	Customer	1
Value of **credit notes** issued in month	Monthly	Past	R	4	Customer	1
Average time to correct **customer problem**	Monthly	Past	R	4	Customer	1
Percentage of **warranty parts** shipped within 48 hours	Monthly	Past	R	5	Customer	1
Listing of **unprofitable customers** and proposed actions to be taken	Quarterly	Past	R	5	Customer	1
Complaints not resolved during the first phone call by a customer	Daily	Current	R	3	Customer	1
Average time from **customer enquiry** to sales team response	Weekly	Past	P	4	Customer	1
Date of next initiative to enhance the senior management team's understanding of **customer needs**	Monthly	Future	R	2	Customer	1
Percentage of **customers** paying >_____% upfront on commencement of project	Monthly	Past	R	3	Customer	1

Percentage of major projects where the first design fully met the **customer's** specifications	Monthly	Past	R	3	3	Customer	1
Average **customer size** by category (category A being the top 20 percent of customers)	Quarterly	Past	R	3	3	Customer	1
Marketing expense as a percentage of revenue	Quarterly	Past	R	2	1	Customer	1
Unresolved **complaints** from **other** customers (not key customers) at end of week	Weekly	Past	P	3	5	Customer	1
Average time to give credit notes for product **quality** problems	Weekly	Past	P	3	3	Customer	1
Service requests outstanding for other customers (not key customers)	Weekly	Past	P	4	4	Customer	1
Number of customer service initial **enquiries** to follow up	Weekly	Past	P	3	5	Customer	1
Number of customers with **outstanding retention** installments	Weekly	Past	R	3	5	Customer	1
Post-project wrap-ups outstanding with customers (major customer projects only)	Weekly	Past	P	3	5	Customer	1

(continued)

279

(*Continued*)

Measure	Frequency of measurement	Time zone (past, current, future)	Result/performance indicator	Strength/feasibility		Keyword	Performance measure category
Date of last **contact** with **key customer** where we are delivering a major project (list by major projects only)	Weekly	Past	P	3	5	Customer (key)	1
Complaints from our **key customers** that have not been resolved within ___ hours, reported to the chief executive officer (CEO) and general managers	24 / 7	Current	P	5	5	Customer (key)	1
Key customer service requests outstanding for more than 48 hours reported to the general manager	24 / 7	Current	P	4	5	Customer (key)	1
Key customer enquiries that have not been responded to by the sales team (over 24 hours old)	Daily	Current	P	5	5	Customer (key)	1
Date of next **key customer** focus group	Quarterly	Future	P	4	4	Customer (key)	1
Date of next visit to **key customers** (by customer name reported to CEO)	Weekly	Future	P	5	5	Customer (key)	1
Number of **key customer complaints** where senior management needed to instigate the remedial action	Monthly	Past	P	5	5	Customer (key)	1

Number of visits made to **key customers** last month	Monthly	Past	P	3	5	Customer (key)	1
Number of variations to contract by **key customers**	Monthly	Past	R	3	3	Customer (key)	1
Number of contacts with each **key customer**	Quarterly	Past	P	4	4	Customer (key)	1
Movement in numbers of **key customers** in last quarter	Quarterly	Past	R	3	4	Customer (key)	1
Number of **key customer** relationships producing significant gross profit (over $____)	Quarterly	Past	R	5	3	Customer (key)	1
Percentage of **key customers** covered by partnership projects	Quarterly	Past	R	4	5	Customer (key)	1
Percentage of key **customers'** business (reported by key customer)	Quarterly	Past	R	5	2	Customer (key)	1
Profitability of business with **key customers**	Quarterly	Past	R	4	2	Customer (key)	1
Timeliness and accuracy of **price quotations to key customers**	Weekly	Past	P	4	3	Customer (key)	1
Weekly sales to key customers by major product lines (no more than five product lines shown)	Weekly	Past	R	3	3	Customer (key)	1

(continued)

(Continued)

Measure	Frequency of measurement	Time zone (past, current, future)	Result/performance indicator	Strength/feasibility		Keyword	Performance measure category
Number of **credit notes issued to key customers**	Weekly	Past	R	4	5	Customer (key)	1
Number of **initiatives** completed from the recent **key customer** satisfaction survey	Weekly for three months post-survey	Past	P	5	5	Customer (key)	1
Number of referrals from **key customers**	Quarterly	Past	R	5	4	New customer	1
Number of **referrals** from other customers (excluding key customers)	Quarterly	Past	R	3	3	New customer	1
Number of initiatives planned for next month, months two to three, four to six, to attract **new customers** to purchase/use our goods or services	Monthly	Future	R	5	5	New customer	1
Date of next initiative to attract targeted **"new customers"**	Quarterly	Future	P	5	5	New customer	1
Number of **new customers** this month	Monthly	Past	R	3	4	New customer	1
Sales to **new customers** by occurrence type (e.g., referrals, promotional drive, prospecting, website, etc.)	Monthly	Past	R	3	3	New customer	1

Number of **confirmed speeches delivered by CEO** to community organizations, conferences, and public forums planned for next month, months two to three, four to six	Monthly	Future	P	5	5	Sales pipeline	1
Number of **confirmed speeches delivered by the senior management team** to community organizations, conferences, and public forums planned for next month, months two to three, four to six	Monthly	Future	P	5	5	Sales pipeline	1
Percentage of successful/unsuccessful **tenders**	Quarterly	Past	R	4	5	Sales pipeline	1
Marketing investment made to develop new markets for **products/services ($)**	Quarterly	Past	R	3	2	Sales pipeline	1
Key donors who have not gifted in last ____ months	Monthly	Past	P	5	3	Sales pipeline	1
Percentage of **sales** that have arisen from cross-selling among business units	Monthly	Past	R	5	3	Sales pipeline	1
Client funds received for investment	Monthly	Past	R	4	5	Sales pipeline	1

(continued)

283

(*Continued*)

284

Measure	Frequency of measurement	Time zone (past, current, future)	Result/ performance indicator	Strength/feasibility		Keyword	Performance measure category
Number of leads generated by agents	Monthly	Past	P	5	5	Sales pipeline	1
Number of **winning tenders** that have created losses	Monthly	Past	R	3	3	Sales pipeline	1
Number of **customer records** over two years old since last update	Monthly	Past	R	4	4	Sales pipeline	1
Number of negative customer ratings on **social media** left unanswered.	Weekly	Past	R	3	3	Sales pipeline	1
Late deliveries / incomplete deliveries to **key customers**	24 / 7	Current	P	5	5	On-time delivery	2
Percentage of **on-time deliveries** (excluding key customers)	Monthly	Past	R	4	4	On-time delivery	2
Percentage of **on-time delivery** (show progress over last eighteen months)	Monthly	Past	R	5	5	On-time delivery	2
Customer orders shipped by express services because of production delays	Monthly	Past	P	4	5	On-time delivery	2
Number of initiatives planned within next three months to **increase on-time delivery** to customers	Weekly	Future	R	4	4	On-time delivery	2

Metric	Frequency	Timeframe	Type			Category	
Orders canceled by reason (limit to no more than five categories)	Weekly	Past	R	3	5	Order processing	2
Order entry error rate	Weekly	Past	P	3	5	Order processing	2
List of **key customers** where time since last order > ___ weeks	Weekly	Past	R	5	5	Order processing	2
Length of **order fulfillment** cycle by major products/services	Quarterly	Past	R	3	3	Order processing	2
Number of **pricing errors** to other customer invoices	Monthly	Past	P	4	3	Pricing	2
Number of **pricing errors** to **key customer** invoices	Weekly	Past	P	5	3	Pricing	2
Number of **defect goods** found during installation (including those that occur within first 90 days of operation)	Weekly	Past	R	5	5	Quality	2
Defects per 1 million ___ (six SIGMA measurement process)	Monthly	Past	R	4	4	Quality	2
Quality problems due to equipment failure	Monthly	Past	R	4	3	Quality	2
Number of **major processes** made fool proof	Quarterly	Past	R	4	4	Quality	2
Number of **defect key products** returned this week	Weekly	Past	R	5	5	Quality	2

(continued)

285

(Continued)

Measure	Frequency of measurement	Time zone (past, current, future)	Result/ performance indicator	Strength/feasibility	Keyword	Performance measure category
Near-miss incidents that could have involved pollution of the environment	24 / 7	Current	R	5	5	Accidents	3
Accidents and breaches of safety	24 / 7	Current	R	5	5	Accidents	3
Vehicle fleet road traffic accidents	24 / 7	Current	R	5	5	Accidents	3
Number of accidents or days lost through accidents (by reason)	Monthly	Past	R	5	4	Accidents	3
Accidents per 100,000 hours worked	Monthly	Past	R	5	4	Accidents	3
Number of lost-time injuries in week	Weekly	Past	R	4	5	Accidents	3
Emergency calls on hold longer than __ seconds	24 / 7	Current	P	5	4	Emergency response	3
Emergency responses which were over maximum acceptable time limit	24 / 7	Current	P	5	4	Emergency response	3
Average emergency response time	Weekly	Past	R	4	4	Emergency response	3
Date of next Health and Safety audit	Monthly	Future	R	5	5	HSE	3
Number of safety inspections planned for next month	Monthly	Future	R	5	5	HSE	3
Health and Safety issues raised and not resolved after two weeks	Weekly	Past	R	5	5	HSE	3

286

Description	Frequency	Time				Category	
Staff **driving** for more than eight hours per day who do not have advanced driving certification	Quarterly	Past	R	3	3	HSE	3
Number of initiatives planned for next month, months two to three, four to six to support **tertiary institutions** that are a source of future graduate recruits	Quarterly	Future	R	4	5	Community involvement	4
Volunteers recruited in month	Monthly	Past	R	5	5	Community involvement	4
Number of employees involved in **community activities**	Quarterly	Past	R	2	2	Community involvement	4
Quarterly donations to the **community organizations**	Quarterly	Past	R	4	5	Community involvement	4
Number of employees involved in up-skilling **local community** organizations	Quarterly	Past	R	4	4	Community involvement	4
Number of external charities supported by company **staff volunteers**	Quarterly	Past	R	3	3	Community involvement	4
Number of **community sponsorship** projects in past 12 months	Quarterly	Past	R	3	5	Community involvement	4
Amount of **emissions** from production	Daily	Current	R	4	5	Environment	4
Entries to **environment/community** awards to be completed in next three months	Quarterly	Future	R	3	5	Environment	4

(continued)

Measure	Frequency of measurement	Time zone (past, current, future)	Result/ performance indicator	Strength/feasibility		Keyword	Performance measure category
Number of **environmental innovations** to be implemented in the next month and months two to three, by location	Monthly	Future	R	3	5	Environment	4
Date of **next environmental disaster** clean-up practice exercise	Quarterly	Future	P	4	5	Environment	4
Date of **last environmental disaster** clean-up practice exercise, by type of exercise	Quarterly	Past	P	4	5	Environment	4
Energy consumed by major plant	Daily	Current	R	4	5	Environment	4
Percentage of current projects that are **environmentally** friendly	Monthly	Past	R	5	3	Environment	4
Number of **environmental innovations** implemented in the past 30 days, by location	Monthly	Past	R	3	5	Environment	4
Environmental satisfaction rating from external survey	Yearly	Past	R	3	3	Environment	4
Number of **environmental** complaints received in a week	Weekly	Past	R	5	5	Environment	4

Percentage of **recycled material** used in production	Weekly	Past	R	3	5	Environment	4
Number of **media coverage** events planned for next month, months two to three, four to six	Monthly	Future	P	3	5	PR	4
Date of next debrief by CEO to **journalists**	Monthly	Future	P	3	5	PR	4
Number of positive **press releases** issued to the papers and journals in the past 30 days /60 days	Monthly	Past	R	5	5	PR	4
Number of positive and negative **articles printed** in the papers and journals in the past 30 days / 60 days	Monthly	Past	R	3	3	PR	4
Number of papers/radio stations who have used key **press releases**	Monthly	Past	R	5	3	PR	4
Number of **photos** (CEO board members, company logo, company premises) in papers last month, months two to three, four to six	Monthly	Past	R	3	3	PR	4
Number of respected **journalists** who have a sound understanding of our operation	Quarterly	Past	R	4	5	PR	4
Waste–scrap, rejects, underutilized capacity, idle time, downtime, excess production, etc.	Weekly	Past	R	4	4	Waste	4

(continued)

289

(*Continued*)

Measure	Frequency of measurement	Time zone (past, current, future)	Result/performance indicator	Strength/feasibility		Keyword	Performance measure category
Percentage of **waste** that is later recycled	Weekly	Past	R	4	4	Waste	4
Waste and scrap produced	Weekly	Past	R	3	3	Waste	4
Weekly **water consumption** compared to weekly production.	Weekly	Past	R	3	3	Waste	4
Candidates (not key positions) who have not responded within 48 hours to their job offer	Daily	Current	P	5	5	Recruiting	5
Key position job offers that are over 48 hours old and have not yet been accepted by the chosen **candidate**	24 / 7	Current	P	5	5	Recruiting	5
Expressions of interest from potential **candidates** that have not been responded to within three days of receipt of interest	Daily	Current	P	5	5	Recruiting	5
Names of short-listed **candidates** for whom the next round of interviews has yet to be scheduled	Daily	Future	P	3	4	Recruiting	5
Feedback on **recruitment processes** from recent recruits	Every employee survey	Past	R	3	3	Recruiting	5

Number of managers trained in recruiting practices	Monthly	Past	R	3	3	Recruiting	5
Number of internal applications for job applications closed in month	Monthly	Past	R	3	3	Recruiting	5
Number of level 1 and 2 managers who were promoted internally	Quarterly	Past	R	3	3	Recruiting	5
Number of candidates for advertised position	Quarterly	Past	R	3	3	Recruiting	5
Number of candidates that come from employee referrals	Quarterly	Past	R	4	5	Recruiting	5
Percentage of hires that accept an offer over competing offers from key competitors	Quarterly	Past	R	5	4	Recruiting	5
Ratio between internal and external recruits for position	Quarterly	Past	R	3	3	Recruiting	5
Turnover of new hires within one year	Quarterly	Past	R	3	3	Recruiting	5
Percentage of key staff who are over ___ years old	Quarterly	Past	R	3	3	Recruiting	5
Date of confirmed psychometric testing of candidates' capabilities	Weekly	Past	P	5	5	Recruiting	5
Recruitments in progress for which the last interview was over two weeks ago	Weekly	Past	P	5	5	Recruiting	5

(continued)

Measure	Frequency of measurement	Time zone (past, current, future)	Result/performance indicator	Strength/feasibility		Keyword	Performance measure category
Known **vacant positions** where job vacancy has not yet been posted on relevant websites	Weekly	Past	R	3	3	Recruiting	5
Positions over _____ level where **check of authenticity** of the qualifications has not yet been done	Weekly	Past	P	4	3	Recruiting	5
Number of **vacant positions** we need to fill by category of importance	Weekly	Past	P	5	5	Recruiting	5
Number of **students** offered internships for the next holiday period	Weekly	Future	R	5	5	Student Internships	5
Number of **students** who have completed internships in the last quarter (trialing potential employees)	Quarterly	Past	R	5	5	Student Internships	5
Employee **absenteeism, by department,** by major reasons	Monthly	Past	R	5	5	Absenteeism	6
Staff who have been ill for over two weeks who do not have a back-to-work program	Weekly	Past	P	3	5	Absenteeism	6
Date of next CEO newsletter	Monthly	Future	P	5	5	Communication	6

Number of processes, procedures, and material added to a knowledge management system last month	Monthly	Past	R	3	3	Communication	6
Number of team meals held where other teams also attended	Monthly	Past	R	3	3	Communication	6
Number of planned CEO **recognitions** for next week/two weeks	Weekly	Future	P	5	5	Recognition	6
Number of CEO **recognitions made** in the past week/two weeks	Weekly	Past	P	5	5	Recognition	6
Number of planned **recognitions** in the next week/two weeks by each manager	Weekly	Future	P	5	5	Recognition	6
Teams with the best **on-time delivery** record (reported to the GMs and made available to all staff in the organization)	Weekly	Past	P	4	4	Recognition	6
Staff with greater than 30 days of **annual leave** owing	Monthly	Past	P	3	5	Staff leave	6
Percentage of staff who have more than ___ days of **annual leave** owing	Quarterly	Past	R	3	3	Staff leave	6
Date of next **staff satisfaction** survey	Monthly	Future	P	3	5	Staff satisfaction	6
Satisfaction with work–life balance (from **staff** survey)	Every employee survey	Past	R	4	3	Staff satisfaction	6

(continued)

(Continued)

Measure	Frequency of measurement	Time zone (past, current, future)	Result/ performance indicator	Strength/feasibility		Keyword	Performance measure category
Percentage of managers who are **women**	Monthly	Past	R	3	5	Staff satisfaction	6
Number of teams who have undertaken internal user **satisfaction** surveys in past six months	Monthly	Past	P	4	3	Staff satisfaction	6
The top 20 with largest number of days **worked overseas** on jobs in past three months (excluding staff relocated)—limit to top 20 with the longest number of days away	Quarterly	Past	R	3	4	Staff satisfaction	6
List of **high-performing staff** who have been in the same position for over two years	Quarterly	Past	R	5	4	Staff satisfaction	6
Employee complaints still unresolved after two weeks	Weekly	Past	R	5	5	Staff satisfaction	6
Number of initiatives implemented after **staff** satisfaction survey	Weekly for four months post-employee survey	Past	P	5	5	Staff satisfaction	6

Number of initiatives implemented in last three months based on **exit interview** feedback	Monthly	Past	P	5	5	Staff satisfaction	6
Staff, in vital positions, who have handed in their notice today notified to CEO.	24 / 7	Current	P	5	5	Staff turnover	6
Length of service of **staff** who **have left** by period of service (less than 1 year, 2 to 5 years, 6 to 10 years, etc.)	Monthly	Past	R	3	5	Staff turnover	6
Turnover of experienced **staff** who have been with the organization for over three years	Monthly	Past	R	4	5	Staff turnover	6
List of managers who have a **high turnover** of **staff** who left within 12 months of joining	Monthly	Past	P	4	5	Staff turnover	6
Turnover of female **staff**	Monthly	Past	R	4	5	Staff turnover	6
Turnover of **staff** by ethnicity	Monthly	Past	R	4	5	Staff turnover	6
Number of **staff** members who **have left** within 3 months, 6 months, 12 months of joining the organization, reported division by division.	Quarterly	Past	R	4	5	Staff turnover	6

(continued)

295

Measure	Frequency of measurement	Time zone (past, current, future)	Result/ performance indicator	Strength/feasibility	Keyword	Performance measure category
Status of the major top 10 **capital expenditure projects** (completed, on-track, behind, at risk)	Monthly	Past	R	5	4	Capital Expenditure	7
Percentage spent of this year's **technology capital expenditure budget**	Monthly	Past	R	4	4	Capital Expenditure	7
Actual hours vs. planned **construction hours**	Monthly	Past	R	3	3	Capital Expenditure	7
Average age of **key assets**	Monthly	Past	R	5	3	Capital Expenditure	7
Free **cashflow** (operating cash flow minus capital expenditures)	Monthly	Past	R	5	5	Cashflow	7
Percentage complete compared to percentage **billed** by major assignment	Monthly	Past	P	5	3	Cashflow	7
The average number of days of production in current key raw materials in **stock**	Monthly	Past	R	5	5	Cashflow	7
Number of current **revenue projects** with all progress payments paid up to date	Monthly	Past	R	3	4	Cashflow	7

Cash-to-cash cycle—length of time from cash out to cash in	Quarterly	Past	R	3	2	Cashflow	7
Debt-to-equity ratio	Monthly	Past	R	5	5	Cashflow	7
Average cost of annual mobile phone calls	Monthly	Past	R	3	3	Cost control	7
Indirect expenses as a percentage of sales	Monthly	Past	R	5	5	Cost control	7
Team's expenditure year to date plus remaining months forecast against year-end target	Monthly	Past	P	4	4	Cost control	7
Average labor cost per hour for direct, indirect, and total labor costs	Monthly	Past	R	2	2	Cost control	7
IT expense as a percentage of total administrative expense	Quarterly	Past	R	3	5	Cost control	7
Organization's credit rating by external agencies	Quarterly	Past	R	5	5	Cost control	7
Average cost of maintaining a customer account	Quarterly	Past	R	1	2	Cost control	7
Administrative expense as a percentage of gross premium	Quarterly	Past	R	3	5	Cost control	7
Staff paid more than 20 hours of overtime in week	Monthly	Past	R	4	2	Cost control	7
Average overtime hours per person (by type of work)	Monthly	Past	R	3	3	Cost control	7

(continued)

297

(Continued)

Measure	Frequency of measurement	Time zone (past, current, future)	Result/ performance indicator	Strength/feasibility		Keyword	Performance measure category
Debtors who have not been contacted within five days of missing their payment terms	Monthly	Past	P	5	5	Debtors	7
Bad debt percentage to turnover	Monthly	Past	R	4	5	Debtors	7
Days sales in **debtors**	Monthly	Past	R	3	5	Debtors	7
Debtors over 30 days/60 days/90 days	Weekly	Past	R	5	5	Debtors	7
Number of times **interest costs** can be covered by EBIT (rolling annual numbers)	Quarterly	Past	R	4	5	Financial reporting	7
Net **surplus/deficit** by major department	Monthly	Past	R	3	5	Financial reporting	7
Return on capital employed	Monthly	Past	R	4	5	Financial reporting	7
Return on net asset value	Monthly	Past	R	4	4	Financial reporting	7
Return on equity	Monthly	Past	R	4	5	Financial reporting	7
Revenues per employee	Monthly	Past	R	3	5	Financial reporting	7
Revenues/total assets (percentage)	Monthly	Past	R	3	5	Financial reporting	7

Revenue by sales team	Monthly	Past	R	5	5	Financial reporting	7
Total assets/employee	Monthly	Past	R	3	3	Financial reporting	7
Value of **work in progress**	Monthly	Past	R	3	5	Financial reporting	7
Number of **policy holder** claims made	Monthly	Past	R	4	4	Financial reporting	7
Value of **policy holder** claims made by category	Monthly	Past	R	3	4	Financial reporting	7
Sales growth rate by market segment	Quarterly	Past	R	4	5	Financial reporting	7
Insurance premiums received from new insurance products	Quarterly	Past	R	4	5	Financial reporting	7
Mark-downs of key products	Weekly	Past	R	3	3	Financial reporting	7
Sales to selling costs ratio	Monthly	Past	R	4	3	Financial reporting	7
Sales made yesterday	Daily	Current	P	5	5	Financial reporting	7
Number of **days of sales** of top 10 products	Weekly	Past	R	5	4	Financial reporting	7

(continued)

Measure	Frequency of measurement	Time zone (past, current, future)	Result/performance indicator	Strength/feasibility	Keyword	Performance measure category
Sales per square foot	Monthly	Past	R	5	5	Financial reporting	7
Gross margin by major business division	Monthly	Past	R	5	5	Profitability	7
Net income by major business division	Monthly	Past	R	4	5	Profitability	7
Profit before interest and tax **per employee** ($)	Monthly	Past	R	4	2	Profitability	7
Products where **gross margin** is > ___ %	Quarterly	Past	R	5	3	Profitability	7
Gross margin of major products	Monthly	Past	R	3	3	Profitability	7
Key product profitability	Quarterly	Past	R	4	2	Profitability	7
Dealer profitability	Quarterly	Past	R	4	4	Profitability	7
Economic value added per employee ($)	Quarterly	Past	R	3	2	Profitability	7
Date of planned **replacement** of a service/product that has now become outdated	Monthly	Future	R	4	5	Abandonment	8
Expected date when major product lines will become obsolete	Quarterly	Future	R	3	4	Abandonment	8
Number of **abandonments** to be actioned in the next 30 days, 60 days, and 90 days	Weekly	Future	P	5	5	Abandonment	8

Number of employees terminated for **nonperformance** or other issues	Monthly	Past	R	2	4	Abandonment	8
Time saved each month through **abandonments** by team (reported monthly featuring top-quartile–performing teams in this area).	Monthly	Past	P	2	2	Abandonment	8
List of **abandonments** in last month by team	Monthly	Past	P	5	5	Abandonment	8
List of meetings that have been permanently **disbanded**	Monthly	Past	P	3	4	Abandonment	8
Number of **reports** terminated this month	Monthly	Past	P	4	5	Abandonment	8
List of major plant and equipment that are in use but past their **expected operational life**	Monthly	Past	R	4	5	Abandonment	8
Number of **contractors** involved in the high profile project	Monthly	Past	P	3	5	Contractor management	8
Percentage of **contractors** to total staff	Quarterly	Past	R	3	3	Contractor management	8
Number of **contractors** who have been employed for over three months	Quarterly	Past	P	4	3	Contractor management	8
Number of IT **contractors** as a percentage of IT employees	Quarterly	Past	P	3	5	Contractor management	8

(continued)

Measure	Frequency of measurement	Time zone (past, current, future)	Result/ performance indicator	Strength/feasibility		Keyword	Performance measure category
Percentage of IT **contractors** to total IT personnel	Quarterly	Past	R	3	3	Contractor management	8
Number of **accounts payable** invoices paid late	Monthly	Past	P	4	5	Internal processes	8
Percentage of **payments** (excluding payroll) where the right amount was paid and on time	Monthly	Past	R	3	3	Internal processes	8
Time taken from month-end to get a **monthly finance report** to the CEO	Monthly	Past	P	4	5	Internal processes	8
Time taken from month-end to get the **monthly report** to budget holders	Monthly	Past	P	4	5	Internal processes	8
Last update of each team's **intranet page**	Monthly	Past	R	3	5	Internal processes	8
Percentage of **hours worked** split into four categories (chargeable, nonrecoverable, administration, other)	Weekly	Past	R	5	4	Internal processes	8
Actual time on compared to **budgeted time** on client	Weekly	Past	R	3	3	Internal processes	8
Number of **overdue reports**/documents required by the senior management team	Weekly	Past	R	4	4	Internal processes	8

Number of **progress invoices** that are due that have not yet been invoiced	Monthly	Past	P	4	5	Internal processes	8
Percentage of **sales invoices** issued on time (within __ days from dispatch)	Monthly	Past	P	4	3	Internal processes	8
Time-recording errors (e.g., time charged to closed or wrong jobs)	Monthly	Past	P	3	3	Internal processes	8
Resource consent returned to originator for rework and resubmission (numbers and dollars)	Monthly	Past	P	4	4	Internal processes	8
Resource consent applications that are now late	Weekly	Past	P	4	4	Internal processes	8
Service-level agreements that are in breach of conditions	Monthly	Past	R	3	3	Internal processes	8
Average resolution time for **IT support tickets**	Monthly	Past	R	4	4	Internal processes	8
Average length of outstanding major **IT requests**	Monthly	Past	R	4	4	Internal processes	8
Number of incidents that have been followed up with a learning session	Monthly	Past	R	4	4	Internal processes	8
Number of unused **software licenses** by department	Quarterly	Past	R	4	4	Internal processes	8
Number of staff with **computers** older than _____ years	Monthly	Past	R	4	4	IT help desk	8
IT service requests closed in month	Monthly	Past	R	4	4	IT help desk	8

(continued)

303

Measure	Frequency of measurement	Time zone (past, current, future)	Result/ performance indicator	Strength/feasibility	Keyword	Performance measure category
Percentage of emails answered by the **help desk** within one day	Monthly	Past	R	2	3	IT help desk	8
Number of **computers** out of action for over __ days	Monthly	Past	R	3	3	IT help desk	8
Percentage of staff who have not sought help or have not been helped by the **help desk**	Monthly	Past	R	3	3	IT help desk	8
Number of outstanding **help desk** requests for assistance	Weekly	Past	R	5	5	IT help desk	8
Number of suppliers on the **accounts payable** ledger	Quarterly	Past	R	2	5	Payables	8
Number of days purchases in **accounts payable**	Monthly	Past	R	2	3	Payables	8
Number of **purchase** invoices disputed	Monthly	Past	R	4	3	Payables	8
Percentage of **accounts payable** invoices processed within __ days of receipt	Monthly	Past	P	4	4	Payables	8
Percent of **large purchases** (greater than $____) from certified vendors	Monthly	Past	P	2	2	Payables	8
Number of unrecorded liabilities over $____ by department noted at month-end	Monthly	Past	R	3	5	Payables	8

Number of suppliers where **early payment** discount is taken	Quarterly	Past	R	3	3	Payables	8
Number of strategic **supply relationships** where long-term agreement is in place	Quarterly	Past	R	3	5	Payables	8
Percentage of **payroll payments** where right amount was paid and on time	Monthly	Past	P	4	4	Payroll	8
Number of **payroll** corrections made after last payroll run	Weekly	Past	R	3	3	Payroll	8
Number of **vacant leadership places** on in-house course (reported to the CEO in the last three weeks before the course)	Daily	Current	P	4	3	Staff management	8
Number of **leadership initiatives** targeted to rising stars to be completed next month, months 2 to 3, months 4 to 6	Monthly	Future	P	4	3	Staff management	8
Date of next **360 feedback** for level 1 and level 2 managers	Monthly	Future	P	3	5	Staff management	8
Number of promotions for high-performing staff planned in the next three months	Monthly	Future	R	3	4	Staff management	8

(*continued*)

306

Measure	Frequency of measurement	Time zone (past, current, future)	Result/ performance indicator	Strength/feasibility		Keyword	Performance measure category
Date of the **next senior executive course** to be attended by senior management	Monthly	Future	P	4	5	Staff management	8
Number of **staff grievances** still not resolved after two weeks	Monthly	Past	R	5	5	Staff management	8
Percentage of staff **performance** reviews completed	Monthly	Past	P	3	4	Staff management	8
Percentage of staff who joined less than three months ago who have had a **post-employment interview**	Monthly	Past	P	4	4	Staff management	8
Percentage of **performance reviews** completed on time	Monthly	Past	R	3	4	Staff management	8
Number of teams who are using **scrum meetings and other agile methods**	Monthly	Past	P	3	3	Staff management	8
Number of **employees** in the organization	Monthly	Past	R	3	5	Staff management	8
Number of managers able to access their department's accounts in the **general ledger**	Monthly	Past	R	3	4	Staff management	8
Number of **mentoring** meetings held last month for rising stars	Monthly	Past	R	4	3	Staff management	8

Number of **mentoring** meetings held last month for other staff	Monthly	Past	R	3	3	Staff management	8
Percentage of employees **below the age** ___	Quarterly	Past	R	2	2	Staff management	8
Percentage of employees with **university education**	Quarterly	Past	R	2	4	Staff management	8
Average employees' **years of service** with company	Quarterly	Past	R	2	3	Staff management	8
Number of **employees certified** for the top five skilled positions	Quarterly	Past	R	3	3	Staff management	8
Number of key positions with **succession plans**	Quarterly	Past	P	4	5	Staff management	8
List of level 3 managers who do not have **mentors**	Weekly	Past	P	5	3	Staff management	8
Number of high-performing staff who do not have a **mentor**	weekly	Past	P	4	4	Staff management	8
List of level 1 and level 2 managers who do not have **mentors** (reported to the CEO)	Weekly	Past	P	5	5	Staff management	8
Percentage of staff **cross-trained**	Quarterly	Past	R	4	4	Staff management	8
Number of **internal promotions** in the last quarter	Monthly	Past	R	4	3	Staff management	8

(continued)

308

Measure	Frequency of measurement	Time zone (past, current, future)	Result/ performance indicator	Strength/feasibility		Keyword	Performance measure category
Key materials that are anticipated to be "out of stock" before next delivery (notified to CEO)	Daily	Future	R	5	5	Inventory	9
Number of days of sales that can be sourced from current stock level for major **inventory** items	Monthly	Past	R	3	3	Inventory	9
Major inventory items where **current stock level** is above maximum level or below minimum level	Monthly	Past	R	4	4	Inventory	9
Number of **days of average sales** in finished goods with inventory	Monthly	Past	R	3	3	Inventory	9
Percentage of **inventory** system records that were tested to be correct to actual quantity held	Monthly	Past	R	3	3	Inventory	9
List of the surplus **inventory** where more than ___ days of sales and/or where last movement was over 12 months ago)	Quarterly	Past	R	4	4	Inventory	9
Number of **stock-outs** in week of major inventory items	Weekly	Past	R	4	5	Inventory	9

Measure	Frequency	Time				Category	
Expected launch dates of the next top five **new products**/services	Weekly	Future	R	4	5	New products	10
Service or **product launches** behind schedule	Weekly	Past	R	4	3	New products	10
Ratio of **new products** (less than ___ years old) to full company catalogue (percentage)	Quarterly	Past	R	3	3	New products	10
Late changes to new major products after design completion	Monthly	Past	R	5	5	New products	10
Revenue from **new products** / services	Monthly	Past	R	4	3	New products	10
Number of profitable **new products** (with quarterly sales over $___ and greater than ___ percentage gross margin)	Quarterly	Past	R	4	3	New products	10
Time taken from initial planning to **new product** launch (major products only)	Quarterly	Past	R	3	3	New products	10
Profits from **new products** or business operations ($)	Quarterly	Past	R	4	2	New products	10
Design cycle time for new products finished this quarter	Quarterly	Past	R	3	4	New products	10
Numbers of **patents** filed and issued that have been incorporated into products	Monthly	Past	R	3	5	Patents	10

(continued)

(Continued)

Measure	Frequency of measurement	Time zone (past, current, future)	Result/performance indicator	Strength/feasibility	Keyword	Performance measure category
Median **patent** age in key products	Quarterly	Past	R	2	5	Patents	10
Numbers of registered **patents**	Quarterly	Past	R	3	5	Patents	10
Date of **prototype** completion	Monthly	Future	R	4	5	R&D	10
Number of **research papers** generated	Quarterly	Past	R	3	4	R&D	10
Research and development expenditure as a percentage of sales from propriety products	Quarterly	Past	R	3	3	R&D	10
Percentage of hours spent on **research and development** by research team (excludes admin time etc.)	Quarterly	Past	R	2	3	R&D	10
Investment in **research and development** ($)	Quarterly	Past	R	2	3	R&D	10
Quality problems in major products attributable to design	Weekly	Past	R	5	3	R&D	10
Number of **new innovations** that will be fully operational in the next month, month two, and month three by department	Monthly	Future	R	5	5	Innovation	11
Date of next **innovation** training session	Monthly	Future	P	4	5	Innovation	11

Date of next major **innovation** with our key services	Monthly	Future	R	4	4	Innovation	11
Number of **innovations** implemented by team	Monthly	Past	P	5	3	Innovation	11
Number of suggested **innovations** from employees by team	Monthly	Past	P	5	4	Innovation	11
Number of **innovations** made to other products (not major products)	Monthly	Past	R	3	3	Innovation	11
Average number of **innovations** implemented per employee per rolling 12 months by team	Quarterly	Past	P	5	3	Innovation	11
Number of **innovations** made to major products in last quarter	Quarterly	Past	R	3	4	Innovation	11
Ratio of **innovations** to suggestions made	Quarterly	Past	R	3	3	Innovation	11
Major **innovations** in the past 18 months showing the degree of success (exceed expectations, met, less than expectations, abandoned)	Quarterly	Past	R	3	3	Innovation	11
Number of changes to **new major products** to correct design deficiencies	Quarterly	Past	R	3	3	Innovation	11
Number of **innovations** that are running behind	Weekly	Past	P	5	3	Innovation	11

(continued)

(Continued)

Measure	Frequency of measurement	Time zone (past, current, future)	Result/performance indicator	Strength/feasibility		Keyword	Performance measure category
Number of **innovations** planned for implementation in 30 days, 60 days, 90 days reported to the CEO	Weekly	Past	P	5	4	Innovation	11
Number of **innovations** that have been copied from competitors	Monthly	Past	R	5	5	Innovation	11
Number of processes that will be integrated avoiding rekeying within next three months	Quarterly	Future	R	3	3	Lean Processes	11
Percentage of customer-facing employees having on-line access to information about **customers**	Monthly	Past	R	3	3	Lean Processes	11
Percentage of employees who have interacted with **customers**	Monthly	Past	R	2	3	Lean Processes	11
Number of **manual transactions** converted to automated electronic feed in last quarter	Quarterly	Past	R	4	4	Lean Processes	11
Number of teams who have updated their policy and procedures manual in last ___ months	Monthly	Past	P	3	5	Lean Processes	11
Production set-up/**changeover** time	Weekly	Past	P	4	4	Lean Processes	11

Number of urgent jobs that **interrupted production**	Weekly	Past	R	5	5	Lean Processes	11
Percentage completed **time sheets** by deadline	Weekly	Past	R	2	4	Lean Processes	11
List of staff who submitted late **time sheets**	Weekly	Past	R	5	5	Lean Processes	11
Cost of operation before **outsourcing** vs. total cost now	Yearly	Past	R	3	3	Lean Processes	11
Number of key suppliers where transactions are totally **paperless**	Quarterly	Past	R	3	3	Lean Processes	11
Number of elapsed weeks invested in the **annual plan**	Weekly	Past	R	3	5	Lean Processes	11
Percentage of **utilization** of owned/leased premises	Monthly	Past	R	4	3	Lean Processes	11
Number of beds **unoccupied** for over 24 hours	Daily	Current	R	5	5	Lean Processes	11
Number of **operations canceled** because of shortage of beds	Daily	Current	R	5	5	Lean Processes	11
Average length of **patient stay** per ward	Monthly	Past	R	3	3	Lean Processes	11
Number of patients active in **clinical trials**	Monthly	Past	R	3	3	Lean Processes	11
Annual expenditure on **health and safety** per employee	Yearly	Past	R	3	3	Lean Processes	11

(*continued*)

(Continued)

Measure	Frequency of measurement	Time zone (past, current, future)	Result/performance indicator	Strength/feasibility	Keyword	Performance measure category
Number of submissions to **industry awards**	Quarterly	Past	R	3	5	Lean Processes	11
Date of last **benchmarking** survey participation	Quarterly	Past	R	3	5	Lean Processes	11
Teams not represented in the **in-house courses** to be held in the next two weeks (reported daily to the CEO)	Daily	Future	P	5	5	Training	11
Number of **training** hours booked for next month, months 2 to 3, months 4 to 6 (in both external/internal courses **by team**)	Monthly	Future	P	4	3	Training	11
Number of **training** hours-booked for next month, months 2 to 3, months 4 to 6 (in both external/internal courses for the **senior management team**)	Monthly	Future	P	4	3	Training	11
Annual average of **training** days by team	Monthly	Past	P	4	5	Training	11
Training days attended this month, by team	Monthly	Past	P	3	5	Training	11
Number of staff who have attended key **training** courses (e.g., leadership, stress management, etc.)	Monthly	Past	P	4	5	Training	11

Measure	Frequency	Timing	Type			Category	Ref
Number of key sales staff not **utilizing the key sales technology**	Monthly	Past	R	3	3	Training	11
Percentage of **staff** meeting continuing professional development requirements	Quarterly	Past	R	3	2	Training	11
Number of staff who have agreed upon **professional development plans**	Quarterly	Past	R	4	3	Training	11
Percentage of **cross-trained** personnel per team	Quarterly	Past	P	3	3	Training	11
Number of staff trained in **first aid**	Quarterly	Past	P	3	3	Training	11
Training hours delivered through tailored **in-house courses** in last quarter	Quarterly	Past	R	5	3	Training	11
Percentage of employees engaged in **further education**	Quarterly	Past	R	3	3	Training	11
Staff who **did not attend** a course due to work commitments	Weekly	Past	P	5	5	Training	11
New staff who have not attended an **induction program** within two weeks of joining (to be reported to the CEO)	Weekly	Past	P	5	5	Training	11
Number of scheduled **interdepartmental** training events	Monthly	Past	R	3	3	Training	11
Number of staff who are completing **external qualifications** supported by the organization	Quarterly	Past	R	3	3	Training	11

(continued)

315

(*Continued*)

Measure	Frequency of measurement	Time zone (past, current, future)	Result/performance indicator	Strength/feasibility		Keyword	Performance measure category
Number of **case studies** relating to mistakes that have been used for training	Monthly	Past	P	3	3	Training	11
Number of staff, by department, who have not received any **training** in the last six months	Monthly	Past	P	5	5	Training	11
Number of hours lost due to **equipment downtime**	Weekly	Past	R	3	3	Maintenance	12
Unplanned versus planned **maintenance expenditure**	Monthly	Past	R	5	4	Maintenance	12
Total value of deferred **maintenance**	Monthly	Past	R	3	3	Maintenance	12
Number of unscheduled **maintenance** calls	Weekly	Past	R	3	3	Maintenance	12
Production schedule delays because of material shortages	Daily	Current	R	5	4	Production	12
Instances where **production tasks** are not being performed on time for key product lines	Daily	Current	R	4	4	Production	12
Time lost due to **production schedule** changes or deviations from schedule	Monthly	Past	R	5	2	Production	12

Description	Frequency	Past/Current	P/R			Category	
The **production** of urgent runs (sign of poor planning) as a percentage of average daily production	Weekly	Past	P	3	3	Production	12
Number of items that make it through **production** without being reworked at any stage	Weekly	Past	R	4	4	Production	12
Average **production** time for top 10 product lines	Weekly	Past	R	4	3	Production	12
Production yield (percentage of product produced fit for purpose over total product produced)	Weekly	Past	R	5	5	Production	12
Improvement in **productivity** (percentage)	Weekly	Past	R	4	4	Production	12
Production cycle time (time in each stage)—use for top five product lines	Monthly	Past	R	2	2	Production	12
Breaches in **IT protocols**	Daily	Current	P	5	5	Security	12
Unauthorized access to computer facilities that has not been fixed to prevent further access	Daily	Current	P	3	3	Security	12
Date of last test of **recovering data** from a back-up held at a remote site	Monthly	Past	P	5	5	Security	12
Number of **virus corrupted computers** this month	Monthly	Past	R	3	3	Security	12

(continued)

(Continued)

Measure	Frequency of measurement	Time zone (past, current, future)	Result/performance indicator	Strength/feasibility		Keyword	Performance measure category
Key systems that have not been **backed up** for over ___ days	Monthly	Past	R	3	3	Security	12
Number of **spam detection failures**	Monthly	Past	R	2	2	Security	12
Number of changes to the programming of major **off-the-shelf applications** used by the organization	Monthly	Past	R	5	5	Systems	12
Number of hours **key systems** unavailable during office hours (list top 10 worst offenders)	Monthly	Past	R	3	3	Systems	12
Number of **current users** of key systems	Monthly	Past	R	5	3	Systems	12
Number of **customizations** planned for each key system	Monthly	Past	R	5	5	Systems	12
Number of days where key systems were not **backed up** at night	Weekly	Past	R	5	5	Systems	12
Average **mainframe response time** by major system	Weekly	Past	R	4	5	Systems	12
Unplanned outages of key systems in week	Weekly	Past	R	3	3	Systems	12
Number of employees trained on ___ system (**advanced technology** only)	Quarterly	Past	R	5	3	Systems	12

Name of unsupported **major systems**, software, or hardware	Monthly	Past	P	5	5	Systems	12
Name of critical processes performed in **Excel**	Monthly	Past	P	5	5	Systems	12
The number of resources (headcount) assigned to manual processes	Monthly	Past	P	5	3	Systems	12
Planned **uneconomic runs** of top 10 machines	Daily	Future	R	3	4	Utilization	12
Utilization of top five IT systems	Monthly	Past	R	5	4	Utilization	12
Spare **Utilization** obtained from adopting lean processes	Monthly	Past	R	3	4	Utilization	12
Number of users of the human resources system	Monthly	Past	R	3	5	Utilization	12
Percentage of time **IT program developers** have spent on actual programming	Monthly	Past	R	4	4	Utilization	12
Outage hours by main system per month	Monthly	Past	R	4	3	Utilization	12
Number of systems that have been integrated with other systems	Quarterly	Past	R	4	5	Utilization	12
Percentage of vehicles consuming more than 10 liters per 100 kms	Monthly	Past	R	3	3	Vehicles	12
Vehicles where mileage is over ___ last month	Monthly	Past	R	2	1	Vehicles	12

(continued)

319

(Continued)

Measure	Frequency of measurement	Time zone (past, current, future)	Result/performance indicator	Strength/feasibility		Keyword	Performance measure category
Managers demonstrating the most success with **project** implementations over past three years, reported to the CEO	Quarterly	Past	P	3	5	Projects	13
Completion of **projects** on time and budget (percentage or dollars of total projects)	Monthly	Past	P	4	3	Projects	13
Number of **projects** finished in the month	Monthly	Past	P	3	5	Projects	13
Number of projects that are managed or staffed by **contractors/consultants**	Monthly	Past	P	4	5	Projects	13
Number of **post-project reviews** undertaken to ascertain lessons learned	Monthly	Past	P	3	4	Projects	13
Date of **pilot testing** completion	Weekly	Past	R	3	5	Projects	13
List of late **projects** by manager reported weekly to the senior management team	Weekly	Past	P	5	5	Projects	13
List of **projects** that are at risk of noncompletion (unassigned, manager has left, no progress has been made in the past ___ months)	Weekly	Past	P	5	5	Projects	13

Measure	Frequency	Timeframe	P/R			Location	Page
Major **projects** awaiting decisions that are now running behind schedule (reported to CEO)	Weekly	Past	P	5	5	Projects	13
Major **projects** in progress without contingency plans	Weekly	Past	P	3	4	Projects	13
Number of **post-project** reviews outstanding (major projects only)	Weekly	Past	P	4	4	Projects	13
Number of **projects in progress**, by project manager, by department	Monthly	Past	P	5	5	Projects	13
Date of next **strategic planning** meetings with key clients and partners	Quarterly	Future	P	3	5	Head office	14
Total headquarters costs/employee (total organization's **staff**)	Monthly	Past	R	3	5	Head office	14
Number of initiatives completed from the recent in-house satisfaction survey on **HQ functions**	Weekly for three months post-survey	Past	P	5	5	Head office	14
Percentage of **head office** staff to total staff	Monthly	Past	R	3	3	Head office	14
Number of **head office** staff time spent out of office with customers, front-line people, noncustomers, by senior manager	Monthly	Past	R	4	3	Head office	14

Index